KNOWLEDGE AND LEARNING IN THE ANDES
ETHNOGRAPHIC PERSPECTIVES

Liverpool Latin American Studies

Liverpool Latin American Studies, New Series 3

Knowledge and Learning
in the Andes
Ethnographic Perspectives

edited by Henry Stobart and Rosaleen Howard

LIVERPOOL UNIVERSITY PRESS

First published 2002 by
Liverpool University Press
4 Cambridge Street
Liverpool L69 7ZU

Copyright © Liverpool University Press 2002

The right of Henry Stobart and Rosaleen Howard to be identified as the editors of this work has been asserted by them in accordance with the Copyright, Design and Patents Act 1988.

British Library Cataloguing-in-Publication data
A British Library CIP record is available

ISBN 0-85323-518-X

Typeset in Plantin by Servis Filmsetting Limited, Manchester
Printed and bound in the European Union by Alden Press, Oxford

Contents

List of Illustrations

Figures

List of Contributors

Astvaldur Astvaldsson is a Lecturer in Latin American Studies at the University of Liverpool. He has published a number of articles in this field and is the author of *Jesús de Machaqa: La marka rebelde.* (Vol 4: *Las voces de los wak'a: fuentes principales del poder político aymara.* La Paz: CIPCA, 2000).

L. Nicole Bourque is a Senior Lecturer in Social Anthropology in the Department of Sociology and Anthropology at the University of Glasgow. Her research interests include syncretism, popular religion, saint cults and agricultural festivals in Ecuador, conversion to Islam in Britain, and transportation and vehicle blessing in Bolivia

Barbara Bradby teaches sociology at Trinity College, Dublin, in Ireland. In 1994–95, she directed a research project on childbirth in Bolivia, sponsored by the European Union, which focused on maternal mortality, through looking at traditions of birth in Quechua- and Aymara-speaking areas, and at migrant women's experiences of hospital birth.

Lindsey Crickmay has a doctorate in Amerindian Studies from the University of St Andrews where she teaches in the Department of Social Anthropology. She has worked in the Bolivian and Peruvian Andes and has published material on weaving, and the christianisation process. She is currently researching tourism in the Andes.

Penny Dransart has taught at the universities of Oxford and London; she is currently Senior Lecturer and Chair of the Department of Archaeology at the University of Wales, Lampeter. Her research interests include textiles, dress and gender. Her monograph, *Earth, Water, Fleece and Fabric* has recently been published by Routledge (2002).

Rosaleen Howard is Senior Lecturer in Latin American Linguistics at the Institute of Latin American Studies, University of Liverpool. She specialises in indigenous languages, oral culture and sociolinguistics of the Andean region. Her publications include *Creating Context in Andean Cultures* (ed.) (Oxford University Press, 1997).

Janet Lloyd completed a doctorate in social anthropology at the Institute of Latin American Studies, University of Liverpool in 1998. She now works with US NGO Amazon Watch supporting Amazonian indigenous organisations in their opposition to natural resource extraction projects on their ancestral lands.

Pedro Plaza Martínez is Lecturer and Researcher on the PROEIBAN-DES Masters Program in Intercultural Bilingual Education, San Simón University, Cochabamba, Bolivia. He completed his PhD in 1998 at the Institute of Latin American Studies, University of Liverpool, and is author of numerous articles on bilingual education in Bolivia.

Henry Stobart is lecturer in Ethnomusicology at the Music Department of Royal Holloway University of London. His co-edited book *Sound* was published by Cambridge University Press (2000) and he is completing a book on Bolivian music for Ashgate. He has toured and recorded widely with the Early/World music ensemble *Sirinu*.

INTRODUCTION

Rosaleen Howard, Françoise Barbira-Freedman
and Henry Stobart

Background to the volume

The chapters collected here are based on papers delivered at a round-table conference held at Darwin College, University of Cambridge, on 30 November–1 December 1996.[1] In the original title of the conference was the Quechua word *watunakuy*, which expresses the idea of a mutual request for information between two parties, a cooperative activity of 'finding out'. In this spirit, the meeting aimed to explore current research into the ways in which Andean peoples create, transmit, maintain and transform their knowledge in culturally significant ways, and how processes of teaching and learning relate to these. The focus was on the diverse ideologies and practices surrounding the production and reception of knowledge, and the activities of teaching and learning, within the many varied sectors of Andean society. The contributions come from researchers in anthropology, sociology, cultural studies and linguistics, including cross-disciplinary approaches, and cover a diverse geographic area from Ecuador to Peru, Bolivia and northern Chile.

Colliding realms of knowledge

A particular feature of Latin American cultural history is the collision of radically different epistemologies, stemming from the early colonial period. In the Andean region, this clash is epitomised by Atahuallpa's reported rejection of the Bible on the square at Cajamarca in 1532. That event is invoked in popular representations of history to this day (see e.g. Millones 1992), and provides a powerful metaphor for the breakdown of communication resulting from the mutual impact of two contrasting systems of knowledge. This communication breakdown, along with political, religious, economic and military aspects of the Conquest, was to reconfigure social structural relationships, providing a framework for the cultural and linguistic hegemony that has operated in the Andes ever since.

---

[1] With the exception of the chapter by Pedro Plaza Martínez, which was commissioned at a later date.

From this reconfiguration has sprung a series of widely recognised dichotomies, at the heart of which is a perceived divide between so-called Western 'scientific' and Andean 'practical' knowledges. This perception, in turn, has tended to be constructed as a hierarchy rather than simply as difference, and has generated a multiplicity of cultural assumptions and stereotypes. But a closer analysis of lived examples, as presented in this volume, suggests more complex and fluid layers of interaction. Even at the momentous encounter between Inkas and Spaniards at Cajamarca, each group had already (mis)interpreted the other's nature and intentions, based on their respective knowledges and expectations (cf. MacCormack 1993). The ideological ground that was to breed the stereotypes was laid from the very outset.

Today, a very different situation presents itself: in light of the cultural *mestizaje* of the intervening centuries, it is often vain, and even invidious, to attempt to unravel Spanish and indigenous elements. On the other hand, the space of *mestizaje* is itself in constant flux: along with the mergings, the boundaries are constantly being redrawn as diverse local identities reposition themselves. This repositioning is part of a hegemonic struggle in which differing perceptions of knowledge play a crucial role, and where the very ontology of knowledge is brought into question. One person's 'knowledge' may equally be another's 'ignorance'. If knowledge is conceived of as 'capital', the potential for lack of knowledge to be perceived as cultural deficiency follows in its wake. From a developmentalist perspective, as Mark Hobart, in his anthropological critique of development, has put it, 'the growth of knowledge entails the growth of ignorance' (Hobart [ed.] 1993: 22, n.1).[2]

Perceptions of ignorance originating in the dominant discourse become interiorised by the people so perceived; a consent in their own ignorance is engendered as hegemonic processes take hold. The Quechua language reveals evidence of this: the term *ñawsa* ('blind') denotes illiteracy in Southern Peruvian Quechua (Cusihuamán 1976) and the term *upa* ('deaf and dumb') is used by Quechua speakers in Central Peru when referring to their inability to speak Spanish or to read and write (Howard-Malverde 1990). These examples suggest that lacking the communicative skills of Spanish-speaking society is constructed as ignorance from the perspective of many monolingual Quechua speakers.

In the last three decades of the twentieth century, both the study of the culture of science and anthropologists' critique of modernisation as a dominant approach to development conceded greater legitimacy to forms of knowledge that do not comply with Aristotelian categories, and are not necessarily codified and stored in literacy. Paradoxically in the information age, 'indigenous knowledge', particularly knowledge of natural resources, has become a new focus of enquiry, both for its epistemological value and for its potential economic worth (Brokensha, Warren and Werner [eds.] 1980;

---

[2] Hobart attributes this point to Richard Fardon (personal communication).

Warren, Slikkerveer and Brokensha [eds.] 1995). 'Local knowledge' has come to be seen as the key to sustainable living in a 'bottom-up' development perspective.

While the aims of indigenous knowledge research have been to achieve a sympathetic, in-depth appreciation of local people's experience, and to promote culturally appropriate adaptations to social and economic change, its political dimensions have been inevitable from the start. 'Battlefields of knowledge', first studied in the Andes by Norman and Ann Long (Long and Long [eds.] 1992) in relation to agricultural development, became increasingly more explicit in the 1990s as 'battles of perspectives' (Sillitoe 1998). At the same time as local expertise and agency were being given new credence within the broad context of the participatory approach to development, 'knowledge' also became a tool actively reclaimed by local people to reconstruct their identity and culture in discourses of resistance.

While not responding to (or reacting against) any particular developmentalist agenda, this volume draws on the recognition that the distinctive, effective practices of resource use among Andean peoples are connected with dynamic tacit ways of knowing. Ellen and Harris's criteria for local knowledge as 'orally transmitted, a consequence of practical engagement reinforced by experience, empirical, repetitive, fluid and negotiable, shared but asymmetrically distributed, largely functional, and embedded in a more encompassing cultural matrix' (1997: 4–5) are validated in this volume, through a focus on both knowing and learning in all spheres of activity. The pursuit is both an intellectual and an applied one, tackling issues of epistemology which have not received direct attention in previous Andeanist anthropological studies.[3]

Alternative epistemologies

From the perspective of the Western intellectual tradition, the question 'what is knowledge?' has been the primordial terrain of philosophy. Establishing what knowledge is from the philosopher's viewpoint is necessarily bound up with the principle of rationality, which in turn is based on logic, a system for testing the validity of thought processes whose evolution can be traced back to Classical times. By way of example we can quote philosopher of education Paul Hirst, who sums up his theory of knowledge as follows:

> The domain of knowledge I take to be centrally the domain of true propositions or statements, and the question of their being logically distinct forms of

[3] This is with the exception of a recent volume of the *Journal of the Steward Anthropological Society* entitled *Structure, Knowledge, and Representation in the Andes*, which contains a section entitled 'The Power of Knowledge' (*Journal* 1997); see also the recent cross-cultural epistemological literature on 'local knowledge', particularly Apffel-Marglin with PRATEC (eds.) 1998, Valladolid Rivera 1998, and Rengifo Vasquez 1998.

> knowledge I take to be the question of their being logically distinct types of true propositions or statements. Certainly we speak not only of knowing truths but also of knowing people and places and knowing how to do things. Detailed analysis suggests, however, that there are in fact only two distinct types of knowledge here, that in which the objects of knowledge are true propositions and that in which the objects are practical performances of some kind . . . (Hirst 1981: 234)

Humanities and social science disciplines owe much to philosophy in the way that their modes of theorising and argumentation have developed over the twentieth century. In particular, anthropologists are much exercised as to whether the tenets of rationality based on the Western logical notion of a 'true proposition', referred to by Hirst, can be seen to hold when they are faced with statements of belief by members of non-Western cultures which do not bear testing against such a principle (cf. Sperber 1982). If the answer is that Western logic does not hold, then the thorny question is raised of how far the doctrine of relativism can help us explain difference.

The dilemma can be somewhat dispelled if we pay attention to the way that epistemic modality works in the grammar of non-Western languages. The case of Quechua is illustrative: here a categorical principle is at work, not to distinguish logically testable knowledge from practical knowledge, but rather to distinguish knowledge of events of which one has direct personal knowledge from knowledge one has acquired second-hand, for example by hearsay, not having witnessed the facts or events for oneself. Quechua speakers are at pains over this distinction, particularly when narrating the past: thus evidential markers and the tense/aspect suffixes combine grammatically to mark the source of knowledge and the truth-value attributed by the speaker to any proposition (cf. Howard-Malverde 1988; for the case of Aymara, see Hardman 1986). The categorisation of knowledge in Andean languages is thus bound up with ontology, leading us to suggest that the distinction between 'indirect' and 'direct' knowledge reveals a dichotomy of 'objective truth' versus 'subjective truth', which it is interesting to compare with Hirst's distinction between 'true propositions' and 'practical performances'.

While, according to the laws of syllogistic logic in the Western Classical mode, 'true propositions' can be said to belong to a relatively objective order of knowledge, 'practical performances' by definition involve the acting subject, and thus constitute a more subjectively constructed kind of knowledge. The status of 'truth', according to rationality criteria, is primarily attributed to the former rather than the latter. In the case of the epistemological principles displayed by indigenous Andean languages, the evidence suggests somewhat the reverse: a proposition based on an indirect (i.e. non-subjective) source of knowledge cannot carry the truth-value that is carried by a proposition based on direct (i.e. subjective, participatory) knowledge; the statement based on indirect knowledge always bears the caveat 'so they say'. In this respect it seems that 'true propositions' and 'practical performances' become intrinsically bound up together in Quechua and Aymara expressions of knowledge, rather than belonging to separate logical domains as in the Western philosophical tradition. A number of the chapters in this volume place emphasis on the interconnections between 'knowing' and 'doing', which will help bear out these epistemological reflections. In sum, it is hoped that this book will encourage a wider recognition that 'truth' and 'knowledge' are indeed culturally relative concepts up to a point, and demonstrate in what concrete ways this is so.

Methods of enquiry into the nature of knowledge in the Western tradition have also been characterised by the use of dialectic. Contradictions are seen to be resolved through processes of reasoning, or, to paraphrase Bertrand Russell, knowledge is sought by question and answer (Russell 1991: 109). Indeed, many earlier philosophers, such as Plato, expressed this reasoning through the model of a dialogue. On the one hand, the model has resonances with the Andean *watunakuy* concept, where dialogue is key. On the other hand, dialectic gives rise to the identification of dichotomies and has as its aim their resolution.

The chapters in this volume highlight a number of such oppositions, which we summarise in a preliminary way as follows: knowledge versus ignorance; scientific versus practical knowledge; collective versus individual knowledge; abstract versus specific knowledge; objective versus subjective knowledge; explicit versus implicit knowledge; outside versus inside knowledge; rational versus relative knowledge; local versus global knowledge. To posit such a set of oppositions is nonetheless problematic. We are talking here of ideological constructs, arising at different periods in history, among different social groupings, in different locations, and at work deep within the consciousnesses of people undergoing processes of social struggle and change. Any such categorisation runs the risk of suggesting an adherence to stereotypes, and may even serve to reinforce them. This is far from our purpose. By drawing attention to these dichotomies, we seek rather to highlight the multiple strands of the debate about the nature of knowledge and learning in the Andes that this book proposes; each contributor shows how these lines of debate are relevant to individual case studies, and the ways in which, in the course of data analysis, apparent oppositions may dynamically break down, merge, and reconverge in contexts of social action. Importantly, moreover, the struggle between experiential and intellectual, dominant and dominated ways of knowing, emerges in this volume as a central focus of social and political differences in the region, at a time when new interpretations of shared knowledge also have profound implications for local power relations.

Layered knowledges

In the Andes, therefore, it is impossible to think in terms of simple dichotomies between modes of knowing. The historical interaction between epistemologies, like that between material aspects of culture, has taken many forms and expressions, from juxtaposition to syncretism, from rejection to inclusion. Part of the Andean specific (itself diverse in its forms) is also the discarded Hispanic, in that past expressions of dominance were successively appropriated by Andean peoples as their own, while they became outmoded in more Westernised sectors of society. Barbara Bradby, for example, shows several historical layers of medical knowledge in relation to obstetric practices, each validating the previous one as more 'Andean', although, as in the case of humoral theories, they are a vestige of dominant Hispanic colonial knowledge. Considerable rationalisation is involved today in appropriating outside practices and fusing them with pre-existing ones, and this has been ongoing since the Conquest; it constitutes a mode of cultural affirmation which, as Grillo Fernández has eloquently put it, 'digests' what is alien rather than hybridising with it (1998: 137).

Multiple media in the creation and transmission of knowledge

In the first chapter, Rosaleen Howard examines ideas about knowing and learning from the perspective of the Quechua language, while seeking to support the premise that 'knowledge' is a 'colonised concept' in the Andes. She takes as her corpus for linguistic analysis the text of the drama *Tragedia del fin de Atawallpa* (Lara 1989), which depicts the Spanish Conquest of the Inkas through the idiom of communication breakdown. Vainly, the Inkas attempt to 'read' the signs, through a series of interpretive strategies familiar to them (divination, dream analysis, oracular reading of the landscape), all of which fail. In addition, they are faced with new communicative codes (the Spanish language, alphabetic writing) which their tried and tested methods of decipherment are inadequate to tackle. In Howard's reading of this play, as in several of the ethnographic studies in this volume (see e.g. Stobart and Crickmay), emphasis is placed on the idea of knowledge as an embodied process, bound up with ontology, bringing about a transformation of the self. As the play unfolds, realisation of the meaning of events is gradually achieved, and the Inkas' world is transformed forever. Howard pays attention to the nature of Lara's text as a problematic source, insofar as it represents an indigenist literary tradition, rather than living bilingual performance; just as the Inkas are portrayed as losing the power to construct their own knowledge, the status of this text as a *mestizo* ('colonised') construct of Andean historical knowledge is necessarily enigmatic. This opening chapter thus highlights the negotiated status of knowledge in the Andes, a theme that recurs throughout the volume.

Lindsey Crickmay's chapter also touches on a number of recurrent themes: she draws our attention to the perceived dichotomy between academic, literacy-based knowledge, privileged in Western cultures, and the practical participatory knowledges that characterise the Andean world, particularly in relation to the millennial skill of weaving. She uses linguistic evidence to develop the idea of a model of Quechua knowledge as dialogue and, in a related way, nurturance. Such nurturing dialogue, or teaching-learning process, may take place between human participants but equally, in a less obvious manner for the cultural outsider, it may be established between the learner and the substance or medium she or he wields in the creative act: between the weaver and the cloth she weaves, between the ploughman and the field he ploughs, and so on. The effect of Western styles of learning, in this analysis, has been to create a distance between processes of acquisition of knowledge and the natural life cycle; as Crickmay puts it, 'we have lost our capacity for dialogue with our sources of knowledge'.

The medium of weaving for the creation and transmission of knowledge is also the theme of Penny Dransart's chapter. In what she characterises as an 'ethnography of colour', Dransart explores the colour perceptions of the people of Isluga in northern Chile, demonstrating how these perceptions evolve within a specific physical and cultural environment (that of highland Aymara llama herders), to be expressed in and through their weavings. The theoretical framework of Dransart's study stresses the symbolic and physiological relationship, or synaesthesia, between vision, whereby colour is perceived, and other senses such as sound. Knowledge of colour in Isluga Aymara culture is shown to be a practical, sensory knowledge which technicians significantly avoid verbalising. Younger generations of women weavers challenge the unspoken rules about culturally acceptable contrasts and complementarities of colour evoked in the weavings of their elders. In a way that appears to confirm Crickmay's argument in the preceding chapter regarding knowing through doing, in weaving practice there is seen to be a deep cognitive engagement with colour that comes about through working with colours rather than talking about them.

Henry Stobart's study of Bolivian panpipe music, seen as a medium for the creation of knowledge among the rural Quechua of Northern Potosí, also emphasises the non-verbalisation of such knowledge, and the importance of a processual model of knowing (as opposed to knowledge *per se*) as dialogue. Firstly, Stobart explores the role of intuition in the Macha Quechua people's experience of the relationship between the human world and the realms of the dead and the animate landscape, respectively. Interaction between these realms, in this case through musical practice, is a path to knowing; and the concept of embodiment is key to our understanding of how this knowing is achieved. Secondly, he examines the specific case of *jula jula* panpipe playing, quintessentially dialogical in its mode of performance: musicians use paired sets of instruments with alternate notes of the scale divided between them; two players then produce an interlocking melody, likened to a reciprocal sequence of enquiry and response (*watunakuy*). Stobart emphasises that music is central to Macha cosmology, bound up with notions of fertility and growth in the human life cycle, as expressed in the emergent nature of the *jula jula* performances, as well as in the agricultural sphere.

Knowledge, power, and authority

Traditionally in the Andes, the creation of community in accordance with cultural norms of society comes about through the system of ritual obligations known as *cargos*, much documented by anthropologists, whereby political-religious authority is achieved and exercised in ritual contexts. Valdi Astvaldsson's chapter particularly illustrates how discontinuation of ritual practices may lead to disunity and radical change in traditional social and political organisation, here in the case of an Aymara-speaking community near Jesús de Machaqa in highland Bolivia. Astvaldsson frames his discussion in terms of Pierre Bourdieu's theory of the 'logic of practice', arguing that the traditional cycle of ritual obligations whereby a married couple were progressively initiated into full adult membership of their community was a context within which their gradually acquired knowledge of the powers of the ancestral gods, on the one hand, and the power of this cultural knowledge for their own socio-political action, on the other hand, mutually reinforced each other in living practice. The author describes how the context of this initiation and learning process has been subject to radical modernisation and partial destructuration, while at the same time highlighting the place of cultural revivalism among educated political activists in Bolivia today. This chapter also contributes to the theoretical debate about types of knowledge, central to the theme of the volume.

Some of the ambiguities and contradictions facing professional indigenous activists are explored by Janet Lloyd, who shows how these individuals draw on, and juggle with, a diverse range of local, national and global forms of knowledge. Her chapter focuses on the case of Luis Maldonado, who was born and bred in a community in the Otavalo region of Ecuador, studied in Cuba, and lived for several years in Holland. While adopting his own immaculate variation on the famous Otavalo dress style, and wearing his hair braided, Maldonado was evidently more comfortable mixing with outsiders, such as the author, than with the indigenous people he represented. Lloyd suggests that knowledge is linked to styles of behaviour and notes how, at workshops, Maldonado's authoritative and assertive style of presentation was resented and felt to be patronising by the indigenous participants, who were accustomed to more indirect and soft-spoken modes of interaction. Yet Maldonado's direct style was crucial to the effectiveness of his negotiations with, for example, government development workers and international NGOs. Despite their mistrust of professional indigenous activists, indigenous people were aware of the need to support their campaigns for local and even national office, so that indigenous voices might be heard on the national and international stage.

Conflicting paradigms of knowledge

In 'Why Nazario is Leaving School', Pedro Plaza Martínez focuses on the ambivalent attitudes of a rural Bolivian community to formal schooling. The contrasted values of the school teachers and community members, and accordingly their very ontologies of knowledge and learning, are brought into sharp relief as Nazario's fate is debated. With the death of his father, should this boy continue his studies at school or abandon them to fulfil his family's responsibilities in the community? While the benefits of literacy and mathematics are recognised by community members as a means 'to defend ourselves', the more influential view seems to be that 'letters cannot be eaten' and are of little value in the 'real world'. In a number of senses, the thousands of hours rural children dedicate to attending school seem to be conceived as a rite of passage in which punishment is condoned by parents and pupils alike, and in which new school reforms which proscribe corporal punishment and advocate games are interpreted as signs of a deterioration, rather than improvement, in teaching quality.

In her chapter, Barbara Bradby highlights the conflicts between the knowledge and practices of traditional Andean midwifery and those of Western scientific medicine. She stresses that the 'local' or 'traditional' knowledges of Andean midwives, which have often been construed as 'cultural barriers' to the implementation of Western medicine, are by no means unique to the region, or static; indeed, as commented above, certain aspects may be traced back to earlier European medical orthodoxies and humoral beliefs. Bradby focuses on a conversation with an urban, yet monolingual Quechua-speaking, midwife, to analyse how local knowledge and identification with traditional rural practices are invoked discursively in opposition to the medical practices of hospitals. For example, the midwife's technique of observing and feeling a woman's hand to tell when she is ready to give birth is angrily contrasted with what she views as the hospitals' invasive practice of vaginal examination ('sticking their hands up'). The midwife acquired her knowledge from her mother, but her own daughter will not follow this trade, which she 'does not understand' because 'she is studying'. Discursively, the associations of formal schooling, with its focus on knowledges mediated in the Spanish language, rule out the very idea of becoming a traditional midwife.

Bradby's paper is this volume's contribution to the all-important area of alternative medical knowledges. The proliferation of manuals of medicinal plant use, made available in health posts and schools in the Andes and used in the training of rural health promotors in some areas (Barbira Freedman and Kroeger 1988), has contributed to the expansion of the production and trade of medicinal plants and plant remedies both in the informal economy and, recently, in the formal economy as well. It is an area of Andean knowing and learning that cuts across boundaries of class and ethnicity in the region as a whole, from the hinterland to affluent residential districts of capital cities. Moreover, the revaluing of traditional herbal curing in the Andes is a central part of current indigenous political agendas.

The final chapter, by Nicole Bourque, concerns agricultural knowledge and the dynamics surrounding the introduction of tree tomato cultivation to an Ecuadorian village. An important conclusion from this case study is that the adoption of external ideas and knowledge is more dependent on the practices of insiders than on the efforts of outsiders. For example, an initiative to introduce modern potato farming methods by members of the Peace Corps, some years earlier, immediately collapsed after the foreigners' departure, but the cultivation of tree tomatoes in the village was initiated by a local individual and has continued to have considerable repercussions. After observing the success and high profit margins achieved by this insider, large numbers of families began to follow suit, and in addition started to apply the fertilisers, fungicides and pesticides required for tree tomatoes to maize cultivation. Bourque demonstrates how such shifts in attitude, and acceptance of new forms of knowledge, depend upon a complex web of social, religious and economic relationships, in which only those new strategies or types of knowledge that are workable within traditional economic and social structures are likely to be accepted and adopted.

Closing remarks and future directions

In principle, *watunakuy* conveys the idea of an equal exchange between parties, where question and answer follow one another in mutual succession. However, in the process of acquiring knowledge, solidarity and competition are never far apart. Indeed, *watunakuy* might also be interpreted in terms of 'competition' – as in verbal or musical exchanges in which participants vie for the upper hand. If we explore the etymology of the English term 'compete' (Latin *competere*, from *com-* 'together' and *petere* 'seek') we find that its semantic range partially coincides with that of *watunakuy* – particularly if we bear in mind that, according to the OED, 'competence' (also from *competere*), which today evokes capacity or ability, historically meant 'rivalry'. The case studies in this book provide a source for reflection on the variously harmonious and conflictive relationships between knowledge, power, communicative media and cultural identities in Andean societies, from within local, national and global perspectives.

The ways of knowing described here are channelled through multiple media. Indeed, the ethnographic evidence demands that we adopt a multimedia approach to communicative strategies in our study of knowledge systems. The medium is intrinsically bound up with the message, and certain kinds of development strategy can lead to conflict over media and the different discourses they generate.[4] A positively framed multimedia

---

[4] In this vein, Denise Arnold and Juan de Dios Yapita have analysed in detail the 'textual struggles' which they see emerging in Bolivia under the impact of recent education reform (Arnold and Yapita 2000).

approach can take many forms. On the one hand it may seek to restore the status of traditional communicative media, such as (in the case of the Andes) weaving, so harshly displaced by the advent of alphabetic literacy. On the other hand, many researchers with first-hand experience of working with indigenous people have noted how elements of high technology merge seamlessly into traditional lifestyles, complementing rather than disrupting the latter.[5] An inclusive model of multimedia communication should make room both for recovering neglected forms of knowledge production and for assimilating new ones. For instance, a topic for future research, although beyond the range of this volume, would be a consideration of the use being made of Internet technology by members of Amerindian language groups and cultures;[6] the significance that this activity has for the future of the languages themselves; and the evolving sense of identity and social status of their speakers, as, at least ideally, new roads for the creation and transmission of knowledge on their own terms, open up before them.

Acknowledgments

The editors are grateful to Darwin College, Cambridge for providing the venue for the conference, and to the Cambridge University Centre for Latin American Studies under its Director, David Lehmann, for hospitality provided.

References

Apffel-Marglin, Frédérique, and S.A. Marglin. 1990. *Dominating Knowledge: Development, Culture and Resistance*. Oxford: Oxford University Press.
Apffel-Marglin, Frédérique, and S.A. Marglin (eds.). 1996. *Decolonizing Knowledge: From Development to Dialogue*. Oxford: Clarendon Press.
Apffel-Marglin, Frédérique, with PRATEC (eds.). 1998. *The Spirit of Regeneration: Andean Culture Confronting Western Notions of Development*. London: Zed Books.

[5] Examples come to mind of an anecdotal nature, but which we believe to be typical of sea changes that are taking place as indigenous peoples adopt and adapt electronic media to their particular contexts: at the 4th Latin American Congress of Intercultural Bilingual Education held in Quito in November 1998, Howard heard tell of Amazonian shamans who enhance their reputation by using mobile phones to communicate with the spirits of the rainforest; Professor Ron Scollon commented recently on the use Inuit fishermen in the Arctic circle make of the same technology, while going about their fishing business in the traditional style (personal communication, 2000).

[6] Many websites already exist; some may be accessed, for example, via http://nativeweb.org/resources/languages_linguistics/indigenous_languages/. Such a study would build on the pathbreaking essays gathered by Hawisher and Selfe (2000), and would raise many questions; for example: Who is building these sites and why? Who visits them and why? Are they helping the status of indigenous languages? Are they in any way contributing to greater social equality for the majority of speakers? and many more.

Arnold, Denise, and J. Yapita. 2000. *El rincón de las cabezas: luchas textuales, educación y tierras en los Andes*. La Paz: Facultad de Humanidades y Ciencias de la Educación, UMSA e ILCA.

Barbira Freedman, Françoise, and A. Kroeger. 1988. *La lucha para la salud en la Amazonía y los Andes*. Quito: Abya-Yala.

Brokensha, David, D.M. Warren and O. Werner (eds.). 1980. *Indigenous Knowledge Systems and Development*. Lanham, MD: University Press of America.

Cusihuamán, Antonio. 1976. *Diccionario quechua Cuzco-Collao*. Lima: Instituto de Estudios Peruanos.

Ellen, Roy F., and H. Harris. 1997. *Indigenous Environmental Knowledge in Scientific and Developmental Literature: A Critical Assessment*. Canterbury: University of Kent.

Grillo Fernández, Eduardo. 1998. 'Development or Cultural Affirmation in the Andes?'. In Apffel-Marglin with PRATEC (eds.): 124–46.

Hardman, Martha. 1986. 'Data Source Marking in the Jaqi Languages'. In W. Chafe and J. Nichols (eds.), *Evidentiality: The Linguistic Coding of Epistemology*. Norwood, NJ: Ablex Publishing: 113–36.

Hawisher, Gail E., and Cynthia L. Selfe. 2000. *Global Literacies and the World-Wide Web*. London: Routledge.

Hirst, Paul. 1981. 'The Forms of Knowledge Revisited'. In S. Brown, J. Fauvel and R. Finnegan (eds.), *Conceptions of Inquiry*. London: Open University Press: 233–46.

Hobart, Mark (ed.). 1993. *An Anthropological Critique of Development: The Growth of Ignorance*. London: Routledge.

Howard-Malverde, Rosaleen. 1988. 'Talking about the Past: Tense and Testimonials in Quechua Narrative Discourse'. *Amerindia* 13: 125–55.

——, 1990. '*Upa*: La conceptualisation de la parole et du silence dans la construction de l'identité quechua'. *Journal de la Société des Américanistes de Paris* 76: 105–20.

Journal of the Steward Anthropological Society. 1997. *Structure, Knowledge, and Representation in the Andes. Studies Presented to Reiner Tom Zuidema on the Occasion of his 70th Birthday*, 25 (1 and 2).

Lara, Jesús. 1989. *Tragedia del fin de Atawallpa. Atau Wallpaj p'uchukakuyninpa wankan*. Cochabamba: Los Amigos del Libro.

Long, Norman, and A. Long (eds.). 1992. *Battlefields of Knowledge: The Interlocking of Theory and Practice in Social Research and Development*. London: Routledge.

MacCormack, Sabine. 1993. 'Demons, Imagination, and the Incas'. In S. Greenblatt (ed.), *New World Encounters*. Berkeley, CA: University of California Press: 101–26.

Millones, Luis. 1992. *Actores de altura. Ensayos sobre el teatro popular andino*. Lima: Editorial Horizonte.

Nader, Laura. 1996. 'Anthropological Inquiry into Boundaries, Power and Knowledge'. In L. Nader (ed.), *Naked Science*. NewYork: Routledge: 1–25.

Rengifo Vasquez, Grimaldo. 1998. 'Education in the Modern West and in Andean Culture'. In Apffel-Marglin with PRATEC (eds.): 172–92.

Russell, Bertrand. 1991. *A History of Western Philosophy and its Connection with Political and Social Circumstances from the Earliest Times to the Present Day*. London: Routledge.

Sillitoe, Paul. 1998. 'The Development of Indigenous Knowledge'. *Current*

Anthropology 39(2): 223–52.

Sperber, Dan. 1982. 'Apparently Irrational Beliefs'. In M. Hollis and S. Lukes (eds.), *Rationality and Relativism*. Oxford: Blackwell: 149–80.

Valladolid Rivera, Julio. 1998. 'Andean Peasant Agriculture: Nurturing a Diversity of Life in the *chacra*'. In Apffel-Marglin with PRATEC (eds.).

Warren, Dennis M., L.J. Slikkerveer and D. Brokensha (eds.). 1995. *The Cultural Dimensions of Development: Indigenous Knowledge Systems*. London: Intermediate Technology Publications.

PART I

*Multiple Media in the Creation and
Transmission of Knowledge*

Yachay: The *Tragedia del fin de Atahuallpa* as Evidence of the Colonisation of Knowledge in the Andes

Rosaleen Howard

The communicative divide between Spanish invaders and Inka holders of power, described by numerous eyewitnesses to the scene at Cajamarca in November 1532, acquired a particular symbolic potency in Andean cultural memory as post-Conquest history unfolded. Over the intervening centuries, the new social classes emerging under colonial and republican regimes have repositioned themselves with regard to the event, evoking the Spanish Conquest of the Inkas in popular culture from diverse political, spatial and temporal standpoints, right down to the present day. One of the best-known examples of such cultural expression is the popular drama generically known as the *Tragedia del fin de Atahuallpa* ('Tragedy of the End of Atahuallpa'; hereafter *Tragedia*), most easily accessible in published form in Jesús Lara's edition (Lara 1989). In this chapter I shall use Lara's text as a focal point around which to explore the way ideas about seeking, acquiring and processing knowledge are expressed in the Quechua language. On the one hand, the play depicts the Spanish Conquest of the Inkas in the idiom of communication breakdown. On the other hand, it raises issues about the ways in which knowledge of history – in particular the Conquest of Peru – is produced in cultural tradition. Accounts of that history vary according to the social, temporal and spatial perspectives of the storytellers, and Lara's text offers a particularly ambiguous view. In spite of, or perhaps because of, its enigmatic origins, and the questions it raises about cultural 'ownership', Lara's version of the *Tragedia* lends itself to analysis from the point of view of what I shall call the 'colonisation of knowledge' in the Andes.

In the course of this analysis, such questions arise as: whose history is this? whose language is this variety of Quechua? and whose knowledge is it expressing? Accordingly, the ways in which Lara's play expresses ideas about knowledge in the Quechua language are not straightforward, or unitary in meaning, but have to be analysed critically.

The social contexts of production of knowledge that I have in mind in approaching my subject are rural and urban provincial areas of Peru and Bolivia where speakers of Quechua and Spanish have for many centuries interacted and merged, in social, economic, and political arrangements generated by colonialism. These are the populations close to whom Lara lived, and among whom, in its many variant forms, the dramatic tradition of the *Tragedia* evolved. These populations display differing degrees of bilingualism; economically they are more or less integrated into the market; and locally perceived cultural distinctions are marked in language by use of terms such as *campesino* (Spanish, 'peasant'), *runa* (Quechua, 'human being'), *mestizo*, and many others. Such distinctions are fluid and contingent, and the difference between self- and other-definition in statements about cultural identity is highly salient. The ethnic and social class labelling adopted by social scientists is always contentious, for it tends to essentialise identities that are by their very nature – due to the often oppressive and unequal social structures in which they have developed – under constant negotiation. However, the fact that such distinctions are perceived by the people themselves, and inform attitudes and modes of interaction between groups and individuals in the Andes, is crucial to our understanding of cultural complexity in the region, and relevant to the present theme.

Yachay: a key word for 'knowledge' in the Andes

Before I enter into the main body of the chapter, a note is in order on the concept of *yachay*, the most frequently used term to refer to knowledge in the Quechua II dialects, and a cognate of the verb *yatiña* in neighbouring Aymara. The derivative noun forms *yachaq* and *yatiri*, respectively, to refer to the Andean shaman or 'knower', give us an idea of the kind of knowledge to which the term may refer in modern-day usage, and study of the word *yachay* from a historical and dialectological perspective reveals a semantic range far beyond what is suggested by the basic English gloss of 'know'.[1]

César Itier reconstructs the etymological intricacies of *yachay* in his analysis of the term *pachayachachiq*, an epithet used for referring to the Inka deity Viracocha in the Quechua prayers recorded by the sixteenth-century chronicler Juan de Santacruz Pachakuti Yamqui (Itier 1993: 151–63). *Pachayachachiq* was broadly glossed by early colonial commentators as 'creator'. However, as Itier demonstrates, the notion of 'creation' in the biblical *ex nihilo* sense is inadequate as a means to define the Andean 'animator' god who, rather than bringing them forth from nothingness, enabled humankind and other elements of the cosmos fully to realise their nature from a latent pre-existing state.[2]

---

[1] The meanings of *yachay* are also addressed by Crickmay and Stobart in this volume.

[2] The term *kamaq* also describes this 'animating' aspect of the Andean creator god; Taylor characterises the concept of 'creation' in pre-Columbian Andean religion as 'la transmisión de la fuerza vital de una fuente animante (*camac*), generalmente un dios regional o un antepasado, a un ser u objeto animado (*camasca*)' ('the transmission of vital force from an animating source [*camac*], generally a regional god or an ancestor, to an animated [*camasca*] being or object') (Taylor 1987: 24; my translation).

This gradual realisation of the full self from a latent potential is here expressed by the verb root *yacha-*. We perceive in this etymology a single conceptual basis which links ideas about knowing with ideas about coming into being.[3] In seeking to reconstruct the semantic categories underlying the form *yacha-*, Itier considers it as composed of two parts (*ya-* + *-cha-*), and concludes that the root *ya-* (and its cognate derivational suffix *-ya-*) contains the idea of 'crossing a boundary' (1993: 154); while the derivational suffix *-cha-* (and its cognate root *cha-*, as found in the verb *chayay* 'to arrive', where *-ya-* occurs as a derivational suffix), has to do with the idea of 'reaching a state of completeness' (1993: 155). He renders the sum of the underlying semantic features of *yachay* as 'completely reaching an objective' (1993: 155).

While I agree with Itier's analysis thus far, I would wish to lay stronger emphasis on the idea of *yachay* as a *transformational* process: to 'know' in Quechua, according to this broader interpretation, has to do with achieving a fuller state of being, in the sense that it is a process through which persons or states of affairs become 'other' than what they were before the process was undergone. On this premise, it is helpful to work with an idea of knowledge as processual 'knowing', occuring in and through subjective practice, rather than as ready established, objectified fact, alienable from the experiential process in which it takes shape, and there to be 'got' in an instrumental way.[4]

I hope that my analysis below of the *Tragedia*, in which the Spanish Conquest is depicted as an event to be gradually realised, interpreted and understood by the Inkas, as their world is transformed forever, will show how this processual – and ontological – idea of knowledge applies in a particular context. My question will be whether the proposed concept of the 'colonisation of knowledge' – that is, the political, social and cultural undermining of *yachay* as an outcome of European conquest – finds expression in the theme and the text of the play. Before moving on to that analysis, however, I wish further to substantiate this key concept of 'colonisation of knowledge'.

The arrival of book-learning in the Andes, as a consequence of European colonisation, had an effect on commonly held ideas about the status of certain sources of knowledge relative to others. The processual, spiritual and practice-based concepts of knowing and learning evoked by *yachay* became challenged, and to some extent demoted, in the face of formal schooling;

[3] Other early colonial texts confirm this; for example the narrator of the Huarochirí manuscript frequently uses the root *yacha-* to describe the acts of 'animation' performed by the culture heroes of the Checa people's origin myths (see e.g. Taylor 1987: 52, para. 6).

[4] Of course, this transformational aspect of knowing is not confined to the Andes, but evokes a certain type of learning process in many cultures, including those of the West. It is also the case that books offer an illusion of the 'fixity' of knowledge that belies the interactive use to which they are often put. However, the transformational connotations of *yachay* in relation to pre-Hispanic beliefs such as those expressed in the Huarochirí creation myths, for example, give the idea of 'knowing' a particular cosmological significance in the Andes.

the ideologies generated by alphabetic literacy and its underside, illiteracy, were critically responsible for fomenting and reproducing over time certain structures of inequality in the evolving colonial and post-colonial social orders. I develop this point in the following section.

Knowledge as a colonised concept in the Andes

In her contribution to an issue of *Bulletin of Latin American Research* devoted to 'race and ethnicity in the Andes', Marisol de la Cadena (1998) convincingly argues that the discourse of racism in Peru is a silent one, which avoids reference to phenotypes, but rather disguises itself in distinctions, drawn in particular by *serrano* intellectual classes interested in underlining their cultural superiority, between the formally educated and those lacking an academic education. She cites a declaration attributed to Javier Prado during his tenure as Dean of the Faculty of Arts at San Marcos University at the turn of the twentieth century, who said: 'Thanks to education, contemporary man can transform his physical milieu and even his race' (1998: 145–46).[5] At a more recent time, and in a less hallowed academic setting, a schoolteacher in a speech to a rural community in Northern Potosí on the Bolivian 'Day of the Indian' of 2 August 1990, picked upon education as the marker that staked out the differences between herself and the community members she was addressing. If it weren't for her education, she said, she and they (the 'indians') would share the same identity: 'As a teacher I don't have pretensions to be from some other nation, I am from your midst. It's just my culture and my education that makes the difference between us' ('ñuqa como profesora mana creekunichu may waq nacionmanta kasqayta, kani qankuna ukhullamantaqa. Solamente culturay educaciónniy ñuqapataqa ruwawan chay diferenciataqa') (Howard-Malverde and Canessa 1995: 243).

De la Cadena's analysis focuses on Peruvian elite *mestizo* discourse, which serves to construct *serrano* legitimacy and power vis-à-vis the *criollos* of Lima on the one hand and the peasants of the rural Cusco hinterland on the other; the Bolivian schoolteacher's words reveal the paradoxes of the *mestizo* stand, whereby simultaneous sameness and difference may seem to be desirable. Both examples highlight the way in which types and degrees of knowledge, particularly that acquired through formal education, to which only the privileged classes have historically had access, serve to articulate social exclusion in Andean society.

To take another example, this time from the discourses of identity of Quechua-speaking *runa*, we find that the idiom of formally acquired knowledge serves in statements of discriminatory self- and other-definition. People in the countryside around Tantamayo (province of Huamalíes, department of Huánuco, Peru), where I worked in the 1980s, had a well elaborated criterion by which they differentiated themselves from bilingual townspeople:

---

[5] De la Cadena further develops this thesis in her monograph *Indigenous Mestizos* (2000).

they referred to themselves as *upa*, a word meaning 'deaf and dumb' in a literal sense, but which they translated into Spanish as *ignorante*. In other areas of their verbal discourse, including mythological accounts, metaphorical lines of association between 'dumbness', Quechua monolingualism, illiteracy, and lack of knowledge were drawn again and again (Howard-Malverde 1990a; cf. Introduction).[6] More recent research which I conducted on ideas about literacy in Northern Potosí also revealed a perception of exclusive interdependency between alphabetic writing and knowledge; several interviewees expressed the view that without literacy they 'knew nothing', and likened illiteracy to 'being like animals' (Howard-Malverde 1998).[7]

The above examples are evidence to suggest that discourse about knowledge in the colonised societies of the Andes has been permeated by an ideology which assumes alphabetic literacy, the Spanish language, and *hispano-mestizo* modes of formal education to be the most authoritative and legitimate means for the production and transmission of such knowledge, to the exclusion of other media.

Lara's *Tragedia del fin de Atawallpa*: the Spanish Conquest of the Inkas as communication breakdown

'What gibberish are you uttering, you wild man? It is impossible for me to make sense of your half-cooked words' ('Imata rimapayajtaj jamuwanki purun runa, manan watuyta atinichu chay mana chayay simiykita') (Lara 1989: 100).[8] This is how the indian interpreter Felipillo translates Pizarro's words to Atahuallpa at one of the many moments in Jesús Lara's published version of the play *Tragedia del fin de Atawallpa* when Inkas and Spaniards puzzle over the nature of their respective adversaries and the meaning of the Spanish invasion for each side. Simply put, Pizarro's speech can be taken as a dramatised retrospective portrayal of the seeds of linguistic discrimination in the Andes. In more complex terms, in addition to its political and economic repercussions, European invasion led to the subordination of indigenous Andean communicative channels: Spanish became the socially dominant code, and alphabetic writing the medium to serve government, law and religion. This usurpation of the means of communication had implications for both the symbolic status and the content of the knowledge produced by the indigenous peoples from that time on. It is therefore not surprising that a dramatised account of the events at Cajamarca and their long-term consequences should deal quite extensively with the theme of communication breakdown, and in so doing make copious use of vocabulary related to

---

[6] Of course, the idea of ignorance is also contained in the English word 'dumb', particularly in US usage.

[7] Cf. Mark Hobart's critique of development cited in the Introduction.

[8] In all extracts from the text, the Quechua transcription is Lara's, while English translations are my own.

cognition: ideas about seeking, acquiring, understanding and processing knowledge.

The social and cultural origins of the play
Before proceeding further, a note is in order regarding the origins and cultural roots of the play. This popular drama is still widely performed, notably in regions geographically removed from Cusco such as the central highlands of Peru and the Bolivian departments of Oruro, Cochabamba and Potosí. In addition to Lara 1989, scripts have been documented and published by Balmori (1955), Millones (1988), and Beyersdorff (1998). Studies of scripts and performances are to be found in Wachtel 1977, González Carre and Rivera Pineda 1982, Kapsoli 1985, Meneses 1985, Burga 1988 (where the 'play' is a dance drama), Millones 1992, Montoya 1993, and Beyersdorff 1993. Flores Galindo (1988: 59ff.) offers interpretation of the tradition in relation to the concept of 'utopia'; Cornejo Polar (1994) takes the *Tragedia* to represent the birth of heterogeneity in Peruvian literature, in its post-Hispanic guise; Chang-Rodríguez (1999), also from the angle of literary criticism, discusses the play's textual antecedents and symbolism; Itier (2000) proposes a radical critique of Lara (1989), which I discuss below.[9]

Lara provides evidence to suggest that the play has been in existence in some form or another since the sixteenth century (Lara 1989: 11–16).[10] The earliest known script to have survived into the present is the one published under the full title of *Tragedia del fin de Atawallpa. Atau Wallpaj p'uchukakuyninpa wankan* (first edition Lara 1957; re-edited 1989) and known as the 'Chayanta manuscript'.[11] My own textual study of this version, confirmed by that of Beyersdorff (1998), suggests that the play's conditions of production owe much to the oral medium. Although scripts such as this were written down, and can be found in the possession of particular individuals in particular communities, actual performances incur improvisation, and comparison across different written versions shows variation which may be the result of such improvisations at different points in time.[12]

[9] Further sources, to which I have not yet had access, include Husson 1997 and Silva-Santisteban 2000 (both cited in Itier 2000).
[10] This evidence is critically examined by Beyersdorff (1998: 193ff.) and refuted by Itier (2000).
[11] The document that reached Lara's hands was dated Chayanta, 25 March 1871 (Lara 1989: 23).
[12] During fieldwork in Pariarca (Tantamayo, Huamalíes, Peru) in the early 1980s, I was shown a partial copy of such a manuscript in the possession of the person in the village who habitually played the part of the Inka; the text was handwritten in an exercise book, and corresponded to his own part only. Had I had time to pursue this further, with the aim of reconstructing the text as a whole, I would have had to track down the other actors, members of the same community, who would, presumably, each have had copies of their individual parts similarly preserved in notebooks; such a project would surely have been a fascinating sociological experience. In Howard-Malverde 1990b I examine the oral history told to me by the same 'Inka' actor, which deals with a related tradition.

The central theme of the play

In her recent monograph, Beyersdorff (1998) details the significant regional variations between different Bolivian versions of the play. Here, a brief synopsis of the main themes will suffice, being my own observations based on the Lara text. The play's dramatic structure can be characterised in terms of the Quechua cosmological model of the *pachakuti* or world reversal: at the start we see the Inkas prior to the invasion, integral in their world, albeit troubled by portents. The action then progresses through the event of the occupation, with its material plunder and spiritual conquest, to the murder of Atahuallpa and the collapse of his power, reaching full circle with Pizarro's return to Spain to be put to death at the hands of the king (an interesting 'pro-indian' twist). The predominant theme is the Inkas' attempt to understand the events that are overtaking them.

As they endeavour to decipher the strange signs and omens that portend misfortune, the Inkas adopt various semiotic and communicative strategies for the production and reading of messages across the cultural and linguistic divide that separates them from the invaders, all of which ultimately fail. They apply procedures from which, normally speaking, understanding should derive, and which should lead to a state of knowledge. These include the reading of natural signs inscribed in the landscape, the interpretation of dreams, oracular supplications addressed to the ancestors, and oral communication in the Quechua language. With the arrival of Pizarro, two further channels for communication intervene: the Spanish language and alphabetic script. The Inkas' inability not only to decipher the messages encoded in these alien media, but also to penetrate meanings inscribed in media familiar to them, is symptomatic of their loss of control over their world. Thus, the demise of their semiotic and communicative systems, and the demise of their social cohesion and political power, can be seen to be mutually entailing.

The conditions of production of the play

Any reading of the play must needs take into account its present-day conditions of production. Nowadays the *Tragedia* belongs mainly to urban *mestizo* popular tradition and performers are bilingual speakers of Quechua and Spanish. If we view the play as an expression of 'colonised identity', such as is displayed in many social contexts in the Andes today, this makes sense. Judged from a present-day perspective, the *Tragedia* is shot through with idealised conceptualisations of the Inka empire, the glorified attributes of the Inka Atahuallpa, and the supposed devastating effect on the native Andean populations of the arrival of the Spanish, their language, technologies, and legal, bureaucratic and ecclesiastical institutions. If we are to understand the meanings that the play has for actors and spectators in the Andes at the beginning of the twenty-first century, we need to recognise these images for what they are: constructs of a colonised, largely *mestizo*, discourse which builds upon an imagined 'golden' Inka past while simultaneously locating itself firmly within the modernising nation with its (today equally reinvented) heritage from Spain.[13]

The language of Lara's text

Jesús Lara's Quechua in the 1989 edition of the *Tragedia* is the most elaborated and lexically rich of all the published versions of the play that I have been able to consult. To my knowledge, it is the only extant script that contains no Spanish at all (cf. Beyersdorff 1998). The speech of the Spaniards is represented by the mere movement of the actors' lips; no sound emerges, and their meaning is translated into Quechua for the benefit of the Inka camp by the interpreter Felipillo. More than this, the Bolivian *quechuista* (by his own admission) made editorial amendments to the text which included modifications to the language.

In order to judge the linguistic attributes of the text, several crucial factors need to be taken into account. Firstly, Lara's is most probably a literary creation, bearing little relationship to living theatrical performances. In the latter, as previously noted, oral tradition and written scripts are intertwined as media for the production and reproduction of different versions of the play. The disconnection of Lara's text from the oral medium means that its language differs blatantly from the speech that would occur in live performances in Northern Potosí, where Quechua and Spanish (and, indeed, Aymara) co-exist. Beyersdorff (1998) makes a convincing case for the exclusively literary genesis of Lara's *Tragedia* by comparing it with scripts more closely embedded in oral production, in all of which the Spanish language is also present.

Secondly, through his editorial activity, Lara was applying certain purist, indigenist criteria typical of his class and of his day. Such *indigenista* literary practices have manifested themselves at various times and places in Andean cultural history; they are part of a bilingual, *mestizo*, elite discourse, whose prime exponent in the present is the *Academia Mayor de la Lengua Quechua* in Cusco. Lara tells us that he altered the spelling of the original document in the process of copying it out by hand (its owner would not permit photocopying), opting for the alphabet agreed by the *Congreso Indigenista de La Paz* (Lara 1989: 24) with which he was more familiar. He refers to the lan-

---

[13] The concept of 'colonised identity' is developed by Tom Abercrombie in his studies of fiestas, ritual, costume and gender relations in Bolivia, whereby he highlights the importance of *cholo* (*mestizo*) identity as an ever-expanding cultural field that absorbs and reconstructs dichotomic 'indian' and *criollo* positions (Abercrombie 1992: 286). Abercrombie comments on performances of the *Tragedia* that take place in Oruro City during Carnival. He sees Oru+eños' interpretations of the play as dichotomising 'indian' and 'Spanish' positions, drawing participants into what he describes as a 'colonial ontogenesis' in dramatised form (1992: 286, 302). These performances suggest an idealised attempt to reconstruct dichotomies which, in real terms, have been continually challenged and transformed into blended cultural positions, as part of the ongoing colonial process. To reiterate, such idealisation suggests an eminently *mestizo* cultural strategy.

guage of the Chayanta manuscript as 'antiguo cuzqueño . . . casi puro' ('ancient Cusqueñan . . . almost pure') by comparison with that of two other manuscripts that came his way (those of San Pedro and Santa Lucía), whose Quechua he describes as 'sensiblemente deformado, casi como el que se usa actualmente entre la población mestiza boliviana' ('clearly deformed, almost like that currently spoken by Bolivian *mestizos*') (1989: 25).[14] These highly evaluative statements (cf. the words *puro* and *deformado*) surely indicate that Lara's approach to editing the text for publication was influenced by purist ideology.

It is thus probable that the Quechua of Lara's edition has been purged of the hispanisms characteristic of contemporary spoken Bolivian Quechua, and adjusted to fit a more standard, 'Cusco-like' image of the language according to Lara's criteria. This idealisation of the language itself can be viewed as concomitant with the idealised cultural images contained in the play: linguistic form and cultural message are mutually reinforcing.

So far, my discussion of likely influences upon the language of the text has taken at face value Lara's own account of its conditions of production: that the manuscript bearing the date 1871 was offered to him by an admirer of his work whom he met fortuitously in a library in La Paz in 1955, and that he copied it out by hand by himself (Lara 1989: 22–23). However, this story rather confounds our attempts to contextualise the ideology expressed in the play. In fact, the ostensible date of the Chayanta manuscript suggests that its authorship predates the indigenism of the first half of the twentieth century which Lara articulated in much of his literary work. In other words, notwithstanding Lara's editorial amendments, there appears to be a certain 'ideological implausibility' in the message of the play, if we take it as indeed a re-copying of a manuscript supposedly authored some eighty years previously. This implausibility demands that my earlier proposition that the text's 'linguistic form and cultural message are mutually reinforcing' be re-examined, and that other possible influences on the text's conditions of production also be considered.[15]

César Itier has developed an innovative theory as to the origins of this text (Itier 2000). His aim is to take issue with Lara's assertion that the nineteenth-century Chayanta manuscript goes back at least as far as the early colonial period, and that it was penned by an indigenous person, as Lara proposes:

[14] This comment is of interest in relation to the difference between the 'Oruro' and 'Chayanta' cycles of the play as identified by Beyersdorff: the Oruro cycle, containing versions performed in Cochabamba and the valleys of Northern Potosí, is bilingual (the Spanish represented as speaking the European language, the Inkas the Andean one); the Chayanta cycle, which belongs to the highlands, and of which Lara's text is a literary offshoot, is distinguished by its exclusive use of Quechua (Beyersdorff 1998: 193).

[15] I am grateful to Henry Stobart for drawing my attention to the contextual problem I am discussing here; and to César Itier for allowing me access to his unpublished work, which provides us with a possible solution, and which I now examine.

[No] es posible ya vacilar en deducir que el autor de la obra tuvo que ser inne-
gablemente indígena. En efecto, sólo un autor indígena pudo reflejar de manera
tan portentosa el funesto significado de la presencia de los españoles para
Atawallpa y para el pueblo entero del Tawantinsuyu . . .

[We] can no longer hesitate to deduce that the author of the work was un-
deniably indigenous. In fact, only an indigenous author could ever give such a
portentous portrayal of the gloomy significance of the presence of the Spaniards
for Atahuallpa and all the people of the Tawantinsuyu . . .
(Lara 1989: 47)

Itier uses philological analysis to demonstrate that, in fact, far from being a
copy of an earlier manuscript which might in turn have derived from an
indian author of colonial times, the *Tragedia* was actually written in the mid-
twentieth century by Lara himself. Far from being 'ancient Cusqueñan',
Itier shows that Lara's Quechua has many features of the modern Bolivian
variety of the language that Lara would have known at first hand (e.g. use of
the tripartite genitive *-pa*, *-paq*, *-pata*, instead of *-pa* and *-paq*, among other
traits) (2000: 4–6). He identifies the purisms in the text, many of which are
neologisms deriving from Spanish colonial efforts to impose new religious
and legal concepts by coining terms in Quechua (e.g. *pampachay*, 'forgive-
ness'; *janajpacha*, 'heaven'; *qhispiy simi*, 'Bible') (2000: 7). Perhaps the most
convincing philological evidence in support of this thesis is the influence of
Spanish syntax on Lara's Quechua, which Itier finds to be pervasive, and to
far exceed the kind of syntactic interference common in the spoken
Quechua of bilinguals in Bolivia. The construction *ama chay uyata churay-
chu*, which appears to be a syntactic calque of *no pongas esa cara* ('don't make
that face'), is an example of the kind of influence he discusses (Itier 2000:
8, citing Lara 1989: 108).

In reaching the conclusion that, despite his assertion to the contrary, Lara
was actually the author rather than the editor of the *Tragedia*, Itier is careful
to point out that this should not be judged as a moral shortcoming on Lara's
part. On the contrary, such literary 'falsification' had intellectual currency
in an era of indigenist cultural militancy, where academic concerns with
'authenticity' had little part to play. Lara's aim would have been to vindicate
the legitimacy of 'Inka literature', to which end a little ruse such as Itier proposes occurred can be seen as quite justifiable. Itier summarises his argument as follows:

A través de sus novelas y sus ensayos, Lara llevaba a cabo un combate ideológico,
casi solitario en Bolivia, dentro del cual la crítica de las fuentes, la dialectología,
la lingüística histórica y el cuestionamiento de los conocimientos establecidos
no tenían pertinencia alguna. Defendió así denodadamente la 'incanidad' de
cuanto texto quechua de autor desconocido cayera a sus manos . . .

Through his novels and essays, Lara conducted an almost solitary ideological
struggle in Bolivia, within which [such academic practices as] the critique of

sources, dialectology, historical linguistics, and the questioning of established scholarship had no place. He thus fervently defended the 'incan' credentials of any anonymous Quechua text which came his way . . . (Itier 2000: 17)

Itier's theory is plausible. However, a considered examination of his evidence is beyond the scope of this essay.[16] For present purposes, his study usefully highlights the enigmatic status of this text as an expression of 'knowledge' about Andean history, from the dual point of view of its linguistic form and its ideological content. However, the issue of authorship, which preoccupies Itier, is crucially distinct from the issue of ownership, and it is ownership that should perhaps most concern us here. A study of Lara's *Tragedia* leads us to ask questions about the ownership of knowledge, the ownership of language, and the ownership of history itself, relative to the Andean case.

The above discussion has led us to no hard and fast conclusions regarding either the authorship or the cultural ownership of the *Tragedia* text. The questions it raises help us to trace the imprint of the colonisation of knowledge in the cultural sphere, providing a necessarily ambiguous backdrop to our application of the concepts of 'knowledge' and 'learning' to the text, which now follows.

The vocabulary of knowing and learning in the Tragedia

'Knowledge' and 'learning' in the *Tragedia* can be examined at two distinct levels: firstly, the vocabulary the play uses for referring to cognitive skills and procedures, as the protagonists attempt to understand and control events; secondly, the level of content, that is, the understanding of history that the play constructs as it unfolds. As I have noted above, language (vocabulary) and knowledge (here, constructs of history) are mutually reinforcing. Their overall status, as articulated in this enigmatic text, defies categorical definition. In this section, I shall examine the Quechua lexicon of knowledge and learning to be found in the text. In the subsequent section, I shall consider the nature of this source as evidence of the colonisation of knowledge in the Andes.

The play opens with Atahuallpa reporting to the Inka princesses on two troublesome dreams he has had, the meaning of which he cannot comprehend; he describes his emotional state as one of extreme sorrow and anguish, and his mental condition as a loss of reason:[17]

---

[16] Itier's proposition may prove controversial in Bolivia, perhaps for ideological reasons not unlike those that gave rise to the *Tragedia*'s composition in the first place. While of a different order, being couched in sound academic arguments, Itier's study is also of interest in the context of a tradition of alleged literary 'falsifications' in Andean intellectual life, recently coming to light. I allude to the recent controversy over the authorship of Guaman Poma's *Nueva Corónica y Buen Gobierno*, which some Italian scholars are claiming to be a Jesuit 'invention' (cf. Ossio 2000); in a different vein, such fictions (whether real or otherwise) bring to mind the literary ploys of Jorge Luis Borges.

[17] The words of interest for the present discussion are marked in italics.

i)   nanaq *llakiy*pimin sunquy   my heart is in painful *sorrow*
       ukhuymin llaqllapayasqa   my emotions are torn apart
       *yuyay*niymin chinkasqanña   my *reason* is lost

       (Lara 1989: 52)

The source of the dream visions is referred to as a *wak'a*. This visionary
experience and Atahuallpa's attempts to apply reason (*yuyay*) in order to
understand it are described in the following passage, containing a number
of verbs referring to the cognitive processes and communicative strategies
by which knowing comes into being:

ii)   uj *wak'a* yanatan *taphya*wan   a *huaca* has *foretold* me a black *omen*
       iskay kutipiñan *layqa*wan   twice it has *cast its spell* on me;
       *muspay*niypi *rikuchi*wan   it has *revealed* to me in my *dream*
       uj *yuyay* p'itiytapuni   *thoughts* that are torn apart,
       mana *rikuy* atinata   that cannot be understood by *looking*,
       mana *rimariy* atinata   that cannot be expressed in *speech*.
       *Chiqa*punichari kanman   might it be *true* indeed
       awqa q'illay runakuna   that enemies clad in iron
       jallp'anchiqman jamunanku   are coming to our land?

       (Lara 1989:54)

As the passage describes, the thoughts revealed in the dream are discon-
nected, impossible to process by the normal channels of thinking (*yuyay*)
and looking (*rikuy*) and impossible to express comprehensibly by speaking
(*rimariy*). The words *taphya* ('omen') and *layqa-* ('cast a spell') convey the
idea that some malevolent force is at work, difficult to control by conscious
means. In the last three lines the question is posed whether what is but dimly
envisioned at this point in the action (the approach of the iron-clad invaders)
will in fact turn out to be reality (*chiqa*). As the play unfolds we follow the
protagonists' attempts to determine the answer to this question. The notion
of truth (*chiqa* literally means 'straight') is tested at various points throughout the play and even in the closing stages the reality of what is happening
is not categorically asserted. On p. 120 Challkuchima queries it as follows:

iii)   *Chiqa*punichus awqa sunk'a   Has it really turned out *true* that
       runakuna kawsayniykita   the bearded enemies will bring
       p'uchukasunqanku kasqa?   your life to an end?

and Atahuallpa queries the existential status of events until it is too late:

iv)   imapitaq rikukunchiq   what is this situation we are in?
       *sut'*ichu *muspay*chu kayqa   is this *reality* or a *dream*?

       (Lara 1989: 122)

   Dreams (*musquy*) and visions (*muspay*) are the principal channels through
which information is being encoded, requiring specialist intervention in
order for the clarity (*sut'i*) of their message to be revealed. In the opening

sequence, Atahuallpa calls upon the shaman Waylla Wisa to dream his dreams for him. Perhaps, with his visionary powers, the wise man might penetrate their message:

v) Waylla Wisa Inka riy
    *puñu*rimuy asllallata
    chay quri wasiyki ukhupi
    icha ari *musquy*niykipi
    *muspay*niyta *sut'icha*waq

    Inka Waylla Wisa go
    and *sleep* a little bit
    in your golden chamber
    perhaps in your *dream*
    you may *clarify* the meaning of my
        vision

(Lara 1989: 58)

Here, three different verbs designate increasing degrees of visionary perception to be attained through slumber: *puñuy*, 'sleep', the initial step necessary for *musquy*, 'dream', to occur, and *muspay*, 'hallucinate', potentially the most revealing level of visionary experience.[18] *Muspay* is the term used for any kind of trance state: it could also be induced by drugs or alcohol – a kind of delirium. Atahuallpa finds himself in the more heightened state of visionary awareness (*muspay*), but impotent to deal with it, dependent on a specialist intermediary to attempt interpretation.[19]

Yet even Waylla Wisa's powers are inadequate to the task. On successive occasions he dreams and is awakened by different members of the Inka's entourage, and each time the visions become a little clearer, but the full import of their message remains beyond reach. The shaman's powers also include the capacity to speak with the mountains (cf. Stobart in this

---

[18] *Muspay* and *musquy* may be etymologically related to *musyay*, meaning 'to learn by auditory means' in the Quechua I dialect I studied in Huamalíes, Peru. If we take the first syllable to be a cognate of the verb suffix -*mu*- marking centripetal direction of the action (cf. Adelaar 1997), we can suggest a semantic content in common for the three verbs, characterisable as 'movement (of cognitive realisation in this case) towards the subject'.

[19] The role of dreams in the play echoes what we know about the divinatory function of dreams in the pre-Hispanic period, as reported by Catholic churchmen such as Arriaga and Hernández Príncipe in early Colonial sources. They refer to the *ministros soñadores*, professional dreamers whose task it was to divine the best course of action for the future by looking into dreams; clearly Waylla Wisa's role is an allusion to this ancient practice. As Bruce Mannheim has pointed out, dreams were recognised by the colonial authorities to be a powerful medium for the expression of pre-Christian religious belief, to such an extent that questions about dreams were included in Catholic priests' confessional manuals of the period, in the hope of eradicating the practice (Mannheim 1987); and Frank Salomon has proposed that the dream sequence experienced by Don Cristóbal Choquecaxa, described in Chapter 21 of the Huarochirí manuscript, illustrates the capacity of dreams to allow for the subconscious persistence of non-Christian religious ideologies, suppressed by would-be converts such as Choquecaxa in their waking hours. In Salomon's interpretation, dream sequences were battlegrounds where conflicting cultural loyalties showed themselves to be ultimately irreconcilable (Salomon 1992). Discussion of the role of dreams and prophecies in ancient Inka religion is also to be found in MacCormack 1991: 285–312, further confirming the roots of the *Tragedia* in historical traditions.

volume), with the *chullpa* ancestors (cf. Platt 1997), and to read the signs in the landscape with the aid of the mythical *anutara* beast, a kind of animal soul companion also with visionary powers. In this sequence Waylla Wisa speaks to the *anutara*:

vi)   Sinchiq munasqay *anutara*   Beloved *anutara*
       [. . .]   [. . .]
       allin karuntan *riku*nki,   you who *see* far into the distance
       *qhawa*chiway ñawiykiwan   make me *look* with your eyes.
       Imaraykuchus *yuy*ani   Why is it that I *think*
       kayman q'iwikamusqankuta   that towards this place are
       mana riqsisqa awqakuna   wending their way *unrecognisable*
                                      enemies
       mana uyarisqa takiywan   with songs *unheard* before
       muyu qarata kunpaspa   beating on great drumskins
       q'illay qinata phukuspa   and blowing on iron flutes

       (Lara 1989: 64)

Here the signs to be read take the form of the invaders' distinguishing traits: their songs and musical instruments. But the usual interpretive techniques – auditory (*uyari*-, 'listen') and visual (*riqsi*-, 'recognise'; *qhawa*-, 'look'; *riku*-, 'see') – are inadequate to deal with the cultural unknown. Applying the methods of *qhawa*- and *riku*-, the shaman with his animal helper looks out over the landscape, reading it like a giant script, but in vain:

vii)   Kayniqta *qhawa*riqtiyri   If I *look* in this direction
       manataq imapas kanchu   there is nothing there
       jaqayniqta *qhawa*rini   I *look* over yonder
       manallataq imapas kanchu   and there is nothing there either
       jaqay waqniqta *qhawa*rini   I *look* to that other side
       manapuni imapas kanchu   and there is nothing whatsoever there
       tukuyninniqtapas *qhawa*ni   I *look* around in all directions
       mana imapas *riku*nchu   and nothing *reveals itself*

       (Lara 1989: 64)

When face-to-face contact with Pizarro and his men is finally made, two further media of communication come into play: a written document handed to the Inkas by the Spaniards, and the Spanish language. The Inkas attempt to decipher the words on the parchment (perhaps an allusion to the *Requerimiento*) using tried and tested decoding techniques appropriate for the media of communication with which they are more familar. Again, Waylla Wisa takes the lead. Notice how in its very poetic structure as well as in the methods of decipherment used, this speech echoes the earlier efforts made by the shaman to read the landscape (Extract vii):

viii)   Ima *nin*chus ari kaypiqa   What does it *say* here
       mana sina jayk'aq pachapas   maybe I shall never

ñuqa *yacha*yta atisaqchu.	be able *to know*.
Kay chirunmanta *qhawa*sqa	*Looked at* from this angle
watwaq sisiman riqch'akun.	it looks like an ants' nest.
Kay waq chirunmanta *qhawa*sqa	*Looked at* from this other angle
chay mayu pata ch'aranpi	it *looks* just the same as
phichiwkunaq chakinpa	the *traces* of birds' feet
*unanchasqa*n kikillan.	on a muddy river bank.
Kayniqmanta *qhawa*risqa	*Looked at* from this direction
*riqch'aku*n ura umayuq,	it *resembles* deer
pata chakiyuq tarukakunaman.	standing on their heads.
Jinallatan *qhawa*qtinchiqri	And if we *look at* it just like this
ura umayuq llamakuna jina	it is identical to upside down llamas
tarukakunaq waqran kikin.	with deer horns.
Pin kayta *unancha*q kasqa.	Who could even *decipher* this.
Mana mana atiymanchu	I should not be able
*unancha*yta, apullay.	to *interpret* it, my lord.

(Lara 1989: 78)

The verb *yachay* appears in this extract, characterising Waylla Wisa's overall aim of achieving knowledge. In addition to the technique of *qhawa-*, the term *unancha-* appears in Extract viii, as it does repeatedly throughout the text. This term has a complex semantic range which deserves particular comment. *Unanchay* means, on the one hand, 'to make a sign': the footprints of birds in the mud are described as *unanchasqa* ('stamped', 'made into a sign'); elsewhere in the play, the insignia of his rank borne by Atahuallpa (the two golden serpents, his golden headdress, golden club and golden sling) are referred to as *unancha*. On the other hand, *unanchay* means 'to interpret a sign' ('mana atiymanchu unanchayta', 'I should not be able to interpret it' says Waylla Wisa in Extract viii). González Holguín (1952: 355) also records this double sided meaning of the verb: 'unanchani. Hazer señales entender, considerar, traçar' ('make signs, understand, consider, trace'). That a single verb can convey both 'to mean' and 'to interpret meaning' suggests to me a two-way relationship between signified and signifier at work in the semantics of the word, indicative in turn of a particular conceptualisation of the relationship between language and knowledge as expressed in the lexicon of the Quechua language.[20]

In other places in the text, the verb *watuy* (cf. the Introduction and Stobart in this volume) alternates freely with *unanchay* in the sense of 'enquire', 'seek out meaning', 'interpret'. In Extract ix Challkuchima makes synonymous use of *watuy* and *unanchay* as he ponders the indecipherable 'scratchings':

[20] Frank Salomon (1982) offered early interpretation of this term, alongside cognate lexical items such as *hamutay* and *yachay* as they appear in the colonial Quechua prayers of Santacruz Pachacuti Yamqui; Regina Harrison has also drawn attention to the interest of *unanchay*, in her extensive discussions of the cognitive processes, related to Viracocha's primordial creative acts, depicted in these prayers (Harrison 1982; 1989: 80); cf. Itier 1993, discussed above.

ix)   Kayri ima yanachawan   With what black substance
      Llimp'isqataj, t'ijtusqataj.   Is this *painted* and *scratched?*
      Manan *watuy*ta atiymanchu.   I am not able to *decipher* it.
      Apay ari Khiskhis Inka   Do take it to Inka Khiskhis,
      sispa wauqechanchijpaman.   Our close brother.
      Ichapas pay *unancha*nman.   Perhaps he could *interpret* it.

(Lara 1989: 82)

These extracts contain but a sample of the full range of vocabulary expressing the strategies of cognition and communication brought to bear by the
protagonists as they struggle to realise the meaning of the events overtaking them. Table 1 summarises this lexicon in such a way as to show the progressive nature of the plot. Reading the columns of Table 1 from left to
right, we see how the action gradually moves from an initial state of affairs
in which the Inkas have life (*kawsay*), power (*qhapaq kay*), and ability to
control their world (*kamay, atiy*), through the failure of their familiar strategies for communication and decipherment, to a final outcome in which
the inevitablity of death (*wañuy*) and demise (*p'uchuy*) becomes clear. The
lexicon referring to the different cognitive and communicative channels
through which knowledge is processed is given in Column II; the media that
encode this knowledge (signs in nature, emotions, dreams, music, speech,
writing, and the *unancha* symbols) are summarised in Column III; the
different agents who attempt interpretation of the signs are assigned to
Column IV; the techniques these agents use for decoding the messages
(visual, visionary and auditory) are found in Column V. The final outcome
(realisation of reality), summarised in Column VI, is seen to be characterised as death and expiry on the one hand, yet with the promise of survival
in memory (*yuyaypi kawsay*) on the other. The disappearance of the Inkas
under the ground (*yaykupuy*; a common theme of many Andean myths) is
the guarantee of their hidden yet lasting influence from the past into the
present and the future.

Colonisation of knowledge? The nature of the source

The text of Lara's version of the *Tragedia* proves to be a rather enigmatic
source through which to access the Quechua lexicon of learning and
knowing. Unlike the language of other scripts that have come to scholarly
attention, whether in performance, in manuscript form, or in printed publications, the 'purified' Quechua unique to Lara's text suffices to suggest that
it is a literary artifice, far removed from the living dialogue performed by
Quechua-Spanish bilinguals in Bolivia today. Furthermore, in theatrical
practice, scripts are the product of collective authorship and subject to
ongoing modifications in use, as they move back and forth between composition and performance at the hands of actors and directors (Beyersdorff

1998: 228–29).[21] By contrast, Beyersdorff suggests, both Lara and the presumed scribe of the 1871 Chayanta manuscript most probably had publication rather than performance in mind when they produced their texts (1998: 229–30).[22]

If it is thus the case that this text does not properly reflect the living tradition, what status can we attribute to its vocabulary, and the concepts underpinning this vocabulary, with relation to ideas about learning and knowing? Whose voice do they represent? In order to consider this question, we need firstly to address Lara's motivation in creating this literary product, deliberately couched in a language far removed from the everyday speech of Bolivian Quechua-Spanish bilinguals. On linguistic grounds alone, we might ask how far it reveals the latter's own conceptualisations of knowledge and history, or rather those of its indigenist editor or author.

Scholars disagree as to the underlying social function of this dramaturgical tradition. Burga, working on the dance dramas of Lima and Cajatambo provinces (Peru), sees it as an expression of indigenous resistance to conquest, variously leading to rebellion or compromise depending on the degree of *mestizaje* of the performers involved (Burga 1988). Saignes disagrees with Burga's thesis, suggesting that this form of drama arose as part of the Jesuit tradition of using theatre for evangelisation purposes, thus as a means to confirm rather than challenge the indian condition of 'vanquished' people, and, in the process, to consolidate alliances between Jesuit orders and local caciques in the early colonial period. Most importantly for Saignes, the Atahuallpa play provides an irrevocably *mestizo* – rather than 'indian' – version of Andean history, bound up with emerging new social identities under the colonial order (Saignes 1990 *passim*). Beyersdorff, drawing on archival research, reaches similar conclusions to Saignes, and elaborates upon the use made of ecclesiastical drama as a doctrinal tool by the clergy (1998: 169–70).

My analysis of the text, above, brought out the way in which the Spanish Conquest is depicted, from the point of view of the Inkas, as an event gradually to be apprehended, interpreted and understood, through a series of communicative and interpretive strategies as the plot unfolds. The quest for *yachay* can be seen as processual: an evolving and irreversible transformation in the Inkas' historical consciousness and worldview. The European invasion of the Andes is presented in this literary rendition as a complete semiotic incompatibility between cultures. And yet we have to read this

---

[21] Beyersdorff's evidence coincides with my own, in relation to the Huamalíes (Huánuco, Peru) and San Pedro (Northern Potosí, Bolivia) traditions, arising from conversations I had with erstwhile performers.

[22] Beyersdorff surmises that the Bolivian priest Carlos Felipe Beltrán may have had a hand in setting the Chayanta manuscript down in cohesive literary form, based on pre-existing scripts, or parts of scripts, which would have come into his possession via performers of the day (1998: 190–91, and citing Rivet and Rodríguez 1947).

(I) Initial state of affairs	(II) Communicative channel	(III) Signs to be read	(IV) Agents	(V) Interpretive techniques	(VI) Outcome
	YUYAY think	*Nature disturbed* YANA black PUKA red	Inkas	TAPUY ask	CHIQA true
	ÑIY say		Spaniards	WATUY enquire, decipher	SUT'I reality, clarity
KAWSAY life	WILLAY tell	*Emotions disturbed* LLAKIY sorrow PHUTIY grief		UYARIY listen	
	RIMARIY speak		Waylla Wisa PUÑUJ APU sleeper lord WILLAJ UMU soothsayer	QHAWAY look	WAÑUY death
	RIKUY see RIKUKUY reveal self	*dream images* AUQA Q'ILLAY RUNA iron-clad enemies	JAMAUT'ANCHIJ our wiseman LAYQA RUNA sorcerer	RIQSIY recognise	
	RIKUCHIY show				
QHAPAQ KAY power	RIQCH'AY appear	PUKA SUNK'A RUNA red-bearded men		SUT'ICHAY clarify	P'UCHUY expiry
	THAPYAY foretell	MANA RIQSISQA unrecognisable	ANUTARA animal with visionary powers		
	LAYQAY cast spell				
KAMAY animation		*Music* MANA UYARISQA unheard before			
	PUÑUY sleep MUSQUY dream MUSPAY hallucinate		FELIPILLO interpreter	YACHAY know	YAYKUPUY enter ground

ATIY ability to act

Speech
ILLAPAJ RIMAY
thunderous language
(of Spaniards)
MANA CHAYAY
half cooked (of Inkas)
THUPA SIMI
ornate language (of Inkas)
QASI SIMI
empty words (of Inkas)

of CHULLPA ancestors

of mountains

of chorus

of FELIPILLO interpreter

Dumbness
UPA
'dumb' state of each side
for the other

ÑUSTAS
chorus of princesses
comment on past
and predict future

YUYAYPI
KAWSAY
live in memory

MANA
QUNQAY
remembrance
(lit. not to forget)

QILLQAY
inscribe, write

Writing
CHHALLA maize leaf

CH'AJCHUSQA sprinkled

T'IJTUSQA scratched
LLIMP'ISQA painted

UNANCHA insignia of
Inka power (golden serpents,
mace, sling, anutara beast)

UNANCHAY
make signs

UNANCHAY
interpret signs

Table 1. The vocabulary of knowing and learning in Jesús Lara's *Tragedia del fin de Atawallpa*.

account with a degree of deconstructive cynicism, for it is, after all, the result of Lara's remodelling. The sequence in which Waylla Wisa attempts to read the parchment (Extract viii above) is an example of the kind of creativity I have in mind: wonderment at the marvels of European alphabetic script is perhaps imputed to the indigenous population in this literary 'reinvention' of the moment of conquest in such a way, whether consciously intended or not, as to stress European superiority (cf. Seed 1991).

That this text is a literary artifice only distantly related to actual dramatised performances, as advanced by Beyersdorff, is likely; that it is an artifice historically elaborated by the Jesuit priesthood out of doctrinal motivations, as surmised by Saignes, is also possible; equally plausible, and a subject for future debate, is Itier's thesis that Lara was its author, and the 'Chayanta manuscript' a fiction. Nor are these three proposals mutually incompatible. If Lara does prove to have been the instrumental author of this particular version of the play, his composition nonetheless has its intellectual roots in an existing popular theatrical tradition, which he doubtless knew at first hand.

An analysis of the language of the play designed to inform a study of the Quechua lexicon of knowledge, such as I have offered here, needs to be appraised with these alternative and yet overlapping views in mind. If indeed the text in itself is an 'impossible chronicle', to borrow an apt concept of Salomon's (1982), this raises the question of whether the vocabulary of knowing, learning and understanding that it contains is in fact an 'impossible lexicon'. Yet perhaps the apparent artificialities of speaking about 'knowing' in this particular language – Quechua – in relation to this particular subject matter – the Spanish overthrow of the Inkas – under this particular editorship (authorship?) – that of the indigenist Jesús Lara – is the crux of what the colonisation of historical knowledge in the Andes is all about. As I suggested at the outset, in spite of, or perhaps because of, the questions it raises about cultural 'ownership', Lara's text is thought-provoking evidence of such colonisation. Herein lie the roots of its 'impossibility': while it portrays the Inkas as losing the communicative power to produce their own historical knowledge, as a *mestizo* ('colonised') construct of Andean history, it is a refracted tale whose teller's position is enigmatic, and in which categorical 'knowledge' of history is inexorably undermined.

Acknowledgments

I am grateful to my co-editor, Henry Stobart, for detailed critiques of earlier drafts of this work; to the anonymous LUP reviewers for their helpful criticism; to Margot Beyersdorff for the gift of a copy of her book (Beyersdorff 1998); and to César Itier for kindly affording me a copy of a forthcoming publication. All of these helped me to shape the chapter into its present form; shortcomings remain my own responsibility.

References

Abercrombie, Thomas. 1992. 'La fiesta del carnaval postcolonial en Oruro: clase, etnicidad y nacionalismo en la danza folklórica'. *Revista Andina* 10(2): 279–325.

Adelaar, Willem. 1997. 'Spatial Reference and Speaker Orientation in Early Colonial Quechua'. In Howard-Malverde (ed.): 135–48.

Balmori, Clemente H. 1955. *La conquista de los españoles*. Tucumán: Universidad Nacional de Tucumán.

Beyersdorff, Margot. 1993. 'La "puesta en texto" del primer drama indohispano en los Andes'. *Revista de Crítica Literaria Latinoamericana* 19(37): 195–221.

——, 1998. *Historia y drama ritual en los Andes bolivianos (siglos XVI–XX)*. La Paz: Plural Editores/UMSA.

Burga, Manuel. 1988. *Nacimiento de una utopía*. Lima: Instituto de Apoyo Agrario.

Chang-Rodríguez, Raquel. 1999. *Hidden Messages: Representation and Resistance in Andean Colonial Drama*. Lewisburg: Bucknell University Press/London: Associated University Presses.

Cornejo Polar, Antonio. 1994. 'El comienzo de la heterogeneidad en las literaturas andinas: voz y letra en el "diálogo" de Cajamarca'. In *Escribir en el aire. Ensayo sobre la heterogeneidad socio-cultural en las literaturas andinas*. Lima: Editorial Horizonte: 25–89.

de la Cadena, Marisol. 1998. 'Silent Racism and Intellectual Superiority in Peru'. *Bulletin of Latin American Research* 17(2): 143–64.

——, 2000. *Indigenous Mestizos: The Politics of Race and Culture in Cuzco, Peru, 1919–1991*. Durham, NC, and London: Duke University Press.

Flores Galindo, Alberto. 1988. *Buscando un inca*. Lima: Editorial Horizonte.

González Carre, Enrique, and F. Rivera Pineda. 1982. 'La muerte del Inca en Santa Ana de Tusi'. *Bulletin de l'Institut Français d'Etudes Andines* 11(1–2): 19–36.

González Holguín, Diego de. 1952 [1st edn 1608]. *Vocabulario de la lengua general de todo el Perú llamada qquichua o del Inca*. Ed. Raúl Porras Barrenechea. Lima: Universidad Nacional Mayor de San Marcos.

Harrison, Regina. 1982. 'Modes of Discourse: The "Relación de antigüedades deste reyno del Pirú" by Joan de Santacruz Pachacuti Yamqui Salcamaygua'. In Rolena Adorno (ed.), *From Oral to Written Expression: Native Andean Chronicles of the Early Colonial Period*. Latin American Series, No. 4. Syracuse, NY: Syracuse University, Maxwell School of Citizenship and Public Affairs: 65–99.

——, 1989. *Signs, Songs and Memory in the Andes: Translating Quechua Language and Culture*. Austin: University of Texas Press.

Howard-Malverde, Rosaleen. 1990a. '"Upa": la conceptualisation de la parole et du silence dans la construction de l'identité quechua'. *Journal de la Société des Américanistes* 76: 105–20.

——, 1990b. *The Speaking of History: 'Willapaakushayki' or Quechua Ways of Telling the Past*. London: University of London Institute of Latin American Studies, Research Papers No. 21.

——, 1998. '"Grasping Awareness": Mother-Tongue Literacy for Quechua Speaking Women in Highland Bolivia'. *International Journal of Educational Development* 18(3): 181–96.

Howard-Malverde, Rosaleen, and Andrew Canessa. 1995. 'The School in the Quechua and Aymara Communities of Highland Bolivia'. *International Journal of Educational Development* 15(3): 231–43.

Howard-Malverde, Rosaleen (ed.). 1997. *Creating Context in Andean Cultures.* Oxford/New York: Oxford University Press.

Husson, Jean-Philippe. 1997. *Une survivance du théâtre des Incas: le cycle dramatique de la mort d'Atawallpa.* Doctoral thesis, Université de la Sorbonne Nouvelle–Paris III.

Itier, César. 1993. 'Estudio y comentario lingüístico'. In P. Duviols and C. Itier (eds.), *Joan de Santa Cruz Pachacuti Yamqui Salcamaygua, Relación de antigüedades deste reyno del Piru.* Cusco: Institut Français d'Etudes Andines/Centro Bartolomé de las Casas: 127–78.

——, 2000. '¿Visión de los vencidos o falsificación? Datación y autoría de la "Tragedia de la muerte de Atahuallpa"'. *Bulletin de l'Institut Français d'Etudes Audines* 30(1): 103–21.

Kapsoli, Wilfredo. 1985. 'La muerte del rey inca en las danzas populares y la relación de Pomabamba'. *Tierra Adentro* 3: 139–76.

Lara, Jesús. 1989 [1st edn 1957]. *Tragedia del fin de Atawallpa. Atau Wallpaj p'uchukakuyninpa wankan.* Cochabamba: Los Amigos del Libro.

MacCormack, Sabine. 1991. *Religion in the Andes: Vision and Imagination in Early Colonial Peru.* Princeton: Princeton University Press.

Mannheim, Bruce. 1987. 'A Semiotic of Andean Dreams'. In Barbara Tedlock (ed.), *Dreaming: Anthropological and Psychological Interpretations.* Cambridge: Cambridge University Press: 132–53.

Meneses, Teodoro. 1985. 'Presentación en forma reiterativa del drama quechua "La muerte de Atahuallpa"'. *Revista Andina* 3(2): 499–507.

Millones, Luis. 1988. *El Inca por la Coya. Historia de un drama popular en los Andes peruanos.* Lima: Fundación Friedrich Ebert.

——, 1992. *Actores de altura. Ensayos sobre el teatro popular andino.* Lima: Editorial Horizonte.

Montoya, Rodrigo. 1993. 'El teatro quechua como lugar de reflexión sobre la historia y la política'. *Revista de Crítica Literaria Latinoamericana* 19(37): 223–41.

Ossio, Juan. 2000. 'Nota sobre el Coloquio Internacional "Guaman Poma de Ayala y Blas Valera: tradición andina e historia colonial". Instituto Italo Latinoamericano Roma, 29–30 de setiembre de 1999'. *Colonial Latin American Review* 9(1): 113–16.

Platt, Tristan. 1997. 'The Sound of Light: Emergent Communication through Quechua Shamanic Dialogue'. In Howard-Malverde (ed.): 196–226.

Rivet, Paul, and Odile Rodríguez. 1947. 'Un apôtre bolivien: Carlos Felipe Beltrán'. *Actes du XXVIII Congrès des Américanistes*: 658–96.

Saignes, Thierry. 1990. 'Es posible una historia "chola" del Perú?', *Allpanchis* 35–36: 635–57.

Salomon, Frank. 1982. 'Chronicles of the Impossible: Notes on Three Peruvian Indigenous Historians'. In Rolena Adorno (ed.), *From Oral to Written Expression: Native Andean Chronicles of the Early Colonial Period.* Latin American Series, No. 4. Syracuse, NY: Syracuse University, Maxwell School of Citizenship and Public Affairs: 9–39

——, 1992. 'Nightmare Victory. The Meanings of Conversion among Peruvian Indians (Huarochirí, 1608?)'. Baltimore: 1992 Lecture Series, Department of Spanish and Portuguese, University of Maryland, Working Papers, No. 7.

Seed, Patricia. 1991. '"Failing to Marvel": Atahualpa's Encounter with the Word'. *Latin American Research Review* 26(1): 7–32.

Silva-Santisteban, Ricardo. 2000. *Antología general del teatro peruano. I. Teatro quechua.* Lima: Banco Continental–Pontificia Universidad Católica del Peru.

Taylor, Gerald. 1987. *Ritos y tradiciones de Huarochiri del siglo XVII.* Lima: Instituto de Estudios Peruanos/Institut Français d'Etudes Andines.

Wachtel, Nathan. 1977. *The Vision of the Vanquished.* Hassocks: Harvester Press.

CHAPTER TWO

Transmission of Knowledge through Textiles: Weaving and Learning How to Live

Lindsey Crickmay

In recent decades the Western world has become increasingly aware that in an age of rapidly expanding technological knowledge many other kinds of knowledge are becoming lost. This preoccupation with loss may manifest itself as nostalgia, New Ageism, or attempts to tap into indigenous knowledge systems in fields such as pharmaceuticals.

Within the field of anthropology there has been an upsurge of interest in the diversity of knowledge systems and how they are learned. This has manifested itself in a considerable literature concerning knowledge in general and indigenous forms of knowledge in particular (Crick 1982; Fardon 1995; Sillitoe 1998), and the definition, learning and transmission of practical skills (Coy 1989; Ingold 1993, 2000; Lave and Wenger 1991; Lock 1993; Pelissier 1991) within such diverse fields as fishing, weaving, blacksmithing and shunting (Palsson 1994; Palsson [ed.] 1993; Aronson 1989; Deafenbaugh 1989; Dilley 1989; Coy 1989; Edelman 1993). In addition several collections have focused on the importance of context in the practice and transmission of knowledge (Howard-Malverde [ed.] 1997; Dilley [ed.] 1999).

In this chapter I will examine the acquisition of one particular form of knowledge: knowledge of weaving practice in a Quechua-speaking community in highland Bolivia in the first half of the 1980s, when I carried out fieldwork in the region. I shall do this through examination of the Quechua concept of *yachay*, 'knowing, knowledge', as described in lexicons of the early colonial period (Santo Tomás 1951; González Holguín 1952) and as observed during fieldwork. *Yachay*, I argue, corresponds to the sense of pre-Enlightenment English-language terms denoting knowledge such as 'craft' and 'cunning'; *yacha-* and these English terms are indicative of learning practical skills through dialogue or interaction with the materials worked upon and of an organic understanding of knowledge and its relation to growth. I contrast this organic knowledge, which can only be learned through practice within the appropriate context, with knowledge gained through study of written texts, which can be gained anywhere at any time and which does not require practical demonstration of understanding for it to be considered learned. I will then describe how weaving is learned by girl children in Quechua villages in the Bolívar area, and my own experience of learning to weave. Such practically based knowledge systems as weaving are in marked contrast to many 'Western' forms: in the West, since the Enlightenment, formal learning has tended to become separated from its social and moral context. I argue that my different experience of learning, in particular its heavy reliance on alphabetic modes of communication, meant that my learning of Quechua weaving practice was also, inevitably, different as well as incomplete. I show that awareness of that incompleteness can in itself lead to positive forms of knowing.

I am aware of the problems of using 'Western' and 'Andean' as categories and that in each case I am considering only one of many available systems of knowledge. In setting up a type of opposition between Western and Andean modes of knowing my aim is to follow the suggestion of Pelissier (1991) and, rather than oversimplifying, to break down the stereotypical dichotomies in which West always emerges as best. I see differences in these categories of knowledge as having less to do with relative capacities for abstract thought – I want to write the instructions down and look at them, Quechua weavers configure the design space and its threads mentally – and more to do with context and the inseparability or otherwise of knowledge and morality, mind and body. Nevertheless, among Western cultures there remains an overwhelming tendency to equate knowledge with completion of formal education and to treat theoretical knowledge as more valuable than other forms. As Ingold notes in his discussion of the practical skill involved in weaving a basket:

> prioritisation of design over execution betrays a ranking of intellectual over physical labour [. . .] and is one of the hallmarks of Western modernity. It divides the scientist from the technician, the engineer from the operative, the architect from the builder and the author from the secretary. (Ingold 2000: 433)

Ingold's comment on the relative values given to different forms of knowledge is pertinent to the Andean area, where alphabetic non-literacy remains widespread and is a common focus of governmental and non-governmental development projects in both Bolivia and Peru. Even when ostensibly packaged as part of bilingual and intercultural education programmes, literacy 'is not being presented as an additional medium for the creation and transmission of cultural knowledge but as the *only* one' (Howard-Malverde 1998: 194).

Concepts of knowing

Yachay

In a collection of articles by the Proyecto Andino de Tecnologias Campesinas (PRATEC), which claims to present 'Andean culture confronting Western notions of development' (Apffel-Marglin with PRATEC [eds.]

1998), one of the organisation's founder members opposes Western ideas regarding the acquisition of knowledge through literacy and formalised education to those found in the Andes. Grimaldo Rengifo Vasquez sees the latter as forming part of a dialogue with nature based on mutual nurturance, 'nurturing and allowing yourself to be nurtured' (Rengifo Vasquez 1998: 172–73, Apffel-Marglin with PRATEC [eds.] 1998: 1).

This interpretation of Andean ways of knowing is supported by definitions of the Quechua term *yacha-*, generally glossed as 'knowledge, knowing' in early colonial and modern lexicons and by studies of its etymology (see also Howard and Stobart in this volume). César Itier proposes that the root *yacha-* derives from a possible prehistorical form **yacha*, made up of a root **ya*, indicative of movement, plus a suffix **-cha*, indicating that the action expressed by the verb is completely realised (1993: 99–101). He applies this understanding to *yachaku-*, literally 'to become involved in knowing', and its colonial gloss 'multiplicar como sementera' ('to multiply like a sown field') (Santo Tomás 1951: 173),[1] suggesting that this gloss should be interpreted 'que una planta llega a su plena desarrollo' ('for a plant to reach its full growth') (Itier 1993: 102). Examples of *yachaku-* used to denote this sense of organic development are also found in seventeenth-century Quechua prayers from the Cajatambo region of Peru.[2] Such an interpretation of the root *yacha-* is congruent with the dialogic nature of the Andean learning process proposed by Rengifo, while 'to multiply like a sown field' links this process to that of progression through the life cycle; one might go further and suggest that in growing to its full potential the plant is 'allowing itself to be nurtured'.

In addition to those related to learning and growing, early colonial glosses for *yacha-* include *yachachi-*, incorporating the 'causative' suffix *-chi*, literally 'to make knowing'; *yachachi-* is glossed as 'criar, hacer de nuevo', 'to create, to make anew' (Santo Tomás 1951: 87). One indigenous chronicler (Pachacuti Yamqui 1993: 208) records the name of the principal Andean divinity as *pachayachachip*, and attribution to *yacha-* of the meaning 'to create' has caused heated debate regarding the possiblity of an Andean 'supreme creator god' prior to the arrival of Europeans and the initiation of the conversion process.[3] 'Creation', however, need not be perceived, as it is

---

[1] Itier (1993: 102) attributes this meaning to González Holguín; however, I found this gloss in Santo Tomás.

[2] For example *mikhuy yachakunqa, pucha yachakunqa, pukyu yachakunqa* (Itier 1992: 1019), *pukyu yachakuchun, yaku yachakuchun* (Itier 1992: 1030), *nina yachakuchun, wamra yachakuchun* (Itier 1992: 1038).

[3] This has consequently been interpreted as 'Creator [*yachachi-* plus the agentive suffix] of the world [*pacha*]' (e.g. Duviols 1977). It might be argued that the Spanish gloss, written prior to 1560, reflects a pre-Enlightenment *European* concept of learning and its imposition on the Andean model, which would support Rengifo's argument concerning the similarity of the Andean and the pre-Enlightenment concepts of learning. More relevant, in view of the above-mentioned debate concerning the creation process, is whether the term of address *pachayachachiq* should be considered as denoting not a divinity that 'created' the world, but one that 'nurtured' it.

in the biblical creation, as 'creation out of nothing', a process in which an actor manipulates an inert substance. Following Itier's interpretation of the root *yacha-* as 'growing to completion', *yachachi-*, 'to create', would mean 'to cause [something] to grow to completion'. Like 'nurturance', this alternative view of 'creation' involves not a unique, perfective action, but a process continuing through time in which what is being created responds by continuing to grow. This interpretation of 'creation' is also congruent with the colonial Spanish gloss *criar*, which can also mean 'to nurture'. As already indicated, it is precisely in terms of 'nurturing and allowing oneself to be nurtured' that Rengifo describes the reciprocal and holistic nature of Andean existence; it is 'nurturance' that he (following a long tradition) contrasts to formal education; it is the meaning 'to teach', i.e. 'to make knowing', with which many of the glosses listed in the early colonial lexicons were concerned (Santo Tomás 1951: 297; González Holguín 1952: 361) and which is the generally accepted usage of *yachachi-* in the present day (Lara 1971: 326; Lira 1982: 337–38).

That the concept of learning is understood in the Andean region as related to experience, to knowing and living as a single process, is supported by further glosses provided for *yacha-* and its derivations in the early colonial lexicons, such as *morar, yachacuni*, literally 'to become involved in living' (Santo Tomás 1951: 171). *Morar* denotes 'living', in the sense of 'dwelling', relating it not to the life process as such but to the place where it is lived; within an Andean aesthetic of everyday life ties with one's community and with the land itself are of primary importance. To settle in one place – for which there is a distinct term, *tiyay* – entails living and learning how to live in that community and its surrounding landscape (see for example Ingold 2000).[4]

In summary, then, the linguistic data provided by the earliest sources on Quechua language and in particular on *yacha-*, 'knowing', describe a process in which the acquisition of knowledge is inseparable from experience of the human life cycle. Knowledge is acquired because and when it is relevant, and increases through experience as a part of growing to maturity. Those who grow up in rural Quechua communities do not learn first and then live, they learn as a part of living; a wise person is one who has lived, one for example who has filled all the positions of authority in his or her local community. It is possible to express this sense of interconnectedness in English by referring not to knowledge, but to learning, in which the outcome of study (learning) is indistinguishable from the process of study (learning).

Living, learning, creating

The concept of *yacha-*, practical knowledge as interactive, as 'nurturing and allowing oneself to be nurtured', and as organic, growing like young crops

---

[4] Santo Tomás (1951: 297) includes an entry '*yachachisca*, experimentado' ('experienced'), indicating that learning had a practical basis in lived experience.

in a field (*multiplicar como sementera*), resonates strongly with Ingold's discussion of skill. In what he describes as a process of *autopoiesis*, Ingold desribes the basketmaker as follows:

> since the artisan is involved in the same system as the material with which he works, so his activity does not transform that system but is – *like the growth of plants* and animals – part and parcel of the system's transformation of itself. (Ingold 2000: 345, my emphasis)

Describing his understanding of the production of 'material culture', Ingold goes on to say:

> According to what I have called the standard view, the human mind is supposed to inscribe its designs upon this surface [of the material to be transformed] through the mechanical application of bodily force – augmented, as appropriate, by technology. I mean to suggest, to the contrary, that the forms of objects are not imposed from above but grow from the mutual involvement of people and materials in an environment. (Ingold 2000: 347)

Ingold's description of the basket emerging through the engagement of the basketmaker with the surface worked upon resonates with pre-Hispanic usage of the Quechua term *qillqa-*. Appropriated as a noun by the Spanish to describe alphabetic writing, its previous verbal usage described the performance of many of the plastic arts, including painting, sculpting, engraving, carving and embroidering (de la Jara 1964: 12), a range of skills in which a design is either brought out of or united with a plain surface (Crickmay 1991: 42–55). That a single term could apply to so many creative skills implies that their function had a conceptual unity:[5] in view of the emergence of design form through the practice of skills denoted *qillqa-*, the term can perhaps be best translated as 'to make visible' or 'to reveal' a latent image which has a communicative rather than a purely decorative function (Crickmay 1991: 43). Such an interpretation also corresponds to Rengifo's claim, when describing the vision of highland Peruvian artisans who can see the form in the natural rock they are sculpting, that 'what is called craft is simply another way of nurturing, of making appear, of generating new forms of life' (1998: 178).

How do Quechua-speaking weavers from Peru and Bolivia, as well as Aymara speakers, with whom they share many cultural concepts, account for and describe the process of skilful creation? Before proceeding I would like to take one further quotation from Ingold:

> the artefact engages its maker in a pattern of skilled activity. These are truly creative engagements, in the sense that they actually *give rise to* the real-world

---

[5] Barbara and Dennis Tedlock (1985) have studied the semantics of the comparable Guatemalan Mayan term *tzib*, adopted to describe alphabetic writing. In addition to the skills included as *qillqa*, *tzib* relates to horticulture and construction of the house, suggesting an interactive and organic notion of the practical skill.

artefactual and organic forms that we encounter, rather than serving – as the standard view would claim – to transcribe pre-existent form into raw material. (2000: 345)

Studies of the acquisition of practical skill do not always make clear whether it is the basic skill or its innovative interpretation which is the truly creative act. Nor, it seems, can weavers, apprentices or anthropologists entirely explain what occurs. In her account of the Quechua community of Sonqo, Catherine Allen relates that when she eventually learnt to spin, her neighbour Basilia congratulated her, saying that she was now *santuyoq*, possessing skill, literally 'possessing the saint' responsible for that skill. Allen compares *santuyoq* to the sixteenth-century usage of *kamayoq* to describe an expert in specialised fields of knowledge, such as the *kipu* (1988: 50). Whether or not this is justified, both *santuyoq* and *kamayoq* describe a 'coming into possession' (*-yuq*) by whoever acquires a skill, not the exertion of control over their materials which the English phrase 'to master a skill' suggests.

In Bolivar, Santa Caterina or Santa Bárbara were approached for help with weaving. Other accounts of acquisition of weaving skill in the Andes suggest a comparable supernatural source among Aymara-speaking as well as Quechua-speaking weavers (Allen 1988, 1997; Arnold 1997: 107). In the Bolivian Aymara village of Qaqachaka the inspiration of weaving is in no way an intellectual process: 'at the precise moment that their heart opens like a bud then spirit flows and they are inspired to weave, grasping the designs from the blood mass in their hearts' (Arnold 1997: 107); 'women explain that their designs are already "just inside their hearts", allowing them to select whichever they wish' (1997: 115).

Franquemont (Franquemont et al. 1992) and Prochaska (1990) both describe a sophisticated mental configuration of space and thread counts during the learning process, but skilled weavers do not draw on these. Describing how weaving is learned in the Quechua community of Taquile, Prochaska writes:

Numbers are very important to the beginning weaver, who will count the threads to pick the different colours for the pattern [. . .] weavers [older girls] on Taquile, as probably elsewhere in the Andes, only rely on counting to weave patterns as beginners. When they advance to weave *chumpis* [belts] and are recognised as expert weavers 'they don't know how to count, because they already know how to weave. Only young girls count.' (1990: 113)[6]

A comparable skill, which has received little attention in the literature, is displayed in the complex designs men knit into their hats in certain Andean communities. When I visited Peru in the summer of 1997 I took the boat

---

[6] Similarly, Peter Gow, in his consideration of painted designs among the Piro of Amazonian Peru (1999), describes the ability of Piro women to imagine the designs they paint on young girls' bodies as part of initiation rituals.

across Lake Titicaca to Taquile Island, where boys begin at around the age of ten to knit the intricately patterned stocking caps they wear. On the trip one of the other visitors had a portable chess set and, seeing the boatman watching him, suggested a game. The game was unfinished when we arrived, but the boatman, even with part of his attention on directing the boat, had evidently proved a challenging partner. Would the ability mentally to perceive spatial relationships and the possible ways that coloured threads might move through space in weaving and knitting be relevant, I wondered, for envisioning the moves of chess pieces across a board?

Connaissance
Today, the Western notion of education typically involves the gaining of knowledge in a location set apart from everyday life: the school or university. Scholars are often isolated from others who seek to acquire or transmit knowledge; generally speaking, knowledge is obtained through the use of only one of the senses, that of sight; knowledge is often unrelated to any present or future practical project. It is seen as a preparation for life, based on the assumption that 'each person is born as an individual in a contractual society that should be understood *before* it is lived in' (Rengifo 1998: 185, paraphrasing Illich, my emphasis). Even where, as in 'flexible pathways to lifelong learning', education continues into adulthood and maturity it is still the case that theoretical knowledge precedes and can be acquired separately from its practical execution. Etymologically the English term for practical knowledge, 'craft', derives from Old English terms for 'power' (*Chambers Twentieth-Century Dictionary*), but today the practical knowledge involved in 'knowing a craft' is not valued in a comparable way to the possession of theoretical knowledge. Practical knowledge is often viewed as second best; 'craft', rather than having connotations of power, may be equated with 'being good with your hands' and by implication 'not good with your head'. Alternatively, craftsmanship may be valued nostalgically as belonging to some idealised, but also less 'developed', past.

Contrasting present Western forms of knowing with those of the Andes, Rengifo argues that, prior to the Enlightenment, Western knowledge was gained through dialogue with nature, as he proposes is the case in the Andes today (Rengifo 1998: 172). Long after the Enlightenment changed the ways in which Western knowledge was categorised and described, English craftsmen retained the ability to see what lay inside the material they used, to visualise its potential, in the way Rengifo describes for today's Peruvian sculptor (1998: 178); just as sixteenth-century Quechua artisans allowed the sculpted, painted, or incised *qillqa* to emerge, these English craftsmen brought out, nurtured, their material's latent potential. In making this comparison I am thinking in particular of two examples, one a factual, the other a fictionalised account, both of men who worked with wood. In his fictional history of a southern English village, *Ulverton* (1993), Adam Thorpe puts words describing the living heart of wood into the mouth of an eighteenth-century joiner, who speaks lovingly of the grain of each tree in terms of its individuality and vitality; the springing grain of the wood to be transformed into a humble gate is reminiscent of Ingold's 'autopoiesis' in the emergence of the basket as a form (Ingold 2000: 345). In his autobiographical *Wheelwright's Shop* (1976 [1923]), written in the early years of the twentieth century, George Sturt describes how he and his father would monitor the growth of individual trees marked for timber, looking for signs that a trunk would be sound rather than 'foxy-hearted'. They would watch how the limbs were formed, seeing in the still living tree the curves of a wheel hub or the angle of a cart shaft. The historical wheelwright and the fictional joiner worked *with* wood; what they did involved a dialogue, a process of interaction between craftsman and medium. This interaction 'gave rise to' the finished articles as the result of a long process, as a woven Quechua textile is the outcome of a process of herding, pasturing, clipping, and spinning which begins when the weaver receives her first sheep from the godparents of her hair-cutting ritual, the ritual by which she first enters the world as a socialised, gendered individual. As members of a fictional sixteenth-century and an actual pre-1918 English village the craftsmen of *Ulverton* and the *Wheelwright's Shop* also belonged to a moral community in which others' judgment of the quality of their work was at the same time a judgment of themselves as moral persons.

Apprenticeship

Can we equate Western knowledge of practical skills today with either that of the English joiner and wheelwright of the past or that of a Quechua weaver? Western craftsmen still study and acquire practical skills through apprenticeship. However, studies of learning within an apprenticeship typically describe a process which differs in several respects from how a Bolivian or Peruvian Quechua child usually learns to weave (Coy [ed.] 1989); such apprenticeships tend to be semi-formal, to take place outside the immediate domestic circle and to result in the ability to produce goods for sale rather than use (Goody 1989; Lave and Wenger 1991). In my view learning to weave is closer to learning to cook, for example to bake bread, as described for the Airo-Pai of Western Amazonia (Belaunde 1992: 179–84).

Palsson, however, argues that apprenticeships, such as that involved in learning to fish, need not be formal (1993, 1994); learning breaks down boundaries between 'them' and 'us'; it should a process of 'actively and intentionally *attending* to the world' (Gibson, quoted in Ingold 1993: 220), to gain enskilment through participation and belonging in the skilled community (Palsson 1993: 123). The perspective taken by these latter studies, like that of Cooper's work on learning to carve wood (1989), suggests the learner's engagement with his or her 'materials'; 'attending' involves a similar interactive engagement to that of 'situated learning' as described by Lave and Wenger (1991: 33). Situated learning implies

[an] emphasis on comprehensive understanding involving the whole person rather than 'receiving' a body of factual knowledge about the world; on activity in and with the world; and on the view that agent, activity and the world mutually constitute each other.

The work of the Norwegian philosopher Jakob Meloe examines the interface between linguistic understanding and practical knowledge; Meloe urges that we should 'situate' ourselves in the context of the word or object we want to understand. In 'Theaitetos' Wagon' (Meloe n.d.: 70–71) he contrasts the different kinds of knowledge we have of what a wagon is when we know all the parts that make it up, and when we know all those parts *and* how they join together to function as a wagon. In order to be able to do that we have to have not only theoretical knowledge of what a wagon is but practical knowledge of how a wagon is used.[7] This example is very relevant to my discussion of the different kinds of learning that the Bolivian Quechua daughter, on the one hand, and the anthropologist, on the other, acquire of weaving. Apprentice craftsmen and anthropologists may both acquire practical skills rather than theoretical knowledge, may learn them through 'mutually constitutive' engagement with their materials and in the appropriate community. However, knowing weaving for a Quechua-speaking girl, like coming to know what a wagon is for a wheelwright, is part of a long process only fully realised through lived experience. Even where the relevant skill is acquired prior to fieldwork, knowledge of such a skill may be seen as 'not appropriate to intellectuals' by those who use it as part of their continuing everyday lives (see e.g. Edelman 1993: 142, 151). When apprenticeship is undertaken as part of fieldwork, the anthropologist's experience of this process is, inevitably, foreshortened. Further, in taking up an apprenticeship anthropologists simply reverse their more usual learning process: instead of going from theory to practice, they practice so that they can subsequently theorise about it, and not for the skill itself.

In the remainder of this chapter I will consider how a young Bolivian Quechua or Aymara girl, such as the daughter of my own teacher, learns to weave and how I myself learned, in order to show that inevitably different kinds of knowledge are gained.

Weaving, living, knowing
Reviewing a number of examples of 'informal' learning or 'socialisation processes' in her article on technology and learning, Pelissier writes:

Learning [. . .] happens for the most part in the course of everyday activity. People do not learn how to build canoes, for instance, in a course on canoe

---

[7] Sturt has a pertinent example: he describes how an apprentice wheelwright built a new and larger model of a wagon, but in doing so changed the 'dish' on the wheels; this meant that the wheels could only turn the cart very slightly before they jammed up against its sides; the lack of dish meant that the wagon could not be moved sufficiently to leave the yard (1976).

building in which they are lectured about the principles of canoe construction; rather they learn it experientially, by helping out in the building of a canoe intended for use, not for purposes of education. Skill, then as well as norms and roles are learned in the doing. (1991: 88)

Similarly, it has been shown for a number of Amerindian cultures (see e.g. Reichel-Dolmatoff 1978; Arnold et al. 1992) that the house can provide a means of both learning and teaching. In their description of the building of an Aymara house Arnold, Jimenez and Yapita describe how this process is part of the acquisition of personal knowledge, while the result is a means of transmitting knowledge that is communally held:

en el transcurso de la construcción de una casa los aymaras reconstruyen su vision cosmológica y la misma casa se convierte en una representación del cosmos, una metáfora del cerro mundo, un axis mundi y una estructura organ-izativa en torno a la cual giran otras estructuras. (1992: 36)

In the process of constructing a house the Aymara reconstruct their view of the cosmos and the house becomes a representation of that cosmos, a metaphor for the World Mountain, an *axis mundi* and an organising structure around which others structures turn. (my translation)

Members of Aymara communities, to apply Howard-Malverde, paraphrasing Keesing (1987: 164), 'do not "read" the meaning-embodying symbols of their culture, but rather they "evoke" them; that is to say, they engage with them and meaningfully reproduce them in an experiental way' (Howard-Malverde [ed.] 1997: 9).

Like housebuilding, knowledge of weaving is transmitted through practical example (see e.g. Crickmay 1991: 73–79; Prochaska 1990: 111). Watching without doing does not constitute knowing. It is not that children, or learning adults, do not first observe their mothers and then try to copy them. Clearly observation and practice cannot be simultaneous where the actions involved are of any complexity. But knowledge of the head, knowing how, is not considered 'knowing' until it is transformed into experiental, lived knowledge. Even where observation and practice are separated in time, observing occurs as part of a particular individual and social context, the age of the child, the place of weaving in the community.

A particular kind of knowledge will be shown at the relevant time in a person's life; learning to weave is related to the learner's biological as well as her cultural life cycle. A woman's ability to weave is one of the ways in which her role complements that of her partner in marriage; young girls should be practising these skills by the time they reach marriageable age. The period when a girl is most productive as a weaver, when she is most innovative in the designs she weaves, corresponds to her own period of greatest sexuality and potential reproductivity. This is reflected in the flamboyance of her designs (Arnold 1997: 114, 117). Women's most creative weaving is done when the earth is also most fertile, especially the rainy season when the earth is green and flowering (Arnold 1997: 108). The textiles the weaver and her family wear display the quality of her work and reflect the personal and moral qualities of the weaver herself; at fiestas, if the woman is helping her partner to sponsor the occasion, the quantity of that work will also be displayed, carried in the *q'epi* ('bundle') on the weaver's back.

Weaving must be performed well or it will not fulfil its function. Weavers often pay special attention to the care with which the 'terminal areas' of the textile, where the weaver has had to put in the wefts with a needle, have been executed. Alongside the many references to weaving terminology in the early colonial dictionaries are references to ways of weaving, such as 'tightly woven', or 'loosely woven' (see e.g. Bertonio 1984: II 94, 259, 313). On my last visit to Taquile Island, where men knit and women weave not only for themselves but to sell to tourists, a friend told me that he and others no longer knitted the patterned caps in the same way. It used to be said that the fabric of a properly knitted cap was so dense that the cap would hold water. Now there are fewer, larger, stitches in a round and the fabric produced is looser. He had recently sold one of the last of the caps he had knitted in the old way and sounded sad and concerned, as though describing more than simply the changing tension of a piece of knitting.

Attention to the lesson: the anthropologist's pursuit of skill
I began this article by contrasting concepts of learning in the Andes with conventional understandings of Western education. Perhaps, then, one possible way to gain some understanding of the complexities involved in Andean systems of learning, living and creating is to consider how my own experience of learning to weave might differ from that of Quechua- or Aymara-speaking beginners.

In showing me how to weave a narrow *chumpi* (woman's belt) my teacher performed the actions over and over again; she did not accompany these actions with words, except when this was to 'tell me the word for'; it was only when I had executed two repeats of a design, one in each of two sets of alternating colours, that my teacher told me 'Yachankiña', 'Now you know it'. I had completed the processes necessary for weaving that figure; nevertheless, perhaps she ought rather to have said 'Now you *should* know it'. I had copied what she showed me, *yacha-*, I had tried to reproduce the bodily movements involved in the weaving process, but could I be said to have either learned or created those designs, to have engaged with the weaving experience, in the sense that *yacha-* has in those contexts?

Since the anthropologist is already formed and shaped by her own life experience, the learning processes she undertakes do not truly replicate those of a child (Okeley 1992: 17). The body movements of another culture do not come readily to an adult, even one who observes 'through all the senses, through movement, through their bodies and through their whole being in a total practice' (Okeley 1992: 16–17). Film of the body movements of Guatemalan children and of two North American adult women learning to weave on a backstrap loom showed that the children's movements were more controlled. This difference, the authors argue, was in part due to the kinds of body movements typical of the two cultures: those of native Guatemalan women are typically restricted, the torso upright, arms close to the sides; this posture is reinforced from babyhood, when children are tightly cocooned, then in activities such as carrying water jars on their heads, when women walk with elbows in and shoulders back, and by their tightly wrapped skirts, in which only tiny steps are possible (Maynard et al. 1999). I experienced similar problems when learning to weave to those described in this study.

A more significant difference, in my opinion, is how complex woven designs are remembered. Older Quechua-speaking weavers around Bolívar would often tell me how many threads the designs take: thirty is a popular figure, and women say many designs 'come out of' thirty threads (Crickmay 1991: 129). Franquemont et al. (1992) have also investigated how women envision threads in order to remember whole designs. What they clearly do *not* do is remember designs by individual rows, as I did; in doing so, I also imagined how I would describe these rows on paper, as knitting patterns are written out for Western knitters. The very different way in which women weavers in the Andean region remember is evident from this description by Prochaska, herself learning to weave in the Peruvian Quechua community of Taquile:

> the adult weavers, who were instructing me as a beginner on the pick-up sequence of a certain motif, first had to pause for a while and count the threads from the picture in their mind in order to tell me. But, as experienced weavers, the girls have reached a higher understanding of the patterns and know each thread individually, as a distinct part of a particular motif. They remember the weaving sequence by 'seeing' the design, and one row becomes a logical sequence to the previous one. Threads are not numbers, but represent the entities themselves. (1990: 113)

I am aware that in rural areas of the Andes sociality is founded on principles of reciprocity, on complementary or alternating opposites, and on a desire to maintain harmony with the cosmos. I know that some the words used by my teacher to describe the weaving process, words such as *tinku-* and *iwala-*, are relevant to this view of sociality as well as to the structure and process of weaving. I can compare the use of *tinku-* and *iwala-* in the context of colour combination to the English verbs 'to clash' and 'to marry' in a similar context, but even though I might comprehend these concepts intellectually this part of weaving lore did not have moral implications for the way I relate to family, friends and neighbours.

In order for learning to be part of development to full potential, to produce the adequacy of fit which Itier proposes for *yacha-*, I should have been learning to weave a belt, not at forty, but at fourteen or fifteen, the age of my teacher's daughter, who sat not far away on the hard earth of the patio, learning a similar lesson. It might perhaps, under certain circumstances, be possible for a Quechua or Aymara woman to come to weaving later in life, but such a middle-aged woman would have already experienced, in other areas, what weaving teaches about their role in society, about appropriate behaviour, about the history of the community and the significance in history and society of the local landmarks. Weaving in the heat of a Bolivian July day did not cause me to recall such images, nor did it bring to my mind the ethics and aesthetics of my own life in a London suburb, its highest buildings and the course of the river between them. The way the colours were arranged recalled neither family relationships nor the foods I am most accustomed to eating. I know that this information is encoded in Andean weavings from a number of different communities, as well as in other aspects of Quechua and Aymara material culture such as the house, because I have read that it is so, in the reported weaving discourse of weavers in widely separated regions of the Peruvian and Bolivian Andes, and in academic journals, and I have tried to write about it myself. Nor, perhaps I should add, does spinning, weaving or knitting in an English or Scottish environment consciously evoke comparable imagery, other than vague thoughts of animals in an unidentified landscape when handling the textures and colours of natural fibres.

Concluding remarks

Though I worked *on* them rather than *with* them I did learn something from handling the materials of the weaving. I also learned something of the aesthetics of weaving in the Andean region, the rules governing which colours can be combined with or placed next to which. Weaving discourse accompanied my attempts at practice: my weaving teacher talked about the relationships between colours as she wound the vertical threads of the warp side by side; she talked about them again as she arranged these colours horizontally into two contrasting sets which would form the upper and lower surfaces of the belt. But as I watched her movements and tried to copy them, how much did I see of what I was looking at?

I succeeded in imitating, *yacha-*, my teacher's design, but I was not able to imitate her means of producing it; I could not perceive that design as a relationship between background and foreground as I believe she did. Most importantly, whether what I learn is lore or manual skill I do not trust myself to 'know' it until I have captured it in written form. Reducing the vitality of handwoven cloth to the fixity of a numerical code, I translated my teacher's actions into counted warp threads and rows of weft. Did I 'know' the design, was I *santuyoq*? While I can imagine what such a dialogue would involve, I did not experience that dialogue, nor did I come to 'possess the saint'.

Does this awareness necessarily lead to negative conclusions about the value of my increased knowledge? Of his own perception of the landscape inhabited by Sami reindeer herders Jakob Meloe (who is at least part Sami himself) writes:

We are foreigners to this landscape. Walking the same tracks as the reindeer herders and looking where they look, we see little of what they see. (There is a sense in which we all see the same when looking in the same direction or at the same lump of matter. But, standing alone, this sense of 'seeing the same' is devoid of practical or moral implications, and so of little use, whether in the moral sciences or in our daily life.) (1988: 400)

For me, learning to weave also lacked practical and moral implications. One day I may learn the difference between an expanse of heather and a Scottish hill but though I know how to weave, it does not seem to me likely that I will fully know weaving.

However, the lack of commensality between my own ways of knowing and those of Bolivian Quechua weavers such as my teacher, Juana, and her daughter seems of more concern to me than to them. When living among Bolivian Quechua speakers I was immediately struck by the importance given to participation. No matter if the beans you sowed did not come out in a straight line, what counted was to take a part in the communal activity. On several occasions after I had participated in long hours of dancing in some *fiesta*, with marked lack of grace, both friends and strangers would nevertheless say to me 'Now you know how to dance'. As Palsson remarks in the context of learning to fish, it is taking, not passing, the test that counts (1993: 123). Knowing what we cannot know can also be revealing. Of the agents' differing perceptions of the Sami landscape Meloe goes on to say (cf. Fabian 1999 on 'misunderstanding'): 'If I have been able to say what it is to be a foreigner to a landscape, and what it is that makes us foreigners to this landscape, then I think we have come as close to knowing where we are as we can hope for' (1988: 400).

Acknowledgments

An earlier version of this paper was presented at the round-table discussion held at Darwin College, Cambridge in November 1997. I would like to thank all those who commented on it at that time as well as the anonymous readers for their very helpful comments and both the editors for their painstaking reading of later drafts and their invaluable suggestions.

References

Allen, Catherine. 1988. *The Hold Life Has: Coca and Cultural Identity in an Andean Community*. Washington, DC: Smithsonian Institution.
——, 1997. 'When Pebbles Move Mountains: Iconicity and Symbolism in Quechua Ritual'. In Howard-Malverde (ed.): 73–84.
Apffel-Marglin, Frédérique, with PRATEC (eds.). 1998. *The Spirit of Regeneration: Andean Culture Confronting Western Notions of Development*. London: Zed Books.
Arnold, Denise. 1997. 'Making Men in Her Own Image: Gender, Text and Textile in Qaqachaka'. In Howard-Malverde (ed.): 99–134.
Arnold, Denise, J. Yapita and D. Jimenez Aruquipa. 1992. *Hacia un orden andino de*

las cosas: tres vistas de los Andes meridionales. La Paz: Hisbol/ILCA.

Aronson, Lisa. 1989. 'To Weave or Not to Weave: Apprenticeship Rules among the Akwete Igbo of Nigeria and the Baule of the Ivory Coast'. In Coy (ed.): 149–62.

Belaunde, Luisa. 1992. 'Gender, Commensality and Community among the Airo-Pai of West Amazonia (Secoya, Western-Tukanoan Speaking)'. PhD thesis, LSE, University of London.

Bertonio, Ludovico. 1984 [1612]. *Vocabulario de la lengua aymara* (Facsimile). Cochabamba, Bolivia: CERES.

Cooper, Eugene. 1989. 'Apprenticeship as Field Method: Lessons from Hong Kong'. In Coy (ed.): 137–48.

Coy, Michael. 1989. 'Being what We Pretend to Be: The Usefulness of Apprenticeship as a Field Method'. In Coy (ed.): 115–37.

Coy, Michael (ed.). 1989. *Apprenticeship: From Theory to Method and Back Again.* Albany, NY: State University of New York Press.

Crick, Malcolm. 1982. 'Anthropology of Knowledge'. *Annual Review of Anthropology* 11: 287–313.

Crickmay, Lindsey. 1991. 'Space, Time and Harmony: The Symbolic Language of Andean Textiles with Special Reference to those from Bolivar Province, Cochabamba, Bolivia'. PhD thesis, University of St Andrews.

Deafenbaugh, Linda. 1989. 'Hausa Weaving: Surviving Amid the Paradoxes'. In Coy (ed.): 163–80.

Dilley, Roy. 1989. 'Secrets and Skills: Apprenticeship among Tukolor Weavers'. In Coy (ed.): 181–98.

Dilley, Roy (ed.). 1999. *The Problem of Context*. Oxford: Berghahn Books.

Duviols, Pierre. 1977. 'Los nombres quechua de Viracocha, supuesto "Dios Creador" de los evangelizadores'. *Allpanchis Phuturinqua* X: 53–64.

Edelman, Birgitta. 1993. 'Acting Cool and Being Safe: The Definition of Skill in a Swedish Railway Yard'. In Palsson (ed.): 140–61.

Fabian, Johannes. 1999. 'Ethnographic Misunderstanding and the Perils of Context'. In Dilley (ed.): 85–104.

Fardon, Richard (ed.). 1995. *Counterworks: Managing the Diversity of Knowledge.* London: Routledge.

Franquemont, Ed, C. Franquemont and B.J. Isbell. 1992. 'Awaq ñawin: El ojo del tejedor. La practica de la cultura en el tejido'. *Revista Andina* 10(1): 47–80.

González Holguín, Domingo de. 1952 [1608]. *Vocabulario de la lengua general de todo el Peru llamada lengua qquichua o del inca.* Ed. Raul Porras Barrenchea. Lima: Universidad Nacional Mayor de San Marcos.

Goody, Esther. 1989. 'Learning, Apprenticeship and the Division of Labor'. In Coy (ed.): 233–56.

Gow, Peter. 1999. 'Piro Designs: Painting as Meaningful Action in an Amazonian Lived World'. *JRAI* 5: 229–46.

Howard-Malverde, Rosaleen. 1998. '"Grasping Awareness": Mother-Tongue Literacy for Quechua Speaking Women in Northern Potosí, Bolivia'. *International Journal of Educational Development* 18(3): 181–96.

Howard-Malverde, Rosaleen (ed.). 1997. *Creating Context in Andean Cultures.* Oxford Studies in Anthropological Linguistics. Oxford: Oxford University Press.

Ingold, Tim. 1993. 'The Art of Translation in a Continuous World'. In Palsson (ed.): 210–30.

——, 2000. *The Perception of the Environment: Essays in Livelihood, Dwelling and Skill.*

London: Routledge.

Itier, César. 1992. 'La Tradición oral quechua antigua en los procesos de idolatrías de Cajatambo'. *Bulletin de l'Institut Français d'Études Andines* 21: 1009–51.

——, 1993. 'Algunos conceptos quechuas prehispánicos: la raíz *yacha-*, sus derivados y *Pacha yachachic*, atributo del héroe cultural Viracocha'. In P. Duviols (ed.), *Religions des Andes et Langues Indigènes*. Provence: University of Provence: 93–113.

Jara,Victoria de la. 1964. *La escritura peruana y los vocabularios quechuas antiguos.* Lima: Imprenta Lux.

Keesing, Roger. 1987. 'Anthropology as Interpretative Quest'. *Current Anthropology* 28(2):161–69.

Lara, Jesús. 1971. *Diccionario qheshwa–castellano*. La Paz: Los Amigos del Libro.

Lave, Jean, and Etienne Wenger. 1991. *Situated Learning: Legitimate Peripheral Participation*. Cambridge: Cambridge University Press.

Lira, Jorge. 1982. *Diccionario kkechuwa–español*. Bogota: Cuadernos Culturales Andinos No. 5.

Lock, Margaret. 1993. 'Cultivating the Body: Anthropology and Epistemologies of Bodily Practice and Knowledge'. *Annual Review of Anthropology* 22: 133–55.

Maynard, A.E., P.M. Greenfield and C.P. Childs. 1999. 'Culture, History, Biology, and Body: Native and Non-Native Acquisition of Technological Skill'. *Ethos* 27: 379–402.

Meloe, Jakob. 1988. 'The Two Landscapes of Northern Norway'. *Inquiry* 31: 387–401.

——, n.d. 'Theaitetos' Wagon'. In G. Skirbekk (ed.), *Praxeology: An Anthology*. Oslo: Universitetsforlaget: 70–80.

Okeley, Judith. 1992. 'Anthropology and Autobiography: Participatory Experience and Embodied Knowledge'. In J. Okeley and H. Callaway (eds.), *Anthropology and Autobiography*. London: Routledge: 1–28.

Pachacuti Yamqui Salcamaygua, Joan de Santa Cruz. 1993. *Relación de antigüedades deste Reyno del Piru. Estudio etnohlistórico y lingüístico de Pierre Duviols y César Itier.* Lima: Institut Français d'Etudes Andines/Cusco: Ceutro de Estudios Regionales Andinos 'Bartolomé de Las Casas'.

Palsson, Gisli. 1994. 'Enskilment at Sea'. *Man* NS 29(4): 901–27.

Palsson, Gisli (ed.). 1993. *Beyond Boundaries: Understanding, Translation and Anthropological Discourse*. Oxford: Berg.

Pelissier, C. 1991. 'The Anthropology of Teaching and Learning'. *Annual Review of Anthropology* 20: 75–95.

Prochaska, Rita. 1990. *Taquile y sus tejidos (Versión Castellano–English)*. Lima: Arius.

Reichel-Dolmatoff, Gerardo. *Beyond the Milky Way: Hallucinatory Imagery of the Tukano Indians*. UCLA Latin American Studies, Vol. 42. Los Angeles: UCLA.

Rengifo Vasquez, Grimaldo. 1998. 'Education in the Modern West and in Andean Culture'. In Apffel-Marglin with PRATEC (eds.) 1998: 172–92.

Santo Tomás, Domingo de. 1951 [1560]. *Lexicon o vocabulario de la lengua general del Peru*. Facsimile. Lima: Instituto de Historia de la Facultad de Letras de la Universidad Nacional Mayor de San Marcos.

Sillitoe, Paul. 1998. 'The Development of Indigenous Knowledge: A New Applied Anthropology'. *Current Anthropology* 39(2): 223–52.

Sturt, George. 1976 [1923]. *The Wheelwright's Shop*. Cambridge. Cambridge University Press.

Tedlock, Dennis and Barbara. 1985. 'Text and textile: Language and technology in the arts of the Quiché Maya'. *Journal of Anthropological Research* 41(2): 121–46.

Thorpe, Adam. 1993. *Ulverton*. London: Minerva.

CHAPTER THREE

Coloured Knowledges: Colour Perception and the Dissemination of Knowledge in Isluga, Northern Chile

Penny Dransart

Since 1986, I have been doing fieldwork in Isluga in the highlands of northern Chile, east of Iquique and adjacent to the frontier with Bolivia.[1] One of the aspects of Isluga culture that immediately attracted my attention was the way in which people use colour, probably because of my own background of having originally trained at art school. As a practitioner in the use of colour, I have long had reservations about Berlin and Kay's (1969) linguistic theory concerning the evolutionary sequence of what they called Basic Color Terms. However, when in November 1996 I presented the paper on which this article is based, a considerable number of scholars of human vision were already extending Berlin and Kay's research. Most of the contributors to the book edited by Hardin and Maffi (1997) (itself an outcome of a conference held in 1992) accepted Berlin and Kay's work on linguistic anthropology. In his chapter, however, Lucy (1997) warned against conflating cognitive and linguistic categories. More recently, Saunders (2000) has published a sustained review of Berlin and Kay 1969, their subsequent revisions and the research of colour scientists who have adapted their premises. She argues that these researchers have established a 'scientific reality [that] replaces ordinary reality with a "data-base" of encodings and theoretical models' (Saunders 2000: 89). In contrast, she perceives colour to exist 'through noticings and reportings as an ensemble of social relations' (Saunders 2000: 93). This is a view with which I have considerable sympathy. Therefore, I wish to begin my chapter by giving the reader

[1] The fieldwork on which this article is based consisted of eight months in northern Chile in 1986, thirteen months in 1987–1988, three months in 1989, short visits in 1995 and 1996, and a further three months in 1997. I wish to thank the Emslie Horniman Fund, the University of Oxford, the British Council, Santiago and the Pant-y-Fedwen Fund for providing financial support. During my fieldwork in Isluga, I was based in the upper moiety of Araxsaya. I wish to thank most warmly the people of Enquelga for their help. In paragraphs two and three, I have changed the names of the people concerned to protect their identity. I have checked the Aymara terms in this work with reference to Aymara-Spanish dictionaries, including Apaza Suca et al. 1984.

some insights into my experiences of ethnographic fieldwork in the Andes, starting with issues that Isluga people have expressed to me without my prompting, as a grounding for developing an analysis of some of the ways in which they use colour, and to which my training has sensitised me.

On my visits to Isluga, people have often expressed their preoccupations about their eyesight to me. During one particular conversation in 1996, Lucia asked me to bring her some binoculars on my return to Isluga. She explained that her eyesight is becoming *pavoso*.[2] Although she can see close up, her eyesight is failing her over longer distances. This makes it difficult for her to identify her animals when she is herding. She attributed her failing eyesight to crying too much when two of her children died. Her mother had warned her then that crying would damage her eyesight.

Lucia's son Edgardo is a slow learner. Now about fifteen years of age, he has a squint and his mother has taken him to an optician in Iquique fairly regularly over the years. At an early age, one of his godparents (a Chilean anthropologist) paid for him to have glasses fitted, and he was practically the first person to wear glasses in his community. In August 1996, Lucia took her son to the optician in Iquique again. In her absence, her son's eye problems were a topic of conversation in the village. One woman commented pointedly that she herself took great care when she was pregnant not to eat hot red peppers (*ají*). On another occasion she addressed her comments to a group of women in a more explicit fashion, stating that you should not eat *ají* when pregnant as it will damage the eyesight of the baby in the womb. The saturated hue and strong taste of the pepper are considered to be dangerous to the foetus.

These concerns expressed by Isluga people have encouraged me to focus on vision in this paper, rather than on the other senses. However, Steven Feld reminds us that perceptual experience has an 'overwhelmingly multisensory character' (1996: 94). He dismisses the point of view expressed by the geographer Denis Cosgrove, who considered the faculty of sight to be particularly important in artistic and literary representations of landscape, as well as in academic geography, a discipline which confers an objectivity on the faculty of sight (Cosgrove 1984: 9). Feld gives an alternative academic history in which places are heard and felt. Nevertheless, citing Ong (1982), he claims that the predominant approach in the West is 'to essentialize vision', while he ascribes 'a presumed centrality' to the senses of sound, smell and taste among non-Western peoples (Feld 1996: 96). He proposes developing an 'acoustemology' in order to re-evaluate sensory ratios. To do this, he sets out to explore 'sonic sensibilities, specifically of ways in which sound is central to making sense, to knowing, to experiential truth' (1996: 97). He reminds us that 'experiencing and knowing place – the idea of place as sensed, place as sensation – can proceed through a complex

---

[2] Isluga people use this adjective for describing things that lack contrast. It is presumably derived from the Spanish verb *apagar*, 'to extinguish' or 'to diminish'.

interplay of the auditory and the visual, as well as through other intersensory perceptual processes' (1996: 98).

In this chapter, I wish to explore the use of colour in herding and weaving, and the way colour is used and talked about – or, more specifically, some of the ways in which certain knowledges concerning colour are transmitted, while others are not divulged – in Isluga. In doing this, I do not intend to imply that the sense of vision is more central to the people of Isluga than their other senses. Nor do I want to characterise the world in a dichotomous fashion; I do not wish to imply that Western peoples are more dependent on certain senses, while non-Western peoples are more reliant on other senses. Paul Stoller has advocated that we practise a sensuous scholarship that enables us to experience the world as 'a wondrous place that stirs the imagination and sparks creativity' (1997: 136). Our senses serve as the means by which we come to know the worlds we inhabit.

Stephen Feld did his fieldwork among the Kaluli in the rainforest region of Papua New Guinea, on the Great Papuan Plateau. He mentions that sound is diffuse in rainforests, and that the Kaluli have developed an 'acute hearing for locational orientation'. Visually, much of the forest is obscured to view, but he points out that 'sound cannot be hidden' (1996: 98). In contrast, my own fieldwork has been in the somewhat arid and treeless highlands of northern Chile. The broad vistas that are exposed to view in Isluga mean that sight is extremely important for locating herds of animals as they work their way around the different pasture grounds available to them. I discovered that the pairs of binoculars I had been taking to Isluga were much in demand as they enabled herders to distinguish between their own and other people's herds from a distance. People know their own animals by using criteria that include recognising the colour patterning of the animals' fleece. Human beings repond to their sensual perceptions within particular cultural contexts. Colour exists in the mind of the beholder where there is light to reflect it, and people's understanding of it in Isluga is brought into play in many arenas of life.

The physiological basis for the importance of vision in humans has been much explored. A widely distributed book that explains the mechanics of vision to a popular readership is Diane Ackerman's *A Natural History of the Senses* (1995).[3] Ackerman says that whereas animals such as bats and dolphins hear geographically, for humans the world is both more 'densely informative' and 'luscious' when perceived through vision (1995: 230). Since 70 per cent of the body's sense receptors are located in the eyes, she suggests that making sense of what we see gave rise to abstract thinking (1995: 230). However, one of the persistent sub-themes in her book is that of sensory

---

[3] Classen (1993: 5) has criticised Ackerman for failing to address how the senses express cultural values. I do not agree with Classen's assertion that 'we' in the West 'are accustomed to thinking of perception as a physical rather than cultural act' (1993: 1). Our cultural responses to perception involve a complex interplay of physiology, psychology and environment.

blending, and she devotes a final chapter to the theme of synaesthesia. Our senses are not always clearly distinguishable one from the other.

At the back of the eye, the retina includes two kinds of photosensitive cells known as rods and cones. There are 125 million thin straight rods that deal with dimness and report in black and white, and seven million plump cones that deal with colours. There are three sorts of cones, which specialise in the primaries, blue, red and green. These rods and cones allow the eye to respond quickly to changing scenes (Ackerman 1995: 233).

Of course I went to Isluga with my own cultural baggage, especially concerning theories of colour. My own background is deeply influenced by my undergraduate experiences at art school and by my five-year period of teaching art in a secondary school in Scotland. At art school, I was taught the twelve-part colour star devised by Johannes Itten (1888–1967), the Swiss author of *The Art of Colour*, which was first published in Germany in 1961.[4] Itten designed the twelve-part star in Weimar in 1921, and it was taught to me as an art student in the 1970s. In his theory of colour Itten listed seven colour contrasts: contrast of hue; light–dark contrast; cold–warm contrast; complementary contrast; simultaneous contrast; contrast of saturation; and contrast of extension (Itten 1970: 32).

Of this list, light–dark, cold–warm, complementary and simultaneous contrasts, and the contrast of saturation are concepts well known and understood by Isluga weavers of all ages, although the terminology would be foreign to them.[5] They have chosen to specialise in these forms of colour contrast in their textiles, using them in specific contexts.

The one contrast that they have not developed to any great extent is that of hue. According to Itten, it is the most simple of his seven contrasts. He explained: 'It makes no great demands upon color vision, because it is illustrated by the undiluted colors in their most intense luminosity' (Itten 1970: 33). Isluga people are aware of its use, however. Contrast of hue is characteristic of the industrially manufactured *awayu* (carrying cloths) made in La Paz (Plate 1). Isluga people buy these *awayu*, which are sometimes sold at the once-a-fortnight Bolivian market on the frontier with Chile at Pisiga.

My discussion of the way Isluga people use colour will relate to their perceptions of the rainbow and their beliefs in the power of red to generate other colours. Before discussing this, I shall first briefly address how anthropologists have studied colour systems in other cultures.

Chromatics

The term 'chromatics' refers to the use of multiple colours expressed as a symbolic system (Helms 1995: 9). Lévi-Strauss's discussion of the

[4] For a comment on the historical and cultural context in which Itten worked, see Gage (1993: 242, 259–63).

[5] In the interests of saving space, I provide more information about these forms of colour contrast as my discussion unfolds, in order to explain them with specific reference to Isluga textiles.

chromaticism of poison in *The Raw and the Cooked* stands at the crux of his argument concerning the relationship between what he calls 'nature' and 'culture'. He argues that lowland South American myths show how native conceptions of fish poison indicate that the division between 'nature' and 'culture' is minimal (1970: 279). Lévi-Strauss sees poison as conjoining nature and culture, but the effect is one of disjunction, because the former depends on 'continuous quantity' and the latter on 'discrete quantity':

> It is not an accident that the Arecuna myth (M145) about the origin of fish poison should include an episode which presents the fragmentation of the rainbow as the cause of the anatomical discontinuity of the living species – i.e., of the advent of a zoological order, which, like the creation of the other realms of nature, ensures that culture has some hold over nature. (1970: 279–80)

In the myths that Lévi-Strauss analyses, combinations of colour occur in both long and short intervals, or in diatonic and chromatic intervals, to use acoustic terms. He advises us, when examining such myths, to ask whether the colours shade into one another in short intervals, or whether they present strong contrasts that take the form of long intervals (1970: 324).

Some authors have taken the colour range to be bounded at either end by black and white. Mary Helms describes the full extent of the chromatic range as 'a multihued enrichment of light sandwiched between the two single, monolithic, and achromatic signs of blackness and whiteness' (Helms 1995: 10). Her treatment of colour relies not only on the work of Lévi-Strauss, but also on Reichel-Dolmatoff's discussion of the Desana of the Vaupés, in Colombia. Reichel-Dolmatoff saw white and black as contrastive sets of 'energies' from which colours emerge in the form of three colour energies, 'white-brilliant-reflection', 'yellow-brilliant-reflection' and 'red strong-brilliant-reflection' (1978: 256). Famously, Berlin and Kay (1969) started their evolutionary sequence from black and white, to which they aggregated colours in successive steps. They argued for the existence of seven evolutionary stages. In their first stage, black and white are the two basic colour terms used in a language; with each successive stage one or more basic colour terms are added (Berlin and Kay 1969: 22–23).[6]

While Lévi-Strauss observes that white and black trade beads were more acceptable than coloured beads in tropical South America (1970: 320), unlike Berlin and Kay and Reichel-Dolmatoff, he does not regard black and white as the basis for an evolutionary sequence. Nor does he bracket the spectra he discusses with white and black, as does Helms. Instead he cites

---

[6] Berlin and Kay treated black and white as if they were 'primary' colours, rather than the total absorption of and the total reflection of light, respectively. In the nineteenth century, Ewald Hering termed black, white and shades of grey as 'achromatic colour' (Wooten and Miller 1997: 69), which to my ears sounds like an oxymoron. The lecturer who went around the studio when I was at art school muttering 'The Impressionists wouldn't have used it!' whenever he found a student attempting to darken a colour mixture with black paint had a profound influence on my attitudes to colour.

Jean-Jacques Rousseau's comments on the derivation of the term 'chro-maticism' from the Greek χρῶμα, which means 'red/colour' (Lévi-Strauss 1970: 280). In Spanish, the adjective *colorado* means 'red'. The bilingual Aymara–Spanish speakers of Isluga sometimes borrow the Spanish term *color* into Aymara as *kulura*. However, I sensed that they found it difficult to speak about colour as an abstract entity in their conversations with me. Indeed, older women would only tell me about colours in a hushed whisper when we were in private. Younger women are more confident about using bright hues in their textiles and speaking about their specific colour choices.

It seems as though older Isluga women share the distrust mentioned by Lévi-Strauss of Bororo women for polychrome clothing; he considers their 'hatred of polychromaticism' to be an extreme manifestation of a general attitude towards colour that is more subtly displayed elsewhere in South America (1970: 321). In highland Isluga, attitudes towards the use of colour have changed rapidly through the different generations, especially in the 1980s (Dransart 1988). The reluctance of elderly women to discuss colours with their daughters and granddaughters has implications for the transmis-sion of knowledge. This reluctance to pass on information has meant that native dye technology is no longer practised in Isluga.

It is of interest to this discussion that Lévi-Strauss incorporates both the fragmentation of the rainbow and the mythic importance of blood-red in his analysis of chromatics. In *The Raw and the Cooked*, he includes a Caduveo myth in which the blood that issued forth from a severed human limb became the source of multicoloured plumage in birds, who were originally all uniformly white, when they dipped themselves or part of themselves in the blood lake (1970: 302). In fact, the most common Aymara term for the colour red is *wila*, which also means 'blood'. I wish to begin my discussion of Isluga people's use of colour with red, and their belief in its generative powers. There are certain contexts in which red, combined with the full light of the day, brings other colours into being.

The generative power of red

Although strong-tasting red food is considered to endanger the vision of the foetus forming in the womb and pregnant women are not supposed to eat it, the colour red is extremely important to Isluga women. Their outermost garment is typically a red shawl. In the past, women dyed homespun yarn red and wove it into a rectangular cloth, wider than it was long, to wrap round their shoulders. They now buy factory-made, fringed shawls, preferably of a red or strong pink colour, from the Bolivian market to keep themselves warm when herding.

The significance of red blood is mythically sanctioned in Isluga. Marcos Castro Challapa told me about a former world age, when the land was all one plain, and the hills did not stand up as they do today (personal commu-nication, 12 January 1997). In the time of *El Inga* ('the Inka'), *El Inga* caused all the hills to stand up, but when he came to Isluga, he was killed by *El Inga español* ('the Spanish Inka'). His blood was put into a jar, and his wife had to wait 15 days before looking. She looked in two days, and *El Inga* was only just forming. Because of this, the hills do not have rich minerals within; there is no silver or tin in the hills of Isluga, unlike those of Iquique.[7]

Other people have described the former world age to me, a world with no order, when people fought with each other. In those days, the daytime was lit by the light of the moon, and where the village of Enquelga is now sited, there was a seething mass of boiling red quinua. In the present world order, day and night are clearly distinguished by the light of the sun and moon, respectively. Daylight brings colours into being, and the people of this world age are able to perceive them clearly in the light of the sun.[8]

Nowadays hills that are bereft of vegetation and whose slopes are highly charged with colour are held in awe in Isluga. In common with other intensely coloured and brilliant items, such phenomena are perceived as being dangerous and possessing ambiguous qualities. Human settlements in Isluga are clustered around the volcanic mountain known as Laram Qawani. Above the vegetation line, its slopes are infused with colour: sky blue, red and yellow. The bright colour indicates that minerals ought to be found within. Colourful hills also acquire a reputation for consuming human beings. Cerro Culebra ('Serpent Hill'), located on the Bolivian side of the border, is described as having a bald head and it is said to have consumed ten Chipaya men who went to mine silver and gold there. According to Don Marcos, 'the hill ate them, they were shouting inside. . .'. He told me a similar story of Wayna Potosí, which is a red, burnt sienna and ochre-coloured hill nearly devoid of vegetation, around which the road meanders to Chiapa, west of Isluga. Ten men were sent to mine silver, tin and iron there: 'they were eaten, the hill ate them' (Don Marcos, personal communication, 19 July 1987). Isluga people pronounce the name of the hill *Wayna P"utusi*, with the stress on the second syllable of the second word. It shares its name with the larger, snow-covered mountain in Bolivia. *Wayna* means 'young man' in Aymara. However, the red hill between Chiapa and Isluga shares its characteristic colour with the famous 'Lady Red Hill' of the mining town of Potosí, Bolivia. In the songs recorded and analysed by Denise Arnold and Juan de Dios Yapita, Qaqachaka women honour *Wila Qull Siñura, Pursil Jamp'atu*, that is, 'Lady Red Hill, Red Toad of Wealth' (Arnold and Yapita 1998). The singers consider the Red Toad of Wealth to bring good luck, and Arnold explains that it is also a term of endearment for the Virgin Earth in the rainy season.

In Isluga myth, the mountain Laram Qawani, which literally means 'the place with the dark blue valley', lacks the seams of precious glittery metals

---

[7] This is a reference to the silver mine of Huantajaya, which is not currently being worked.

[8] The previous world age came to an end in a cataclysmic reversal known to many Andean societies past and present in the concept of *pachakuti* (see, for example, Randall 1982) or the *muntu t'ijrasiniw* ('the world turned upside down or inside out') among the Laymi of Boliva (Harris 1987: 96).

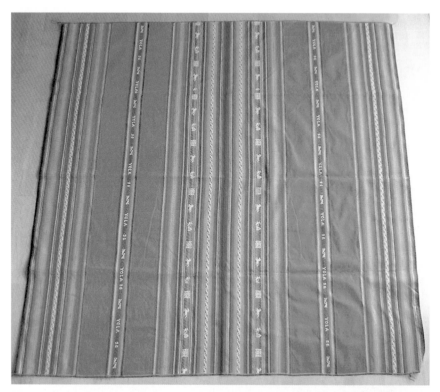

Plate 1 Industrially manufactured *awayu* bought at the Bolivian market, Pisiga. It attempts to copy some of the colour contrasts used in Isluga, but the saturated colours employed give the initial impression of a contrast of hue.

Plate 2 *Wayñu* ceremony in Isluga, 1987. The male alpaca has ear tassels (*wantilurita* and *sombreros*), a neck piece (*wistalla*) and dyed *chimpu* fleece tied along the spine.

Plate 3 Industrially spun, synthetic yarns arranged in orange, pink, blue and green *k'isa*. Bought at the Bolivian market, Pisiga.

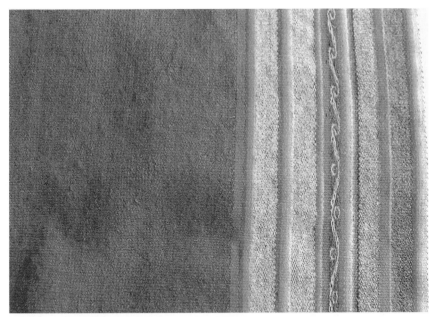

Plate 4 Carrying shawl, *awayu*, woven by Luisa Castro Castro when she was a teenager.

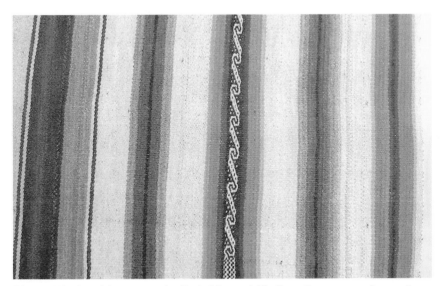

Plate 5 Blanket, *iqiña*, woven by Soria Mamani Challapa from yarns of natural alpaca fleece arranged in *k'isa*. The light beige is spun from llama fleece.

Plate 6 Blanket, *ch'usi,* woven by Soria Mamani Challapa from softly spun yarns of natural alpaca fleece arranged in *ch'ulla k'isa.* The light beige is spun from llama fleece.

that vein hills elsewhere in the Andes.[9] Instead, Isluga people associate the thermal waters, which issue out of the ground two kilometres from Enquelga, with the volcano and its irascible fumaroles of steam. They have an alternative name for the hill: *jiwq'ir qullu*, because it produces steam (*jiwq'i*).[10] Their hill lacks the strong redness that is characteristic of awesome and fabulously rich hills elsewhere in the Andes.

Traditionally, bright colours have been eschewed in everday life in Isluga. Clothing especially was largely plain in colour. Men typically wore *vicuña*-coloured ponchos, and women a black or very dark brown dress tightly belted at the waist. Men wear belts, too, but the bright colours are worn next to the body, hidden beneath the outermost garments. Even in women's dress, the bright red borders of the belts are partially hidden by the folds of the upper part of the dress. The contrast in such garments is between undyed and dyed colours – *k'ura* and *p"ana*, respectively, in Aymara. In effect, weavers are exploiting simultaneous colour contrasts, using Itten's terminology. Itten explained that when we focus on a given colour, the human eye requires its complementary colour, and in its absence, it will generate it spontaneously (1970: 52). He stressed that this effect arises in the eye of the perceiver; it is not one that can be photographed. The large expanses of natural colour juxtaposed with intense red, or sometimes other hues, in Isluga textiles serve to generate simultaneous colour contrasts – the strong red will spontaneously generate green in the mind of the beholder. Undyed grey llama and alpaca fleece is often chosen for the broad plain area in the middle of a carrying shawl (*awayu*) or small rectangular cloths for carrying coca leaves or money (*inkuña*). In these textiles, the neutral grey appears to be tinged by the complementary colour to the stripe that borders it. In turn, the simultaneous contrast intensifies the brightness of the red used in the border.

There is, however, a time of the year when an abundance of bright colours is employed ritually to invest the herd animals with symbolic garments. The ceremony is called the *wayñu* in Isluga, meaning, literally, 'song' or 'dance'. It is designed to enhance the fertility of the llamas, alpacas and sheep. Elsewhere in the Andes, the rite is referred to the marking or the flowering of the herd animals. Each family in Isluga has its own date for the ceremony, usually between New Year and Carnival (which begins on the Saturday before Ash Wednesday), for the celebration of the family's herds of llamas and alpacas. In my understanding of the ceremony, the effectiveness of the ritual stems from the combination of performing sad and mournful-sounding music with the use of strong, bright colours (Dransart 1997: 88).

A large part of the ceremony is spent in 'dressing' the animals with

[9] Miners have prospected for sulphur in the hill.

[10] Gabriel Martínez has argued that Jiwq'ir Qullu is the common name of the hill, while Laram Qawani is its secret name (1976: 315). This is perhaps an attempt to fit Isluga naming systems into a pre-existing anthropological mould. The name Laram Qawani is known throughout the Qaranqas region (Torrico Prado 1971: 77). Isluga people use the different names to refer to different aspects of the hill (Dransart 1991: 115–16).

earpieces known as *sarsillu*, which are tassels of coloured woollen yarns, neckpieces called *wistalla*, the Aymara term for a small pouch in which coca leaves are kept, and *chimpu*, which consists of dyed but unspun rovings of alpaca or llama fleece. Nowadays, *chimpu* is red, pink, orange or yellow in colour. Elderly women do not approve of the inclusion of yellow for this purpose. Evidently, they see colours associated with redness as being more appropriate for *chimpu*, which is tied onto the bodies of the llamas and alpacas. The term *chimpu* means 'mark' in Aymara, and it is used in a gender-specific fashion. Clumps of *chimpu* are tied to the fleece that grows from the withers of female llamas and alpacas, while pieces of *chimpu* are tied to locks of fleece along the spine of male animals.

Different colour choices are made for the ear tassels. Four types of *sarsillu* are made for different categories of animal. The first type, *tilantir sarsillu*, is made for the guide animals of the herd (Plate 2). They are usually mature female llamas unaccompanied by young animals, and they are known by the Spanish term *adelantero*, which is pronounced *dilantir* or *tilantir* in Isluga. The second type of earpiece is made for the female llamas and alpacas of a reproductive age. It is called *tama*, the term for 'herd' in Aymara. The other two types are known as *wantilurita* and *sombreros*, or flags and hats, both terms being borrowed from the Spanish: They are designed for the male animals.

The arrangement of colours selected for making these tassels appears to be highly significant. Red predominates in the *tama* tassels. To make them, red yarn is wrapped around the fingers of the left hand, two loops around three fingers, six loops around two fingers and a further two loops around three fingers (Figure 1). This tassel is tied in place on a long piece of white yarn called *jinchu ch'anka* ('ear yarn', see Dransart 1991: 200). Next the maker groups the six short loops into three groups of two and, using a lark-spur knot, ties two strands of three different coloured yarns from each of the three groups. To complete the tassel, the turns of the long loops are cut. The colours chosen for the three groups of pendant yarns may be pink, green and bluish green, or light pink, darker pink and green, or orange, green and pink. These choices express different types of contrast, such as warm–cold (red and orange are warm colours, but green is cold[11]), and light–dark (pink is light red, and the bluish green is darker than green). The complementary contrast between red and green is also present in some of these tassels. Symbolically, the position and dominance of red in the *tama* tassels suggests that it is believed to generate the other colours.

Tama tassels are hung from the ears of the female llamas and alpacas of

[11] In conventional language used in the West, blue and green are 'cold' colours, while red and orange are 'warm' colours. John Gage observes that these linguistic habits run counter to 'common sense' since the blue part of a flame heats most effectively (e.g. the high-energy, short-wave blue flames of a gas cooker), and the even higher ultraviolet energy waves, which human eyes cannot see, burn skin. He comments that in the West the classification of colours as warm or cold seems to go no further back in written record than the eighteenth century (1993: 8).

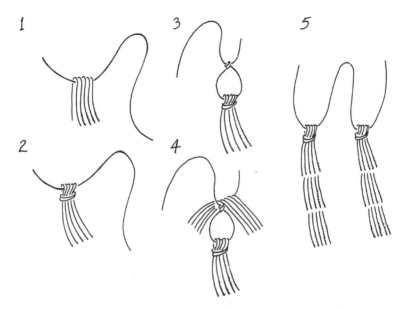

Figure 1a Diagram showing the making of *tilantir sarsillu*.

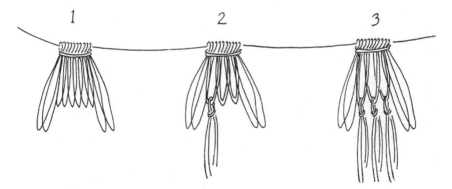

Figure 1b Diagram showing the making of *tama sarsillu*.

a reproductive age. Ritually enhanced by the *wayñu* ceremony, they will go forth to generate lineages of animals. The ceremony serves as a rite of passage for the herd animals, for animals that are approaching their sexual maturity have notches known as an owner's mark cut into their ears. While women participants in the ceremony are responsible for piercing the ears of the llamas and alpacas by stitching the *jinchu ch'anka* ('ear yarn') through the animal's ear with the aid of a needle, it is men who are responsible for cutting the notches. Both these actions produce blood. The men's cutting action produces a flow of blood in recognition of the approaching sexual maturity of the young animals, but in subsequent years women's stitching produces droplets of blood of the same colour that predominates in the *tama* tassels. Arnold and Yapita recognise the connection between blood and flowers in a discussion of the flowering and marking of sheep in Qaqachaka. A woman commented to them: 'the blood flows and the marking follows from generation to generation, following the material blood-line' (Arnold and Yapita 1998: 170, my translation). Qaqachaka women sing about crimson red and pink flowers, just as Isluga *tama* tassels are red and support pink and other coloured pendants.

Tassels designed for the mature female animals who guide the herds, and the male animals, are configured by a different colour system. Colours of different hue are selected, arranged in short intervals of lighter or darker gradations. Green, orange and pink are commonly used in these tassels. Blue is rarely used, and purple is never selected. This arrangement of colour is termed *k'isa* in Isluga. These chromatic gradations in colour are used in conjunction with the mournful songs. It is intriguing to note Lévi-Strauss observes that chromaticism in Western music is also associated with a sense of ambiguity and sorrow: 'The chromatic style is well suited to express grief and affliction' (1970: 281). Isluga people themselves admit to the sadness of the music that the men play on mandolins and that they sing during the ritual investiture of the herd animals. The couple who host the ceremony often become tearful as the event progresses. It is only when the last day of the ceremony ends, and darkness falls, that the music becomes joyful and people dance around a bonfire. The saturated colours, which are so powerful during the daytime that they have to be accompanied by sombre music, are not so threatening as the light fades. Saturated colours are pure and intense (Itten 1970: 55), but with the arrival of nightfall, even colours of maximum intensity are diluted.

K'isa

As explained above, the *k'isa* is an arrangement of colour graded in little steps to form a narrow sequence from light to dark, or *vice versa*. It is an abstraction of colour and light, or one might say that it is light refracted and embodied in coloured yarns. Verónica Cereceda has compared the Isluga *k'isa* with the 'mirror' of a rainbow, because it is not an exact copy (1987: 215). Women incorporate these stripes of colour executed in plain weave in their textiles, especially in carrying shawls and blankets.

Weavers tell me that it is important that the colour in a textile should 'sing out'. They take particular care in choosing the colours for the *k'isa*. Colour combinations in a textile that do not set up sufficient contrast in the eye of the beholder are criticised as being dead and like lead (*qaqa*). The *k'isa* that are woven by the women are the counterpart of the music led by the men in the llama corral during the *wayñu* ceremony. However, in some parts of the Andes, the Aymara term *k'isa* means 'wrinkled fruit', or fruit that is sweet and over-ripe.[12] The almost overbearing sweetness of the colours is the counterpart to the dirge-like character of the music performed when the llamas and alpacas are ritually dressed with highly charged coloured 'garments'.

In the past, spinners used to buy aniline dyes in the once-a-fortnight Bolivian market. They dyed yarn spun from sheep's fleece to introduce the colour accents in their weavings, which were largely woven from naturally coloured camelid fibre yarns. Industrially spun acrylic yarns are also available in the market, and increasingly they have been employed to weave the *k'isa* in a textile (Plate 3). They are more colour fast than yarns dyed with aniline dyes. With the easy availability of colour in different tones, the *k'isa* are becoming wider as they are formed from a greater number of little steps than previously. The intervals between the colours are becoming shorter. Nowadays, weavers aim to find five, six, or sometimes even seven, tones of one colour to make a *k'isa*.

On asking a group of Isluga weavers what they thought was the most beautiful detail they were capable of weaving, Verónica Cereceda reports that they all agreed that the *k'isa* was the most beautiful part of a textile. One of them told her, 'The *k'isas* are its light' (Cereceda 1987: 184, my translation). In her description of the visual characteristics of these colour formations, Cereceda emphasises the light–dark contrasts. A 'complete' *k'isa* is one that traverses from light to dark and back to light again in little tonal steps of the same hue.[13] However, weavers mostly use combinations of 'half' *k'isas* known as *ch'ulla*, the Aymara term for 'one of a pair'. They arrange these half *k'isa* around narrow pattern bands and at the edges of a textile, or between the colourful lateral bands and the wide natural coloured main part of the textile, which is known as the 'body' of the textile (Plate 4).

As mentioned above, with reference to the ear tassels worn by female guide animals and male animals, the *k'isa* also exploit complementary and cold–warm contrasts. These colour contrasts are developed to a greater extent in woven blankets and carrying shawls. The colours used in *k'isa* are

[12] In Isluga, the term that is used for sweetness is *muxsa*. The adjective has been discussed by Platt among other terms of a symmetrical and oppositional character (1987: 96–97). One of the other adjectives he considers is *q'ayma*, and its meaning of 'lacking in salt' (in both a literal and a metaphorical sense). Henry Stobart has discussed the language of taste that the Quechua speakers of Ayllu Macha, Bolivia, apply to melodies and potatoes; both are considered to be insipid (*q'ayma*) when they belong to the old generation, but 'sweet' when they emerge from the new generation (1996: 429). It is of relevance to the present discussion on synaesthetic effects that an Aymara dictionary definition (Apaza Suca et al. 1984:188) lists a visual term among the meanings of *q'ayma*: 'faded (clothing)'. One of the most striking examples of such effects was recorded by Arnold in a song performed at a house-roofing ceremony in Qaqachaka, of an Inka house constructed from adobes of sugar stuck together with paste of *aji* (Arnold 1992: 55 and 73).

[13] Cereceda offers a list of different types of *k'isa* (1987: 190–95). The weavers I have consulted with sometimes use the terms she lists, but according to my data, what she calls a *k'isthapita* is light rather than dark at the centre.

pink (which is a light form of red with a slightly violet tinge), green and orange.[14] Blue *k'isa* are sometimes also used, but traditionally blue was only used in a narrow stripe at the junction between the lateral bands and the body of a carrying shawl. Weavers have expressed to me their uneasiness about using blue, and its associations with sadness.[15] Yellow is never used as an independent colour in Isluga textiles. Like blue, its use is constrained by culturally specific restrictions.[16] It is the colour of death (*amaya*). Occasionally, the setting sun suddenly turns the land and the air yellow. This phenomenon is referred to as *amaya*, and people rush inside when it happens, especially the young and sick.

Such colour choices demonstrate that Isluga weavers use colours optically because they base their palette on the red, green and blue lights of the spectrum. To put it technically, they select prismatic, non-corporeal colours, but paradoxically they have to express these colours by using pigmentary, or corporeal colours in the form of dyed yarns. Among prismatic colours, the primaries are red, green and blue. In contrast, painters' and dyers' colours are pigmentary colours, and the primaries are red, yellow and blue (Itten 1970: 16). Such colours are absorptive; when they are mixed in certain proportions, they produce black. In contrast, the mixture of prismatic colours results in white light. When white light is dispersed through a prism, it is refracted into a spectrum of colour, which, starting with the red, passes through orange, yellow, green, blue and violet. The only colour not represented in the spectrum is purple, which, significantly, Isluga weavers do not use in their textiles. It is also significant that they have chosen green rather than yellow to use in their *k'isa*. A green *k'isa* is often paired with an orange *k'isa*, and sometimes with a pink *k'isa*. These colour contrasts are very nearly complementary ones.

Since the 1980s, teenage girls have increasingly been using the contrast of orange and blue *k'isa* in their weavings. Orange and blue are complementary colours because they are diametrically opposed to each other in a colour circle (Itten 1970, Fig. 3). Itten describes such complementary colours as

---

[14] In Aymara, the colour term for the pink configuration is *liriu* (the term is borrowed from the Spanish *lirio*, for an 'iris' or 'white lily'), for the green it is *ch'uqña*, and for the orange it is *jaruma*. The pinkness of the *liriu k'isa* is considered to contrast sufficiently with the blood red that is often selected for the main part of the lateral band in a carrying shawl.

[15] María Flores admitted to me that 'blue is sad', and that it can bring about a death. The first time she used it in a traditional women's dress (*urk"u*), she introduced it into the hem, which was hidden under her left arm when she wore it (personal communication, 26 February 1987). Alison Spedding Pallet has suggested that the colour blue is associated with liminality by Aymara speakers, which may explain why women harvesting coca leaves in the geographically distant valleys of Nor and Sud Yungas in Bolivia use a sky-blue cloth tied to the waist (1992: 67, 82–83).

[16] On one occasion, I was sitting with the late Natividad Castro Challapa at the fortnightly market on the Bolivian–Chilean frontier, when a girl walked past wearing what Doña Nati thought was too much yellow. She turned to me, saying 'You shouldn't wear yellow, or you will bore your husband'.

being opposite, yet the one requires the other: 'They incite each other to maximum vividness when adjacent; and they annihilate each other [. . .] when mixed' (1970: 49). Prismatic colour contrasts yield white when mixed together. Teenage girls are apparently aware of such effects, because they have introduced further modifications into the carrying shawl. Formerly, the body of the textile was woven from fairly dark natural brown or grey camelid fibre yarns. Through time, weavers have been selecting lighter greys, beiges and even white. However, white camelid fibre is often tinged with a creamness or a greyness. Teenage girls have started to weave carrying shawls made entirely from synthetic yarns, using a brilliant white for the body of the textile. They are reproducing the colour spectrum in their weavings; the white of the body of the textile is interrupted by the narrow stripes of complementary colours which appear as if refracted through a prism.

Isluga textiles express a very sophisticated colour theory. It is, moreover, a theory that is not explicitly verbalised. Confronted with the silence of their elders on the subject of colour, teenagers have been developing colour schemes that display their awareness of prismatic colours. This has not always met with approval.

In February 1987, Marina Castro Mamani was weaving a loom length of a carrying shawl designed to have colourful lateral stripes along the side selvedges, as well as three inner stripes, all flanked by k'isa.[17] A couple visiting her family's home said the shawl must be a matrimonial one, and they commented on the amount of money that had gone into buying the synthetic yarns. Unlike yarns spun from the fleece of her own animals, Marina had to buy them in the market. Other people were more forthright in their comments; one woman said 'This carrying shawl is ugly', using the Spanish term *fea*. Marina's mother, the late Gabriela Mamani Challapa, thought this comment was unfair, saying how well the shawl was woven. However, in the late 1980s I observed that the adjective *fea* was frequently applied by middle-aged and elderly weavers to describe the colourful weavings of teenage girls. They praised the technical skills of the young women, but what offended them was the over-abundance of saturated, dyed colour.

Verónica Cereceda, whose fieldwork in Isluga predated mine, also noted that some women had problems accepting the overuse of k'isa in textiles. In the upper moiety (Araxsaya), women referred to the textiles of Manq"asaya (the lower, or 'inner' moiety) as having too many k'isa (Cereceda 1987: 195). However, blankets may be woven in Isluga from warp yarns that are entirely dyed. Cereceda illustrates such a blanket (1987: 193), adding in her caption the words: 'Continuity without rupture is perceived as dangerous (absence of articulation = asociality)'.[18] In her interpretation, the design of the blanket is organised in such a fashion that the succession of k'isa set up an

---

[17] In Isluga, carrying shawls are woven from two loom lengths which are later stitched together.

[18] My translation.

ambiguity in the eye and mind of the beholder. She maintains that when we see the blanket, we perceive a continuity, but logically we are confronted by a discontinuity, consisting of slight, minimal differences. This, she says, is the only thing that keeps *k'isa* on the side of culture; they are classifiable but they offer only minimal distinctions that may be perceived (1987: 195). Cereceda's argument is couched in Lévi-Straussian terms, and it rests on the premise that Isluga people recognise a distinction between nature and culture.[19] From my experiences of living with Isluga families, I am not so convinced that they draw distinctions in such terms.[20] Cereceda does not ask why Isluga women choose to weave such dangerously coloured, 'asocial' blankets with which to protect their family members when sleeping. It is perhaps significant that Isluga houses in the past did not have windows. In the dimness inside the house and under the darkness of night, all colour distinctions are diminished. 'For all Colours will agree in the Darke', Francis Bacon observed (1892: 11). Only when the blankets are brought into the light of day do the colours 'sing out'. The young women who expanded the 'traditional' colour schemes in Isluga are not considered to be asocial, or even pre-social. They have a long weaving apprenticeship, and their mothers continue to teach and assist them until they leave home to work elsewhere, or until they marry. In a sense, their mothers are complicit in helping their daughters to extend their colour awareness. Older women are now including blue where they would not have done so before, and they are also extending the *k'isa* in their textiles.[21]

K'isa are representations of a natural phenomenon, but rainbows also exist outwith Isluga culture and society. They provide weavers with the colours with which to configure their textiles. However, they are held in awe; a young weaver warned me that you should not point at a rainbow.[22] In Misminay, near Cuzco, Peru, the rainbow has been described as a manifestation of 'chthonic or celestial forces' that take the appearance of a giant double-headed serpent rising up out of a subterranean spring and plunging its other head into a distant spring (Urton 1981: 93). Rainbows are, in Urton's analysis, indicative of the fertility within the earth.

[19] See also Cereceda 1978: 1029–31. Paradoxically, Lévi-Strauss himself admitted that no gulf exists between 'nature' and 'culture', and that the boundary between the two is 'permeable' (1970: 275).

[20] Equally, I do not regard perception and thinking to be separate mental activities, as Cereceda seems to imply when she contrasts *la mirada* ('the gaze') with *el pensamiento* ('thinking').

[21] It is interesting to note that the woman who criticised Marina's weaving for its overuse of colour had sons at that time, but she did not yet have a daughter, and was therefore not training someone to weave.

[22] The comment was made by Lucrezia Castro Mamani on 3 February 1997. For a discussion of woven representations of rainbows in Isluga belts, see Dransart 1988: 46–48 and Figs. 9, 10a and 10b. Rainbows are believed to be able to enter a person's stomach. However, the woven representations take the form of a pointed zigzag, in contrast to the curved character of the natural phenomenon.

In the past, the Isluga *k'isa* did not take the form that it has today.[23] Cereceda observes that there is little evidence for anything similar in Aymara weavings of the nineteenth century (1994: 66). However, Isluga weavers have told me that not only stripes consisting of little, graduated steps of the same hue are called *k'isa*. They also apply the term to narrow plain weave stripes of different colours. This colour arrangement is common in pre-Hispanic and colonial period textiles (Dransart, in press). It was used in Isluga by women who are now in their seventies and eighties.

K'isa in camelid fleece

Camelid fibre is the basic raw material that spinners and weavers transform into yarn and fabric. It is pigmented; the colours of fleece are corporeal, but they are modified by the fall of light. Isluga people have extended the concept of *k'isa* to apply it to natural as well as dyed colours. With the development of the configuration in the form of small tonal steps, it has become possible to organise natural colours in a similar fashion. An extensive *k'isa* from white to black passes through the various tones of brown, as follows:

Janqu	White
Janqu q"usi	Light fawn
Q"usi	Fawn
Wari q"usi	Light brown (like *vicuña*)
Paqu	*Vicuña* colour
Ch'umpi	Brown
Ch'ar ch'umpi	Dark brown
Ch'ara	Black

When there is a large number of llamas or alpacas in a herd, herders resort to some less frequently used terms in order to distinguish between their animals. *Liriu q"usi* is used for a very light brown tending towards pink; and *chupika*, for a resonant reddish brown which is often seen in alpacas in Isluga.[24] Both these colours are, of course, undyed, or *k'ura* colours. When I asked Soria Mamani Challapa to explain the colour *liriu q"usi* in further detail, she described it as a light *p"ana* colour. In other words, she ascribed qualities associated with dyed colours to this undyed natural colour.

Tones of grey may also be arranged in a *k'isa*, from light to dark:

Janqu	White
Janqu uqi	Very light grey
Chilka or *chuchi*	Light grey, *azucarina* in Spanish

[23] Elsewhere in the Andes, the term *k'isa* is used differently. Among the Laymi of Bolivia, the Aymara-Spanish term *k'isado* ('sweetened') refers to the symmetrical disposition of colours around a central pattern band or at each side of a shawl (López, Flores and Letourneux 1993: 99).

[24] *Chupika* is another Aymara term for red or scarlet.

Uqi	Grey
Ch'ar uqi	Dark grey
Ch'ara	Black

Camelid fleece may also appear to be half grey, half brown; *ch'uñup"uti* is a dull colour, not particularly prized. It resembles the colour of cooked *ch'uñu* potatoes, which are freeze dried in the Andes to preserve them, and this process turns them blackish-buff in colour. More favoured grey colours are *kupala*, a light colour named after *kupala* resin used for medicinal and ritual purposes; *q'illuwari*, a slightly yellowish grey colour, which, like *chilka* (the name of a plant that grows at a lower altitude than Isluga), is sometimes translated into the Spanish *azucarina*; and *chinchilla*, a dark grey like the fur of the chinchilla. Other variations employed for black are *ch'iyara* and *ch'ar aceituna*, from the Spanish for 'olive'. In Isluga there is a greater variety of grey colours in alpacas than in llamas, which tend to be a darker grey or *ch'uñup"uti* coloured. In all, Doña Soria recognises eighteen different natural colours of fleece. She exploits these colour characteristics in many of her weavings (Plate 5).

There is an extensive colour terminology that herders and weavers can call upon to describe the colour of a given fleece (Dransart 2002: 104–107). However, colour perception varies from person to person, and there may be disagreement between people in deciding on what colour to call a particular fleece. Much may depend on the intended use of yarn spun from such fleece, since the natural colours of llamas and alpacas have very specific roles in the traditional garments of Isluga. For example, the *vicuña* colours of *wari q"usi* and *paqu* are traditionally used for men's ponchos, but *janqu*, *ch'umpi* and *ch'ara* are used in bags called *wayaqa*. The same brown yarn may be called *paqu* if it is woven into a poncho, but *ch'umpi* if it is used in a *wayaqa*. Depending on the tension of the spin or ply angle in a yarn, the same colour of fleece may look slightly different in colour, as a more tightly spun yarn will not reflect the light in the same manner as a loosely spun yarn (Plate 6).

Concluding comments

Urton observes that the seven colours of the rainbow may correspond with Western classical and medieval beliefs in numbers, in which the numeral seven is accorded astrological, alchemical and religious importance (1981: 87). When he asked Misminay people how many colours there are in a rainbow, he received various answers. He considers the dominant colours in Misminay rainbows to be red and blue, and that, in specific circumstances, rainbows can be classified as either 'red' or 'blue', the former being 'female' and the latter 'male' (1981: 89). I agree with Urton that it is important to consider how colours are perceived in specific cultural contexts, but, like Constance Classen (1993), he may be overemphasising the cultural at the expense of physiological, psychological and environmental aspects of colour perception.

At the other extreme, Berlin and Kay (1969) argued that colour vocabulary is innate rather than culturally determined. The book was a reaction against ultra-relativism, and it made a case for an evolutionary process in the degree of elaboration of colour terminology in different societies (Morris 1979, note 16). In response to the book, John Bousfield argued that what is at issue when different cultures perceive the same spectrum is how it is cut up and classified and how it is encoded into language (1979: 205–206).[25] He argues that 'the rules of classification do not reflect the categories; rather the categories are sustained through the application of rules which themselves form part of complex social practices' (1979: 216–17).

I accept this claim, but I think that my study of how Isluga colour perceptions are expressed in textiles and my own art school training raise some interesting questions.[26] My training enables me to observe at least some of the colour contrasts Isluga weavers use. Following Urton's comments that chopping up the rainbow into seven colours might tell us more about the classification of colour in Western societies than about rainbows, one might suggest that Itten's scheme of seven colour contrasts also corresponds with culturally specific notions regarding the numeral seven. There may be more subtleties in Isluga textiles to which my training has not yet sensitised my colour perception. In any case, the full colour spectrum includes ultraviolet, red, green and blue light. Of this spectrum, human eyes can only perceive red, green and blue light.[27] Other animal species, such as Brimstone butterflies and starlings, are able to see these colours as well as ultraviolet (Institute of Contemporary Arts 1973: 34).

In my own folk model (received from my art school training), black and white are not 'colours'; black objects absorb all colour wavelengths, while white ones reflect them all. I therefore do not accept Berlin and Kay's evolutionary sequence of what they call 'basic colours', as it begins with black and white. An art-historical analysis of Isluga material culture, if one could imagine a depressing situation in which the people themselves were no longer able to talk about it, would almost inevitably highlight the importance of the blood-red hue that plays such a prominent role in wayñu and in textiles, particularly along the edges. However, the term wila ('blood') does not correspond to one of Berlin and Kay's basic colour terms because the term is not an abstract one. One might well find oneself in the paradoxical quandary in which Saunders found Berlin and Kay to be in their treatment of Zuñi colour terms: their linguistic criteria and 'foci' did not mesh (Saunders 2000: 87).

[25] A well known case in point is the term glas in both Gaelic and Welsh, which means 'blue', but which encompasses the adjacent colour values of blue and green in the spectrum, as it also applies to grass.

[26] See Saunders 2000: 89 for a comment on the Bousfield article.

[27] Human beings are sensitive to light waves of about 400–780 nanometers or millimicrons, while insects are receptive to ultraviolet light waves with a peak of 350 nanometers (Itten 1970: 15; Institute of Contemporary Arts 1973: 34).

There is in any case a complex interrelationship between dyed and undyed *k'isa* in Isluga. Cereceda (1978: 1035n) reports that the ultimate contrastive colour pairing in Isluga is between white (considered to be 'male') and all other colours (considered to be 'female'). Her own groundbreaking work has focused on interpreting the interplay of light and dark contrasts in Andean textiles (Cereceda 1978, 1987: 184–200, and 1990).[28] In Isluga myth, the present world order came into being when white daylight shone on the shadowy redness of the previous world age and produced the colourful distinctions of the present age. Symbolically, red contains the potential for refracting into all the colours of the spectrum. However, as noted, Isluga people apply the non-abstract term for blood to the colour. It is possible that people's reluctance to speak about colour in a direct fashion has encouraged the development of a range of alternative terms so as to avoid naming strong colours. If people have strong taboos against naming colours, this would invalidate the efforts to establish evolutionary linguistic sequences.

There are indications in the literature of the fundamental importance of the colour red in other Andean communities. Denise Arnold has discussed the transmission of ancestral substance in Qaqachaka, Bolivia, in the form of red bloodlines (matrilineal kindreds) and white male kindreds that are conceived of as paired red and white pathways, streams of tears, or ribbons, respectively (1988: 191–206, 1992: 99). She explains that incest beliefs focus on blood ties, the expiation of 'blood-guilt' and the character of the taboo on sexual and marital relationships between brothers and sisters. Interestingly, incest is referred to by the Aymara terms *larama* ('blue') or *ch'unq"a* ('green') in Qaqachaka (Arnold 1988: 196). At a symbolic level, it constitutes a 'middle pathway', and on the physiological plane it introduces the complementary colour contrasts required by the mind, which, in the presence of red, will spontaneously generate its complement, green (Itten 1970: 49).

Urton's discussion of rainbows includes beliefs that they can enter the human body, making contact with the subterranean spring from which they rise. He cites Lira (1946): 'waters from which rainbows arise have small, colorful deposits [*colorcitas*] which can enter the body; if these waters should enter the body, one's urine will be rainbow coloured' (1946: 89). The colours of the rainbow in the urine are, in effect, produced by refraction through the prism of the red deposits. There is a need to examine the cultural as well as the physiological conditions of such knowledges that concern colour. What Cassandra Torrico stresses is that although semiotic codes (she was referring to the design principles of light and dark in weavings) may be similar between different ethnic groups, 'there are differences in the messages transmitted by each ethnic group' (no date).

[28] A fine study inspired by the work of Cereceda is Cassandra Torrico's manuscript on the woven sacks of Ayllu Macha, Bolivia. It addresses the semantic universe of Macha weavings, as expressed largely in terms of light–dark contrasts.

This ethnography of colour has shown that older women in Isluga choose not to talk about colour. Younger women learn about it through their own observations of natural phenomena and how they have been represented in the weavings of other women. Consequently, there are implications for understanding the transmission of knowledge in Isluga. In 1977, Bloch presented a conundrum. He suggested that if we believe in the Durkheimian proposition that categories of understanding and systems of classification are social in origin, then 'this leaves the actors with no language to talk *about* their society and so change it, since they can only talk *within* it' (1977: 281). In Isluga, changes in the weaving of textiles are due at least partly to the response of young women to the *silence* of their mothers and grandmothers, who refused to talk about strong colour and dye technology. I am reluctant to regard this negation of verbal communication as part of Bloch's category of 'systems by which we hide' the world (Bloch 1977: 290). However, following Ellen's argument (1979: 19), it suggests that there is no all-embracing, undifferentiated worldview integrated through symbolic classification in Isluga.

Dan Sperber has argued that the act of transmitting a representation tends to transform the representation (1985: 75). He distinguishes between mental and public representations. The former are psychological, while the latter have to do with the interface between the brain and its environment. Like Bloch, Sperber argues that different types of representation achieve rationality in different ways. Sperber suggests that everyday empirical knowledge is developed under strong conceptual, logical and perceptual constraints. Other forms of mental representations (such as religious beliefs) involve other cognitive abilities that are developed with greater flexibility, especially the capacity to form representations of representations (1985: 83). The Isluga *k'isa* is an excellent example of a representation of a representation. One might say that Isluga people's experience of their herding and weaving activities deeply colours their knowledge of the world and is mediated through those very practices of herding and weaving. More than that, the reproduction of *k'isa* in textiles demonstrates that young women in Isluga make public and communicate their own representations of the representations of rainbows that their mothers and grandmothers have been weaving. Older women produce their own variations by responding to their daughters' reproductions when they transform their own practices to share in the enhanced knowledge concerning colour perception.

References

Ackerman, Diane 1995. *A Natural History of the Senses*. New York: Vintage Books.
Apaza Suca, Nicanor, K. Komarek, D. Llanque Chana and V. Ochoa Villanueva. 1984. *Diccionario aymara–castellano. Arunakan liwru aymara–kastillanu*. Puno: Proyecto Experimental de Educación Bilingüe.

Arnold, Denise. 1988. 'Matrilineal Practice in a Patrilineal Setting: Rituals and Metaphors of Kinship in an Andean Ayllu'. Doctoral thesis, University of London.

——, 1992. 'La casa de adobes y piedras del Inka: Género, memoria y cosmos en Qaqachaka'. In D.Y. Arnold, D. Jímenez A. and J. de D. Yapita, *Hacia un orden andino de las cosas*. La Paz: Hisbol/ILCA: 31–108.

Arnold, Denise, and J. de D. Yapita. 1998. *Río de vellón, río de canto: cantar a los animales, una poética andina de la creación*. La Paz: Hisbol/ILCA.

Bacon, Francis. 1892. 'Of Unity in Religion'. In *Bacon's Essays and Colours of Good and Evil*. London: Macmillan and Co.: 8–13.

Berlin, Brent, and P. Kay. 1969. *Basic Color Terms: Their Universality and Evolution*. Berkeley and Los Angeles: University of California Press.

Bloch, Maurice. 1977. 'The Past and the Present in the Present'. *Man* NS 12: 278–92.

Bousfield, John. 1979. 'The World Seen as a Colour Chart'. In R.F. Ellen and D. Reason (eds.), *Classifications in their Social Context*. London: Academic Press: 195–220.

Cereceda, Verónica. 1978. 'Sémiologie des tissus andins: les *talegas* d'Isluga'. *Annales: Economies, Sociétés et Civilisations* 35(5–6): 1017–35.

——, 1987. 'Aproximaciones a una estética andina: de la belleza al *tinku*'. In J. Medina (ed.), *Tres reflexiones sobre el pensamiento andino*. La Paz: Hisbol: 133–231.

——, 1990. 'A partir de los colores de un pájaro . . .'. *Boletín del Museo Chileno de Arte Precolombino* 4: 57–104.

——, 1994. 'Notas para una lectura de los textiles tarabuco'. In J. Dávalos, V. Cereceda and G. Martínez, *Textiles Tarabuco*. Sucre: Asur: 47–88.

Classen, Constance. 1993. *Worlds of Sense: Exploring the Senses in History and across Cultures*. London: Routledge.

Cosgrove, Denis. 1984. *Social Formation and Symbolic Landscape*. London: Croom Helm.

Dransart, Penny. 1988. 'Continuidad y cambio en la producción textil tradicional aymara'. *Hombre y Desierto: una Perspectiva Cultural* 2: 41–57.

——, 1991. 'Fibre to Fabric: The Role of Fibre in Camelid Economies in Prehispanic and Contemporary Chile'. Doctoral thesis, University of Oxford.

——, 1997. 'Cultural Transpositions: Writing about Rites in the Llama Corral'. In R. Howard-Malverde (ed.), *Creating Context in Andean Cultures*. Oxford Studies in Anthropological Linguistics. New York and Oxford: Oxford University Press: 85–98.

——, 2002. *Earth, Water, Fleece and Fabric: An Ethnography and Archaeology of Andean Camelid Herding*. London: Routledge.

——, In press. 'Iconografía en el arte textil del sur del Perú y del norte de Chile: algunas consideraciones sobre las formas figurativas y abstractas'. In S. Arce Torres (ed.), *La arqueología de la costa sur peruana*. Ica: Museo Regional.

Ellen, Roy. 1979. 'Introductory Essay'. In R.F. Ellen and D. Reason (eds.), *Classifications in their Social Context*. London: Academic Press:1–32.

Feld, Steven. 1996. 'Waterfalls of Song: An Acoustemology of Place Resounding in Bosavi, Papua New Guinea'. In S. Feld and K.H. Basso (eds.), *Senses of Place*. Santa Fe, NM: School of American Research Press: 91–135.

Gage, John. 1993. *Colour and Culture: Practice and Meaning from Antiquity to Abstraction*. London: Thames and Hudson.

Hardin, C.L., and L. Maffi (eds.). 1997. *Color Categories in Thought and Language*. Cambridge: Cambridge University Press.

Harris, Olivia. 1987. 'De la fin du monde. Notes depuis le Nord-Potosi'. *Cahiers des Amériques Latines* 6: 93–117.

Helms, Mary. 1995. *Creations of the Rainbow Serpent: Polychrome Ceramic Designs from Ancient Panama*. Albuquerque, NM: University of New Mexico Press.

Institute of Contemporary Arts. 1973. *Illusion in Nature and Art*. Ed. K. and R. Campbell. London: Duckworth and Company.

Itten, Johannes. 1970. *The Elements of Color: A Treatise on the Color System of Johannes Itten Based on his Book The Art of Color*. Trans. E. van Hagen. New York: Van Nostrand Reinhold.

Lévi-Strauss, Claude. 1970. *The Raw and the Cooked*. Trans. J. and D. Weightman. London: Jonathan Cape Ltd.

Lira, Jorge. 1946. *Farmacopea tradicional indígena y prácticas rituales*. Lima: Talleres Gráficos 'El Condor'.

López, Jaime, W. Flores and C. Letourneux. 1993. *Laymi Salta*. La Paz: PAC–Potosí and Ruralter Editores.

Lucy, John A. 1997. 'The Linguistics of "Color"'. In Hardin and Maffi (eds.): 320–46.

Martínez, Gabriel. 1976. 'El sistema de los uywiris en Isluga'. *Anales de la Universidad del Norte (Homenaje al Dr Gustavo Le Paige S.J.)* 10: 255–327.

Morris, B. 1979. 'Symbolism as Ideology: Thoughts around Navaho Taxonomy and Symbolism'. In R.F. Ellen and D. Reason (eds.), *Classifications in their Social Context*. London: Academic Press: 17–138.

Ong, Walter. 1982. *Orality and Literacy: The Technologizing of the Word*. London: Methuen.

Platt, Tristan. 1987. 'Entre *ch'axwa* y *muxsa*: para una historia del pensamiento político aymara'. In J. Medina (ed.), *Tres reflexiones sobre el pensamiento andino*. La Paz: Hisbol: 61–132.

Randall, Robert. 1982. 'Qoyllur Rit'i, an Inca Fiesta of the Pleiades: Reflections on Time and Space in the Andean World'. *Bulletin de l'Institut Français d'Etudes Andines* 11(1–2): 37–81.

Reichel-Dolmatoff, Gerardo. 1978. 'Desana Animal Categories, Food Restrictions, and the Concept of Color Energies'. *Journal of Latin American Lore* 4(2): 243–91.

Saunders, Barbara. 2000. 'Revisiting Basic Colour Terms'. *Journal of the Royal Anthropological Institute* NS 6: 81–99.

Spedding Pallet, Alison. 1992. '¿Por qué las yungueñas usan *mitiña* celeste? Una aproximación al simbolismo de colores en el mundo andino'. *Revista Pumapunku* 3: 67–89.

Sperber, Dan B. 1985. 'Anthropology and Psychology: Towards an Epidemiology of Representations'. *Man* NS 20: 73–89.

Stobart, Henry. 1996. 'Los wayñus que salen de las huertas: Música y papas en una comunidad campesina del Norte de Potosí'. In D.Y. Arnold and J. de D. Yapita (eds.), *Madre melliza y sus crías. Ispall mama wawampi. Antología de la papa*. La Paz: Hisbol: 413–30.

Stoller, Paul. 1997. *Sensuous Scholarship*. Philadelphia: University of Pennsylvania Press.

Torrico, Cassandra. No date. 'Living Weavings: The Symbolism of Bolivian Herders' Sacks'. Unpublished manuscript.

Torrico Prado, B. 1971. *Indígenas en el corazón de América*. La Paz and Cochabamba: Editorial 'Los Amigos del Libro'.

Urton, Gary. 1981. *At the Crossroads of the Earth and Sky: An Andean Cosmology*. Texas: University of Texas Press.

Wooten, Bill, and D. Miller. 1997. 'The Psychophysics of Color'. In Hardin and Maffi (eds.): 59–88.

CHAPTER FOUR

Interlocking Realms: Knowing Music and Musical Knowing in the Bolivian Andes

Henry Stobart

In this chapter dedicated to the music of a rural community of *ayllu* Macha, northern Potosí, Bolivia, I wish to approach knowledge in terms of sensibility and as a process of interaction. Such sensibility concerns embodied ways of knowing, such as socially relevant behaviour and sensory understandings, which are often difficult, and sometimes all but impossible, to verbalise.[1] Andean music is not unique in this sense; as Derryk Cooke has observed more generally, 'the thoughts which are expressed to me by a piece of music are not too indefinite to be put into words, but on the contrary too definite' (1959: 12, cited in Blacking 1995: 36).

When we speak of 'knowing' a particular piece of music or genre it is generally the experience of embodying the sounds – and to some degree 'emplacing' ourselves through them – to which we refer, rather than to any technical knowledge of the music.[2] We seem principally to remember and reproduce melodies as sequences of embodied gestures without any mental representation of, for example, intervallic, rhythmic or metric structure. Several writers have compared this embodied experience of music to dancing. In the words of Roger Scruton:

> In responding to the meaning of a piece of music, we are being led through a series of gestures which gain their significance from the idea of a community that they imitate, just as do the gestures of a dance . . . As we move with these elements, therefore, we are led by our sympathies into a wholly new totality: a musical bridge is created, spanning distant reaches of human life. (Scruton 1993: 201, cited in Frith 1996: 266–67)

The musical 'bridge' invoked here by Scruton emphasises the way music is able to connect people and places as interlocking realms. No musical

---

[1] See Feld 1994: 93–94 on the problems of verbalising precise musical understandings. It is also important to stress that verbal interaction is often less concerned with the exchange of information than with the interactive processes through which individuals constitute themselves and communicate their sensibilities as social beings (see Bauman 1977: 11).

[2] See Feld 1996 and Stokes 1994 for discussions of emplacement through music.

performance, personal practice on an instrument, or even private listening to a recording, is ever a truly independent act. Such activities automatically connect us with a multiplicity of social relationships, past experiences and places. Music is in constant dialogue with its past, its potential future, and the cultural spaces it creates and articulates. However innovative or individualistic musicians may attempt to be, their creativity always operates in dialogue with learned social and cultural norms – an unavoidable characteristic that has deeply frustrated a number of twentieth-century composers.

Before accepting the idea of music as essentially dialogical, it is important to remember that, to the contrary, in many cultures music is presented in terms of individual expression. This is particularly evident in the widespread reference to individual musicians or composers in discourse about music or marketing, and in the existence of societies to protect the rights of composers and performers as the individual creators of music. However, during fieldwork in the rural Andes I discovered that music was generally presented in terms of an interface or bridge between people or realms of being, where individual musical creativity and knowledge were subsumed within broader notions of knowledge, dialogue and community. The very concepts of a 'composer' or 'soloist' were not only absent but also often actively discouraged, where equality of opportunity, consensus, and the idea of community were stressed above individual competence (see also Turino 1989: 4).

Although music is the focus of this chapter, it is important to stress that our analysis of musical knowledge cannot and should not be neatly separated from other forms of knowing. As Hoffman has pointed out, 'musical knowledge is based on the same epistemology which underlies and pervades the entire culture' (1978: 69). Furthermore, during my fieldwork among the Macha, my hosts did not approach knowledge as the exclusive realm of humans. Instead, human knowledge was presented as just part of a much wider sphere of knowledge. According to this same epistemology, I was told that all music, even that from commercial recordings, is acquired from ambiguous non-human beings, such as the *sirinus* ('Sirens') or *satanas* ('Satans'). The emphasis was thus shifted away from the idea of individual human creation or talent and instead focused on ideas of dialogue with sources of knowledge beyond the individual, in which musical creation and performance are dependent upon the interlocking of different realms. Similarly, my Andean host rejected the notion of innate musical talent, arguing instead that – as with other skills – musical competence is dependent upon dedication of time and energy.

Implicit in the idea of dialogue is the existence of an 'Other', and in the case of the *sirinus* or *satanas* this 'Other' is identified with the non-human world. However, this identification of powers emanating from beyond the individual may also be an acceptance that the stature and creative potential of the knowledge generated through dialogue is somehow greater than that of the individual human actors participating in the exchange. This is made particularly evident in one of the main themes in this chapter, the use of 'interlocking' or 'hocket' technique in panpipe performance. For this technique, two people are required to perform a melody, and alternate notes of the scale are divided between their paired instruments. The two players both bring their individual powers and knowledge to bear on this musical dialogue, but the resulting melody, its emotive power, potential for transformation and the sense of understanding it conveys is, in a very real sense, more than just the sum of the parts.

The inter-animation of the players participating in this musical dialogue, expressed by the unification of their distinct but complementary sounds in melody, contrasts vividly with the silence of their disengagement. Such musical dialogue necessitates the active exchange of energies whereby the participants are transformed and the potential for transformation is invoked in other realms. For example my hosts often referred to the power of music to influence weather conditions or plant growth (Stobart 1994). Here, however, I wish to focus on the transformation of the actors themselves, as a form of learning process and activation as social beings. Similarly, in this volume, Lindsey Crickmay has described traditional modes of learning in the Andes in terms of 'an interactive dialogue between learner and teacher', in which the teacher may be a person or a 'thing', and in which both learner and teacher are transformed through their dialogue.

Yacha- : knowledge as mutual transformation

Concepts of dialogue and mutual transformation appear to be implicit in the very construction of the Quechua verb stem yacha-, meaning 'know'.[3] Yacha- might be approached as a combination of the two verbalising suffixes: -ya- (for intransitive verbs) and -cha- (for transitive verbs).[4] The distinction between these verbalising suffixes is evident, for example, in combination with the word tuta ('night'), where tuta-ya means 'become dark' and tuta-cha 'make something dark'. The combination ya- + -cha- thus suggests both (a) taking on form, becoming something, as the transformation of the subject, and (b) acting upon something (or someone) else, the object. This implicit dual action and mutual transformation in the process of knowing, as both constructive and interactive, seems most relevant to wider discussions of knowledge and, in particular, to the theme of this chapter.

Rather than presenting this linguistic distinction in terms of 'evidence', I wish to use it to highlight certain points relevant to this chapter and to approaches to knowledge in general. Firstly, as the very presence of these Quechua verbalising suffixes also appears to imply, knowledge is active and principally concerns process and transformation rather than some notion of

---

[3] For a fuller analysis of the meanings and further perspectives of yacha- see Howard and Crickmay in this volume.

[4] It must be stressed that the precise linguistic distinction between Quechua roots and suffixes remains unclear.

static mental entities, a point that is by no means uniquely relevant to the Andes (Keller and Keller 1996: 159; Hobart 1995: 51). Secondly, knowledge is not an independent entity, it is always relational or in dialogue. Alan Fogel has made a similar point from the perspective of psychology. He argues that 'the human mind and self must be understood as evolving out of the historical process of personal relationship formation between self and other individuals' (1993: 4). Reacting against the idea of the 'disengaged first-person', which has dominated so much modern scholarship, the philosopher Charles Taylor suggests that 'a great deal of human action happens only insofar as the agent understands and constitutes himself as integrally part of a "we"' (1991: 311).[5]

For Western cultures the views of Fogel and Taylor remain controversial, but it is likely that many rural Andean people would find their approaches extremely natural. Indeed, the idea of twinness is important to many Amerindian cultures, where single objects or beings are often considered incomplete when outside a dialogical relationship typically represented by pairing (see e.g. Diamond, Cronk and von Rosen 1994: 29). This is vividly expressed among the Bolivian Macha by the concepts of *yanantin* and *tara*. According to Tristan Platt, the word *yanantin* can strictly be translated as 'helper and helped united to form a unique category' (1986: 245), and is used to refer to paired objects which belong together, such as ears, eyes or shoes, and which alone would be incomplete or *ch'ulla*. The implicit dialogue or sociality at the heart of human life was also emphasised to me by the widespread assertion that the souls of the dead are *ch'ulla*.[6] Indeed libations for the departed souls of the dead are always drunk from a single vessel, while those for the living are typically drunk from paired cups, one for each hand.[7]

The word *tara* also implies a double aspect, such as two people walking together, and is used to refer to the rich vibrant timbre of certain wind instruments (Stobart 1996: 70–71). *Tara* richly evokes notions of productivity, exchange, balance and harmony, and is contrasted with the word *q'iwa*, which is applied to thin, clear musical timbres and is said of people who are mean or cowardly, or of objects or concepts which imply dissonance, imbalance or mediated contrast. For example, *q'iwa* was described as 'half-man, half-woman', said of small children who constantly cried, and categorised as *ch'ulla* – single, without its partner (Stobart 1996: 70–71).

[5] By extension Taylor claims that identity, rather than simply being defined in terms of our individual properties, also 'places us in some social space' (1991: 311).

[6] This incomplete or *ch'ulla* dimension was associated with the journey of the soul from the world of the living to the 'land of the souls' (*alma llajta*), where the soul is socialised once more as it joins the community of the souls. Only the *condenados* ('condemned') never complete this journey and remain *ch'ulla*, trapped between these worlds.

[7] This use of paired cups was described to me as *yanantin*. A further quadripartite or mirror image also implied by *yanantin* is highlighted in the use of paired wooden 'bull cups' (*turu wasus*) for ritual drinking, where a pair of oxen is carved in the centre of each cup.

Both the concepts *yanantin* and *tara* seem to stress the centrality of dialogue and exchange to human life, where such interaction involves mutual transformation, exchange and the growth of knowledge through life.

Before moving on to discuss contemporary musical practices I would like to consider briefly a representation of Andean music from seventeenth-century Peru. Through the use of paired figures, once again this image seems to invoke pairedness, dialogue, and the idea of a musical bridge, communicating between sharply contrasted realms of knowledge and modes of being.

Guaman Poma's musical bridge

Guaman Poma's drawing *canciones y musica* (Figure 1) appears, without explanation, at the beginning of the section dedicated to pre-Hispanic Andean music in his mammoth 1189-page *Nueva Corónica y Buen Gobierno* (1980[1615]: f. 316). Drawn around the year 1600, undoubtedly this image's mode of representation was strongly influenced by European drawing and emblem book conventions (Austern 1999). We have little sense of how representative it may have been for other Andean people or of how artistic conventions and the artist's imagination may have shaped the plastic language of this fascinating drawing. Guaman Poma was highly educated, idiosyncratic and ambiguously positioned between elite Andean and colonial Spanish cultures. For sure, this image should be interpreted with extreme caution. However, its placement at the start of Guaman Poma's section on music, followed by descriptions, drawings and song texts presenting a variety of musical contexts and traditions from the four quarters of the Inka Empire, seems to imply a special status and possibly a wider relevance for Andean music in general.

What, then, is Guaman Poma telling us about music and knowledge through this image? Firstly, the presence of paired male flautists and paired naked women is particularly striking, with their contrasted but also interlocking iconographic realms. The active flute playing or singing by one partner within each pair and evident silence of the other suggests the idea of dialogue or musical exchange between equals. I shall consider similar forms of interaction later between *jula jula* panpipe players in terms of the active accumulation of cultural knowledge through life. The paired men and women are situated at opposite extremes of the drawing, the men perched high on a cliff and the naked women partially submerged in swirling water, suggestive of a waterfall. Sexual attraction is suggested by the women's naked bodies, but any attempt to approach by the men would presumably result in plunging from the cliff and certain death. Thus, the gulf between the men and women is not only a matter of gender but also one of mortal separation, which only music seems able to bridge. Distinction in gender and implicit sexuality is further emphasised by the plastic language of the drawing, in which the solidity of the men's high,

Figure 1 *Canciones y musica*, by Guaman Poma de Ayala (1980 [c.1615]: f. 316).

rocky cliff contrasts with the swirling fluidity and formlessness of the water in which the women are submerged.[8]

The men appear calm, as though lost in thought or day-dreaming,

---

[8] See Cereceda 1987: 149–54 for a detailed analysis of the plastic language of this drawing.

whereas the expressions of the women, especially the uppermost, seem crazed, as if in a state of extreme agitation. While the lower woman apparently sings and points a single forefinger upwards towards the sun, the upper (silent) woman points directly at the lower (silent) man, suggesting some form of communication. This image is immediately reminiscent of contemporary rural accounts of the communication of new melodies from the *sirinus* or *sirenas*, musical beings that may take a variety of forms and are typically said to reside in waterfalls.[9] A number of men have told me how, while listening to the low-pitched *booo booo* of the waterfall, new melodies have entered their heads as if in a dream. These 'phantom' melodies[10] are at first 'indistinct' (*charpu*), but gradually acquire increased definition so that the players are able to play them on their instruments.

There are many further aspects of this fascinating drawing that I hope to develop elsewhere. However, for the purposes of this chapter I wish to stress two contrasted forms of musical dialogue: firstly, exchanges between sharply contrasted realms (the men and women of the drawing), presumably representing the communication of musical knowledge from beyond the (living) human sphere; and secondly, exchanges between apparent social equals (within each gendered pair in the drawing).[11]

Whether or not Guaman Poma intended to convey this distinction through his drawing, I wish to use it here to distinguish two seasonally contrasted forms of musical dialogue encountered today among the Bolivian Macha. The first form of dialogue, which bridges sharply contrasted realms, is evocative of that between the living and the souls of the dead, as invoked by my hosts to bring about agricultural reproduction. The local assertion that the souls of the dead (*almas*) constantly sing and dance *wayñu* music in the 'land of the souls' (*alma llajta*), which is perpetually green, helps to explain why the regenerative powers of the ancestors are invoked to encourage plant growth during the rainy growing season by performing *wayñu*. In turn, the arrival of the year's new fruits is heralded by new *wayñu* melodies collected from the *sirinus* or *satanas* during the weeks leading up to Carnival. Thus, through musical dialogue these ambiguous musical beings bridge the gulf between the living and the dead to bring new life (and, as we shall see, 'thought') into the realm of the living.

The second form of dialogue, between the apparent social equals in the drawing, is evocative of the balanced interlocking or dialogue technique used between paired *jula jula* panpipe players. As in the case of the paired

---

[9] Cereceda (1987: 151) and Turino (1983: 111–12) have also identified similarities between this picture and contemporary accounts of *sirenas* (or *sirinus*) in several parts of the Southern Andes.

[10] As evocatively described by Claudio Mercado (1996: 56).

[11] While I have identified certain resonances between this image and contemporary descriptions of the *sirinus*, it is important to point out that the few individuals of *ayllu* Macha to whom I have shown this image have not made this connection. However, these same people, although not accustomed to such forms of iconographic representation, have also typically described *sirinus* as residing at waterfalls, as seductive, mortally dangerous, and the source of all music.

flautists depicted in Guaman Poma's drawing, one partner is always silent while the other sounds his instrument. *Jula jula* panpipes are played during the harvest season and dry winter months, a time that, according to certain local song texts, is linked with youth and evokes notions of development and the accumulation of knowledge through life.

In many ways the use of interlocking technique in panpipe performance is a paradigm case of what Taylor has described as 'dialogical action' (1991: 310). He notes that, in relaxed, intimate exchanges in conversation, 'the "semantic turn" passes over to the other by a common movement', felt by both partners together sharing a common rhythm. Bores and compulsive talkers 'thin this atmosphere of conviviality' because they are impervious to this rhythm. In the case of interlocking panpipe performance the shared rhythm of the dialogue is prescribed by the melody, which in turn may be seen to represent the players' shared knowledge and mutual understanding.

As Taylor also points out, the modes of understanding and sensibilities involved in such interactions are rarely articulated verbally (1991: 308). Social and sensory coordination through music (like dancing together to a commonly perceived rhythm and pulse) undoubtedly plays a crucial role in the creation of group feeling, a form of knowledge that is too precise for words. Similarly, the idea that all such sensory understandings are controlled by intelligence, which somehow resides 'inside the animal' pulling the strings of action, would seem nonsensical (Ingold 1993: 431). Rather, a large proportion of our knowing actions and interactions in the world are performed by the whole body, such that 'our understanding is itself embodied' and responsive (Taylor 1991: 309).[12]

These notions of knowledge, as embodied and sensorial, inherently processual, dialogical, interactive and transformative, are all especially relevant to music, which, as an increasing number of scholars have come to accept, is not simply something that happens *in* society. It is perhaps better to approach it as a performance medium – among others – through which many of the most fundamental aspects of socio-cultural knowledge are actively created, recognised and articulated (Seeger 1987: 140; Stokes 1994: 2).

Before going on to consider the two seasonally contrasted examples of dialogue in turn, I shall include a short overview of musical practices in a rural community of *ayllu* Macha, northern Potosí, Bolivia, where I carried out fieldwork in 1990–91 (nine months), 1993 (three months), 1996 (three months), and during several subsequent visits.

---

[12] For example, when I am about to play a piece of music, which I know from memory, it is often my fingers and their sensory knowledge of the instrument that lead the way, rather than conscious memory. However, in certain other music learning or performance situations I rely upon conscious knowledge and symbolic representation. It would seem that it is necessary to consider both of these opposing theoretical perspectives 'in a dynamic view of culture that emphasises the process of learning in public contexts through private reflections and sedimentations and the process of anticipating and governing behaviour on the basis of prior knowledge' (Keller and Keller 1996: 172).

Figure 2 The author's host hamlet in Macha territory showing homesteads and community church, tower and cemetery.

Music and knowledge in an Andean community

My Quechua-speaking host family live in a hamlet of some 60 souls, at an altitude of about 4100 m (Figure 2), and survive principally from the cultivation of potatoes and barley, and herding llamas and sheep. Several men supplement this essentially subsistence agriculture by migrant work for several months each year, typically as builders' labourers or porters in the larger towns of the region. Musical performance is deeply interwoven with agricultural activity. Although perhaps difficult to grasp for outsiders, in many ways musical knowledge is agricultural knowledge and vice versa. For example, the seasonal alternation of musical instruments, musical genres and tunings is one of the principal ways through which the ritual calendar is defined, made known and experienced. Almost without exception, every man knows how to play four types of musical instrument: the *jula jula* panpipes and mandolin-like *charango*, which are restricted to the dry winter season, and the *pinkillu* flute and the *kitarra*, a local guitar, of the rainy growing season. A few men also possess the specialist knowledge and technique required for playing *siku* panpipes (Figure 3), which are mainly confined to the patronal festivals of early spring (September–October).

Women do not play instruments, but are the principal singers and creators of song poetry. As such, they articulate a somewhat separate but complementary and interlocking sphere of musical knowledge, which – like the

Figure 3 *Siku* panpipe players with a *bombo* (bass drum) in the llama coral during an animal sacrifice on the eve of the feast of Guadalupe (September).

men's – is deeply integrated with notions of production and reproduction (see also Arnold and Yapita 1998).[13] The complementary nature of these gendered realms of musico-productive knowledge was sometimes made particularly explicit. For example, once when I recorded a young man singing to his own strummed *charango* accompaniment, he apologetically explained that the music was incomplete without a woman's voice.

Relatively little music-making takes place outside the context of feasts. Yet, during such festivals, when music is played almost constantly, musical performance is one of the principal means through which people come together and are actualised as a community (cf. Stokes 1994: 12). However, with different musical genres and moments in the seasonal cycle 'community' comes to mean different things. For example, during the rainy growing season, which is defined musically (but only loosely by actual weather conditions) as November (All Saints) to March (Carnival), the focus tends to be on the immediate hamlet. Thus, during Carnival, dancing and singing to the hamlet's *pinkillu* flute consort is usually performed in the llama corral of each family's homestead.[14]

[13] Following cohabitation with a man, leading to marriage, women's singing is usually prohibited except during weddings and Carnival.

[14] As a result of a variety of tragic circumstances, during one Carnival I attended, community relations had broken down to such a serious degree that no music was performed in the hamlet nor communal visits made to individual households by singers and dancers. As many people stressed to me at the time, the community had literally become dysfunctional. There was no music and consequently no community.

However, during the feast of the Holy Cross (*cruz*) in May, the harvest season, 'community' comes to mean a series of larger-scale political affiliations, within the broader ethnic group or *ayllu*, which are again invoked through musical performance.[15] For this feast, men from several affiliated hamlets come together to perform *jula jula* panpipe music, thereby identifying themselves as a significant socio-political unit or 'community'. These ensembles, each playing their own emblematic melody, often enter into aggressive confrontations with one another on their pilgrimage journeys to the local town of Macha. Yet, after converging on the town, ensembles sharing higher levels of political affiliation often come together to perform a special stamping dance to *charango* accompaniment, taunting and some-times entering into ritual battle with affiliated 'communities' from other districts. Thus, most people's sense of identity and political affiliation is, to a surprisingly large degree, constructed, known and maintained through musical performance and sensibilities.

The annual repetition of the various musical genres, each connected to and creating a particular context, also instils a sense of history and serves as an important mode through which cultural knowledge and sensibilities are both grasped and transmitted. When we examine musical discourse and practices in more detail, the importance of music as a medium through which understandings of the world are constructed, renewed and trans-formed is heightened still more.

Intuition: knowledge from beyond

As noted above, my Andean hosts approach human knowledge as just part of a much wider realm of knowledge, including that of the animated land-scape. This is emphasised below in a fragment from a conversation with my host's brother Francisco. He is most explicit about the animated quality of the mountains, their immense knowledge/power, and their ability to speak.[16] Having allegedly been struck by lightening several years earlier, Francisco is gradually learning to become a *yatiri* – a type of shaman. At the time of our conversation he was doubtful whether his power/knowledge was adequate to make the mountains speak.

F. Ah, runajina paykuna [jurq'us]. Parlankupis kikillantaq i? Kikinta parlanku a. Ichari pero . . . parlachisun karqa . . . ichari faltan, ichari mana, ichari watapaq [. . .] parlachisunchis. Faltayuq nuqa . . . Paykuna yachanku a. (Tape 9b: 82).

F. Yes, they're like people [the mountains]. Also they speak in the same way, don't they? Perhaps though . . . we'll make them speak . . . perhaps it will fail,

[15] See Platt 1986: 236 for explanation of the various nested levels of political affiliation within the *ayllu* Macha. Also see Allen 1988: 107 for a discussion of the meaning of *ayllu*.

[16] Following the lead of Foucault, it seems especially appropriate to connect power and knowledge in this example (Fardon 1995: 5).

perhaps not, perhaps next year [. . .] we will be able to make them speak. I can't
do it yet . . . They [the mountains] really know.

Not only is the landscape attributed knowledge that is normally inaccessible
to humans but so are certain animals, rendering them ambiguous and
potentially dangerous. For example, I was told that parrots know everybody's names and that foxes know about future agricultural production – for
which their cries and movements serve as prognoses. The ambiguous nature
of the parrot may be understood better when it is explained that names may
be used to cause harm in witchcraft and for this reason they are often with-
held from strangers. For example, Francisco, whom I now count as a close
friend, gave me a false name during my first recorded interview with him.
In respect to this belief, the name Francisco, like certain others in this text,
is a pseudonym. However, I am torn by very contradictory feelings in
making such ethnographic decisions. Withholding knowledge of names
might equally be construed as discrediting and rendering anonymous or
'Other' the very individuals whose cultural practices and views I am
attempting to describe and evoke in my text.

    The idea of rendering 'Other' is by no means limited to the practice of
ethnography. For my Andean hosts 'Other' is perhaps primarily understood
in terms of powerful hidden knowledge, which may typically mean that it is
either possessed by other social groups, for example in their songs (Seeger
1993: 32), or somehow embodied in the animated landscape. Such dangerous but also often potentially creative powers are typically termed *sajra*
(*saxra*), a word that has sometimes been translated as 'secret' (Platt and
Molina, in Harris 1982: 71 n. 28) or 'unknown' (Huanca 1989: 103; Harris
1995: 120). When used in reference to individuals, *sajra* usually conveys an
almost exclusively negative sense, such as a person with a spiteful or evil
nature. However, non-human beings classed as *sajra* are often identified
with the Spanish loanwords for 'devil' (*diablo*) or 'satan' (*satana*). In the
rural Andes such 'satanic' beings should not be interpreted as purely negative (see Harrison 1989: 47–48; Silverblatt 1987: 178), as in more institution-
alised Christianity, but rather in terms of the power of radical
transformation, which is potentially either creative or destructive. I wish to
highlight the crucial association and inseparability between accessing
knowledge from this ambiguous 'Other' realm, as a form of dialogue, and
the idea of transformation. This idea is particularly vividly invoked in discourse concerning musical creativity.

Instrumental music, music as instrumental
I have already stressed how knowledge and understandings of the world are
generated, articulated and maintained through musical performance. The
idea that music is also instrumental to bringing about concrete transformations in the annual cycles of production and reproduction is emphasised in
the insistence that, for certain genres, new melodies must be acquired and
performed each year. My host stressed that melodies from previous years are

q'ayma ('tasteless' or 'insipid') and, as he put it, 'unable to do anything'. Elsewhere, I have described how the growth cycle of potatoes is directly linked to that of the new *wayñu* melodies of the rainy season (Stobart 1994). As the new generation of potato tubers begins to take form on the roots of the parent plant, new melodies surface, conveyed to humans, it is claimed, by the *sirinus* ('sirens'). These new *wayñu* melodies are performed until the end of Carnival (March), after which they must not be heard again until the following November, when *pinkillu* flutes are brought out and sounded once more, invoking the powers of the dead and devils to bring the rains and stimulate plant growth (Stobart 1994; Harris 1982). In this way music, acquired through dialogue with another realm, is instrumental in the annual transformation of the landscape and cycles of reproduction.

In the following extract, Francisco vividly conveys the idea that *wayñu* melodies are a form of knowledge that is 'taught' to humans by the *satanas* ('satans' or 'devils'). I had drawn his attention to the contrast in musical structure between the highly regular six-syllable couplets of dry season songs and the irregular verse structure of rainy season *wayñu* songs.[17] He explains the irregularity of *wayñu* in terms of a sequence of different melodies taught by the *satanas*, each with a distinct and unique form.

F. Paykuna satanasmantajina. Ichari satanas. Wak wayñu ya esta chayachin. Wakin wakin waktaña, yachachinankutaq. Wakin wak wayñu, wakin wakwan kay takishanku ya. Wakin waktaña yachallantaq. Chayrayku jina chayqa. (Tape 9a: 285)

F. It's like they're from the *satanas*. Probably the *satanas*. Just like that they deliver a different *wayñu* tune. Another, another, and then another, they teach. They are singing, some with another *wayñu*, and some with another one. Other people know another one. That's why it's like that.

In this context, music is presented in terms of a bridge or medium of communication that interlocks different realms. As I have already noted, several individuals told me that *all* music is derived from the *sirinus*, which are included in the same category as the *satanas* (cf. Turino 1983: 96). The widely reported ability of these musical beings to adopt a variety of different forms, thus embodying the very notion of transformation, emphasises the power of their music to invoke transformations in other spheres and represent a bridge between different realms or states of being. Thus, despite its immense importance as an identity emblem and the objective view that it is humanly organised (Blacking 1973), my Andean hosts present music as the expression of contact or dialogue with another realm. I now wish to

---

[17] In this case I was alluding more particularly to the songs accompanied by the *kitarra*, a local rainy season guitar (Stobart 1994), rather than those performed with *pinkillu* flutes. Both these rainy season genres are termed *wayñu*, a word that conveys many meanings in Andean societies (Leichtman 1987; Arnold 1992; Dransart 1997: 85–91).

demonstrate how such dialogue is also presented in terms of a form of knowledge. Indeed in a more general sense, focusing on European traditions, Jacques Attali has also described music as an 'instrument of understanding' in that 'it prompts us to decipher sound as a form of knowledge' (1985: 4).

The idea of music as a means of understanding, or knowledge, was forcefully brought home to me by Alberto Senega, who comes from a rural community near to that of my hosts. In our rather drunken conversation in Spanish, recorded in a bar in the village of Macha, Alberto had already emphasised the immense danger of the *sirinus*. He was happy to take me to visit these dangerous musical beings, at the waterfalls, springs or rocks where they are typically said to live, but he was adamant that he could not accept any responsibility for my safety. Perhaps sounding a little incredulous, I asked Alberto why people insisted on visiting the *sirinus* to collect new melodies if this practice is so dangerous. Exasperated by my failure to understand, in the following example, Alberto explains that collecting music from the *sirinus* is critically important to understanding as it 'creates solutions' and 'brings about all ideas'.

> H. Si es muy peligroso para ir a los sirinus porque saben ir la gente?
> A. Mira! Escuchame la cosa! Esto de nosotros, para Carnaval la gente de nosotros ¿no ve? Como esta materia hace solucionar pues. Hace como ésta, hace llegar todo el pensamiento.
> H. De los sirinus?
> A. Exacto pues!
> H. Todo esta cosa va entrar . . . ?
> A. . . . en la cabeza de nosotros, como lo quieres asistir pues. (Tape 2b: 83).

> H. If it's so dangerous to go to the *sirinus*, why do people go?
> A. Look! Listen to me, this is how it is! For us, for us people at Carnival, you see? Like this matter it creates solutions. Like this it creates, it brings about all ideas.
> H. From the *sirinus*?
> A. Exactly!
> H. All this enters . . . ?
> A. . . . in our heads, in the way you want to visit them.

This response to my question is particularly interesting as Alberto presents the musical knowledge of the *sirinus* in terms of ideas or understandings which seem to extend well beyond any narrow notion of music as a separate, autonomous or irrelevant sphere of activity. Rather than relegating music to the position of an optional extra, or mere entertainment, he seems to suggest that the *sirinus* music resides at the very core of human understanding. The identification of the *sirinus* with wider notions of intuition seems to suggest that they are seen to creatively bridge and connect different realms of knowledge. This notion of intuition reiterates the local importance

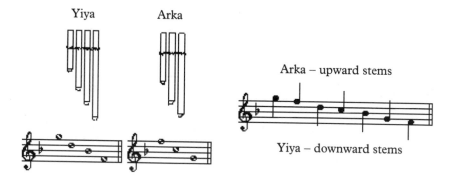

Figure 4 *Jula jula* scale showing division of pitches between paired panpipes.

given to knowing 'how' rather than knowing 'why'.[18] Similarly, Ester Grebe-Vicuña discovered that Tarapacá musicians in Chile disclaimed knowledge of a music theory, instead attributing such knowledge to the *sereno* (*sirinu*) (1980: 186)

Interlocking panpipes: the sounds of enquiry

I shall now turn to dialogue between approximate social equals, as expressed in *jula jula* panpipe music, which, like many other panpipe genres of the Southern Andes, is played using so-called 'interlocking' or 'hocket' technique (Figure 4). This dialogic method of performance, where alternate notes of the scale are divided between paired (half) instruments, requiring two players, is an immensely practical performance solution. Especially in the case of the largest panpipes, this technique provides time both to manipulate instruments and to breathe between melody notes. In turn, it enables the creation of greater volume of sound and diminishes physical demands, enabling the extended performances demanded during fiestas.

Besides the practical advantages to such a technique, interlocking vividly evokes a sense of ritualised dialogue. Greg Urban has interpreted (verbal) ritual dialogues from other parts of South America as models for social interaction and, in particular, solidarity (1986: 381). They occur, he notes, in contexts involving maximum social distance between the participants and high likelihood for conflict (1986: 372). Among the Shuar-Achuar, for example, such dialogues are used to establish solidarity between members of a war party and to key them up for battle (1986: 380). Like the examples described by Urban, *jula jula* panpipe performance precisely concerns solidarity and conflict, as though stressing Taylor's point that 'we define

---

[18] Compare Diamond, Cronk and von Rosen, who cite testimonies from members of First Nation communities of northeastern America. To ask 'why' is treated as evidence of failure to learn (1994: 9).

Figure 5a *Siku* panpipe melody: asymmetrical interlocking between paired panpipes. The *primeros* sound five notes (three distinct pitches) before the *segundas* enter. Key: seven-tube *primeros* in spaces of stave; eight-tube *segundas* on lines

Three-tube arka set (upward stems)

Four-tube yiya set (downward stems)

Figure 5b *Jula jula* panpipe melody: strict/symmetrical dialogue between paired panpipes. Each change in pitch involves alternation between players. Key: three-tube *arka*: upward stems; four-tube *yiya*: downward stems.

ourselves partly in terms of what we come to accept as our appropriate place within dialogical action' (1991: 311). Extending this idea, I shall also approach the musical dialogue in *jula jula* performance as a model for the exchange and accumulation of knowledge.

However, I would be hesitant about making a similar claim for other panpipe genres. It should be stressed that although interlocking technique is widely used in panpipe performance in the Southern Andes, the strict dialogue found in *jula jula* performance appears to be quite rare. In other panpipe genres, a single player may sound several different pitches consecutively before his partner sounds a note (Figure 5a). By contrast, for the case of *jula jula* panpipes, a single player cannot change to a differently pitched pipe without a note from his partner being sounded first (Figure 5b). For this reason, I wish to suggest that the interlocking of paired *jula julas* might be classed as strict or symmetrical dialogue, while that of other panpipe genres, such as *sikus*, might be classed as asymmetrical (Figures 5a and 5b).

Whereas *siku* panpipes have no particular association with physical conflict, *jula julas* are intimately associated with ritual battles called *tinku*. Many hundreds of players, in ensembles sometimes exceeding several dozen men, converge on the village of Macha at harvest time for the Feast of the Holy Cross (May 3).[19] The male players typically wear fighting dress, including ox-hide helmets (*monteras*) based on those of the Spanish *conquistadores*, and it is common for taunting *jula jula* music between rival bands to lead to scuffles or even full-scale fighting. Following arrival in Macha, *tinku* fighting takes place between paired men from rival factions, often specified to be of similar age and strength.[20] (Later, fighting sometimes degenerates into full-scale stone-throwing battles between the principal rival factions.) It is significant that the discourse surrounding *tinku* fighting, which the men anticipate with immense excitement and which rarely concerns personal disputes between individuals, seems less concerned with defeating the opponent than with expressing personal bravery in the face of the 'Other'. In the days following *tinku*, I encountered no talk of winning but many men proudly paraded their broken noses, blackened eyes and torn lips – vivid evidence of their personal courage and, by extension, integrity.

The conflation of personal integrity with courage, in what might be construed as a highly barbaric ritual practice, may seem hard to reconcile for the outsider. However, a person who does not wish to participate in *tinku* is likely to be described as *q'iwa*. This word not only refers to a thin timbre and notions of dissonance (as discussed above) but also to a person who is cowardly, mean, or – as Francisco implied to me on one occasion – lacking in knowledge.[21] People who have integrity and are socially competent are expected to assert themselves by giving, or making exchanges, whether as help or in combat. Similarly, the use of interlocking in *jula julas* performance would seem to emphasise the centrality of dialogical action, as a form of shared agency (Taylor 1991: 311).

Watunakuy: the language of interlocking

I discussed the interlocking between the four-tube *yiya* (Sp. *guia* 'guide') and three-tube *arka* ('follower')[22] panpipes of the *jula jula* ensemble with Don Adrian, who was widely considered the oldest and most knowledgeable man in the district. He described this technique with two words that, on my

---

[19] In other parts of northern Potosí *jula julas* are also played at Easter, and several feasts associated with planting in October. *Tinku* is by no means confined to feasts in which *jula julas* are played, but many people would identify a strong connection between the two, particularly in the context of the harvest feast of *Cruz* (3 May).

[20] In some parts of northern Potosí I have also witnessed women fighting in *tinku*. I have never seen this at the Feast of the Holy Cross in Macha; however women and children do fight one another during the evening on Good Friday. As one man explained, Christ has died so there is no order in the world and even women and children fight.

[21] My own lack of desire to participate in *tinku* seemed to be accepted, both because I was an outsider and because there was no equal for me to fight. It seems quite possible that this may have been related to my lack of locally relevant cultural knowledge and relative linguistic incompetence.

[22] See Sanchez 1996 for a detailed discussion of these terms.

Figure 6 Moche panpipes, strung together (Kutscher 1950: 31).

recording of our conversation, sound like *watanakunku* and *qhespinakunku*. Both these Quechua words incorporate the suffix *-naku-*, which refers to reciprocal action. In classical Quechua, *qhespinakunku* may be translated as 'they save each other'. According to Pedro Plaza, to whom I am indebted for his help in translating and interpreting these words, this apparently implies that 'one without the other would die out', there have to be two. Indeed, if we are to treat sound as a primary expression of life, as it appears to be approached by my hosts (Stobart 1998: 581–82), the continuity of sound in a melody created through the use of interlocking technique becomes an immensely powerful metaphor for the continuity of life itself.

Don Adrian's other word, *watanakunku*, may be literally translated as 'they tie each other', suggesting that through their action the paired panpipe players bind one another together into an interdependent unit.[23] It is intriguing to observe that several images from the Moche culture, of the northern coast of Peru, depict paired panpipe players with their instruments connected by a piece of string, presumably implying the use of interlocking technique (Figure 6). However, it must be stressed that the few Moche depictions of paired panpipe players should not necessarily be taken as evidence for the widespread use of interlocking technique in the pre-Hispanic Andes.

[23] It is perhaps significant that the word *wata* also means 'year'.

To my ears, on repeated listenings to the recording of our conversation, Don Adrian appears to say *watanakunku*. However, when my host helped me transcribe this tape he automatically inserted the word *watunakunku*, meaning 'they ask questions to each other', which Pedro Plaza also assures me would be more usual in this context.[24] As Pedro Plaza also stressed, the presence of the *-naku-* suffix means that this would entail a double cycle of 'questions' and 'answers', a two-way enquiry. The sense that the participants somehow bind themselves together through their mutual interaction still seems to be implied, as the word *watu* also means 'string'. Once more this implies the notion of solidarity also noted for the ritual (verbal) dialogues described by Urban (1986).[25]

When we consider the mutual enquiries of *watunakunku* in the context of the melodic structure and the dance formation of the *jula jula* ensemble, the idea of this performance as a model for the dialogical growth of knowledge becomes considerably more compelling. *Jula jula* melodies, I was told, always pass from left to right, which means from the short tubes on the player's left to the long ones on his right.[26] Indeed most tunes from this region start on the shortest pipe of the four-tube *yiya* instrument and end, one octave lower, on the longest pipe of the three-tube *arka* instrument.[27] Thus, melodies pass from small to large – a growth cycle involving a doubling in size (as a descent in pitch of one octave) that suggests development from child to adult (Stobart 1998: 594–96). While elsewhere I have related this melodic movement to physical growth it would also be appropriate to consider this transformation, resulting from questions and answers, in terms of the growth of knowledge.

[24] Ideally I would have liked to question Don Adrian on this point again; however, I am sad to report that on a more recent visit I found him extremely deaf and very confused.

[25] I am most grateful to Rosaleen Howard for her comments concerning the linguistic relationship between *wata-* and *watu-* and for drawing my attention to a tantalising potential link with the river *Watanay*, as follows: 'In the *Diccionario Quechua–Español–Quechua* of the Academia Mayor de la Lengua Quechua, the roots *wata-* ("year") and *watu-* ("enquire, diagnose, predict") have semantic features in common in certain contexts: thus *watay* is glossed as "amarrar, ligar, fijar con cuerda alguna cosa" ("tie, fix something with cord") and the noun *watu* "cordon, pita, cuerda, hilo retorcido" ("cord, string, thong, twisted thread") gives us the transitive verb *watuchay* "amarrar, atar, fajar, encordelar" ("tie, bind") (Academia 1995: 729–31). Thus, at one level of their respective complex meanings, the words *watunakuy* and *watanakuy* might be said to be homonyms. The variable pronunciation and interpretation to which the words are treated in your data also suggest that, for certain purposes of meaning, the semantics of the two words coincide. It is enticing to see as relevant to this argument, that the river in Guaman Poma's "musical bridge" drawing [discussed above; see Figure 1] is the river *Watanay* (spelt *uatanay* by Guaman Poma).' (Personal communication).

[26] In a variety of other contexts movement to the right was linked with passage through life, and presumably the growth and acquisition of knowledge this implies. In contrast the souls of the dead (*almas*), as a sort of mirror image of the living, were said to travel to the left.

[27] Throughout the northern Potosí region *jula jula* melodies always end on the longest tube of the three-tube *arka*. However, while always beginning with the four-tube *yiya* instrument, in other parts of the region it is quite common for melodies to begin on one of the middle tubes.

As I noted above, the interlocking technique used in *jula jula* performance, unlike that of many other panpipe genres, is a symmetrical or strict form of dialogue. In this genre a player may only move to a different pitch (tube size) after his partner has sounded a note – which may be thought of as simultaneously a reply (to his earlier question) and a new enquiry. Accordingly any transformation in size in the growth cycle from child to adult, invoked by *jula jula* melodies, may only take place through dialogue. In other words, without dialogue, development or growth (in knowledge) are impossible. Thus, the music may be seen as a presentation of transformation and the very process of learning and acquisition of understanding.

Elder and younger brother

Several scholars report that the paired instruments used in certain forms of panpipe interlocking are considered male and female (Baumann 1996: 31; Grebe-Vicuña 1980: 254). However, when I enquired whether a gender distinction was recognised between paired *jula jula* panpipes this was always denied.[28] Instead, the four-tube *yiya* and three-tube *arka* were described as *kuraq* ('senior') and *sullka* ('junior'), and related to the idea of two brothers, an elder and a younger. This emphasises the process of transformation as exchanges through time, rather than the more static imagery implied by gender or other dualistic oppositions.[29] In a similar vein, Bourdieu has pointed out the danger of ignoring the temporal element in the analysis of gift exchange, where strategies of delay are constitutive of meaning, and where to reciprocate immediately would be tantamount to non-acceptance (1977: 6). The importance of time is patently clear in the case of music, especially that played using interlocking technique, in which each participant must know where to place his note in the melody. In describing this very point to me, Don Adrian focused precisely on the necessity of knowledge – albeit of a more skill based variety –for timing exchanges correctly: 'Mana yachaspaqa pantanku. Yachaqpurarí kawal "pun pun" ninku a' ('Those who don't know [how to play] make mistakes. Between those who know they play accurately "pun pun" [onomatopoeic sound of *jula jula* music]').[30]

It is always the four-tube *yiya*, or 'senior', that initiates the melody (asks the first question) and three-tube *arka*, or 'junior', that plays the last note (gives the final answer). However, in the course of the melody the reciprocal action implied by -*naku*- in the word *watunakunku* seems to suggest that the roles of 'senior' and 'junior' are constantly reversed, such that each

---

[28] Thomas Turino also observes that no gender contrast seems to be recognised between paired panpipes in Conima, Peru (1993: 43).

[29] Max Peter Baumann gives the Quechua word *purajsikinakuy* for panpipe interlocking, which he translates as 'we catch up with each other' (1996: 32), evoking a vivid sense of movement through time.

[30] The -*pura*- suffix (*yachaqpura*) conveys the sense of 'among equals'.

Figure 7 *Jula jula* panpipe players dancing in a file.

'answer' is simultaneously a new 'question'.[31] The implication would appear
to be that learning is not construed as a one-directional process, as knowledge passing from guru/teacher to disciple/student, but rather as a two-way
process in which both participants acquire knowledge through mutual dialogue.[32] Certainly this is the case in music learning, which mostly takes place
informally in musical interaction among peer groups.[33]

Moving ahead in knowledge

A *jula jula* ensemble typically includes some twenty to fifty players with
paired sets of instruments in five sizes and tuned in octaves, so that the
melody is sounded in five parallel octaves (Figure 7). The principal dance
of the ensemble consists of a long snaking single file called *wayli*.[34] An adult
man, with the largest four-tube instrument, who is specified to be coura-

[31] In his analysis of the terms *ira* (which is comparable to the Spanish-derived *yiya*) and
arka in the context of dialogue between paired panpipes, Walter Sanchez (1996: 89) cites two
dictionary entries by Torres Rubio (1966 [1616]). He notes that *Irckastha* is translated as *responder al que enseña* ('respond to one who teaches') and *Arcayastha* as *responder al que enseña, u otra
persona mayor* ('respond to one who teaches, or to another senior person'). Not only does this
highlight the aspect of knowledge transmission in this exchange, but also suggests that both
partners are teachers (and learners).

[32] See the Platonic notion of dialogue discussed in the Introduction to this volume.

[33] Compare descriptions of peer group music learning in Bulgaria (Rice 1994: 44).

[34] Other more specific terms for this serpentine dance are *link'u-link'u* or *q'iwi-q'iwi* (Stobart
1998: 589).

geous and a good fighter, dances at the head of this file, flanked by two unmarried young women with flags.[35] Immediately behind him comes a man with the largest three-tube instrument. The other players, with a variety of sizes, follow in single file, usually in no strict order. Finally, at the back or tail of this serpentine dance, which is explicitly compared to a snake, comes a boy playing the smallest instrument.[36] Typically this boy holds the four-tube and three-tube pairs together, as an *iraskillu*, enabling him to play the complete melody.

When elders leading the ritual wished the *jula jula* ensemble to start playing it was to the boy that they directed their requests and following his first few notes the other instruments gradually joined the melody. Thus, in the organisation of the *wayli* dance, with its 'strong man' at the head and boy at the tail, we are presented with a growth cycle from childhood to adulthood. Each player follows the path of those before, and by implication adopts the cultural practices and acquires the cultural knowledge of his elders and ancestors.

The dance also evokes a double hierarchy in which the adult man at the head leads the dance but the boy at the tail leads the melody, the sounds and gestures of which ultimately motivate the dance to move forward. Like the *wayñu* tunes of the rains, the origin of the *jula jula* melodies used for this dance is typically attributed to the *sirinus* or *satanas*. With this melody there is a sense that, alongside his own youthful animation and desire for knowledge, the boy carries the gift of the intuitive understandings and animation of the *sirinus*. Through the course of the performance and passage through the dance this is culturally shaped, socialised and transformed into dialogue, as a presentation of the acquisition of knowledge and necessity of dialogue on the path through life.

The sense of melodic movement across the seven pitches of the *jula jula* melody is also seemingly evoked in the words of the following dry season song, recorded during the Feast of the Holy Cross when *jula julas* are played. The seven pitches seem to suggest seven stages of knowledge acquisition, alongside movement through the *wayli* dance, from childhood to adulthood:[37]

> Silu patitasman urqhurishallan
> Ima cielopata aswan altuspata
> Qanchis ventanayuq chayman altuspata
> Celeste punkuyuq chayman alawana. (Tape 34a: 250)

---

[35] These are the only women who participate in this dance.

[36] Several people described this role of a boy at the tail of the dance. However, in practice I only witnessed a boy dancing in this position on a few occasions. These seemed to be of special ritual importance, such as when the cross was carried out of the *calvario* on the eve of the Feast of the Holy Cross in May.

[37] If the seven tubes of the *jula jula* panpipes are thought of in terms of a Russian doll, with the shortest and narrowest at the heart, the movement of the melody would indeed be 'out from within', as in the first line of this song.

Bringing it out, up to the sky
The top of the sky higher and higher[38]
Right up to the place with seven windows
We must give praise at the place with the sky-blue door.

I discussed the words of this song with Francisco in the context of *jula jula* music, linking the 'sky-blue door' with the idea of revelation or release, to which I inadvertently introduced a religious dimension.[39] Francisco was adamant that the song text had absolutely nothing to do with a Christian sense of revelation. Instead, he explained it with the following words:

F. Tukuy ima wasis ruway munan, ya astawan yachay munan. Ya . . . mana . . . urayman ni munanchu, ni adelantar munanchu qhipaman. Ya astawan ñawpaq yachayman, tukuy imata . . . takiyta, tukuy ima hasta . . . a chay chayqa. Porque entonces payqa altuspatitasman.

F. He wants to build houses and everything, now he wants to know more. No, he doesn't want to go down, nor does he want his progress to fall behind. Now, much earlier I would know, everything . . . to sing, everything . . . Yes, that's how it is . . . Because then he reaches the upper floors.

Francisco's explanation conveys the idea of moving forward and getting on in life, where to 'build houses' seems to relate to acquiring status as the male head of a household, and thus independence from the parental home. Building houses, like the many other tasks expected of a mature and respected adult man, both requires knowledge and brings knowledge into being (cf. Crickmay in this volume). Thus, as Francisco points out, progress in life – as 'accumulated sociality' – is directly related to increase in knowledge, they go along together.[40] Similarly, in his overview of South American cultures, Lawrence Sullivan has observed that many societies 'recognize the singular role human knowledge plays in personal and social formation' (1988: 375). In a variety of senses this same idea of learning and transforming into a knowledgeable person or *yachaq* though dialogue seems to be beautifully expressed through *jula jula* panpipe performance.

Conclusions

In this chapter I have presented two rather different but connected forms of knowing, both with rich musical resonances. The first is a form of creative or intuitive grasp on the world, which brings solutions or understanding to the existential situations with which living beings are presented. Such

[38] Literally: 'what sky top is higher'.

[39] I made this connection due to the association of the number seven with perfection in Christian symbolism (Hulme 1909: 11).

[40] I am grateful to Rosaleen Howard for her suggestion of the expression 'accumulated sociality'.

ontological knowledge invokes powers from beyond the realm of living humans in the form of music, as a source of life itself. There is a sense that the music of the *sirinus*, which is linked with the ability to understand, feel, desire and act in the world, resides at the heart of every living being.[41] It is this power and desire – taking the form of a melody or 'path'[42] – which propels living beings forward in a quest for knowledge and thereby for reaching their potential. In a sense this knowledge is precisely our potential as living beings, which helps to explain why the powerful musical knowledge of the *sirinus* is linked with prophecy, and while potentially life-giving and inspirational it may also be fatally dangerous or lead to insanity.

Secondly, I considered this same quest for knowledge through life, animated by the *sirinus* music, in terms of the interlocking technique between paired panpipe players in *jula jula* performance. Through reciprocal musical enquiries and responses the players bind each another into shared networks of mutual understanding and knowledge, and in the process transform one another. The image that emerges is of knowledge not as a fixed or static entity but rather as an interactive process and mode of mutual transformation, with a strong temporal dimension. Foucault has linked knowledge with power. From the perspective of this rural Andean music it is tempting to link knowledge with transformation, or more accurately, knowing with transforming (see also Howard, Crickmay and Astvaldsson in this volume).

More generally, the ability of music to communicate between different realms, invoking a multiplicity of 'interpretative moves' (Feld 1994: 85–91), and serving to 'transform experience', might even be seen as one of its most universal characteristics (McAllester 1971: 380; Nettl 1983: 40). It is by no means exclusively in the Andes that music has been approached as a bridge which simultaneously connects and divides people, ideas, places and objects – and the feelings they arouse – across time and space. Yet, as others have also noted, such musical knowing is often too precise for, or simply incompatible with, words. Furthermore, musical knowing is not just about music. Its language of sensibilities informs, shapes and reflects many other aspects of behaviour and knowledge.

In the Andean examples I have described, the quest for knowledge and 'solutions' does not appear to direct the subject's attention inwards to

---

[41] I am hesitant to restrict this to human knowledge as, for example, foodcrops are sometimes said to weep like a human baby if not cared for appropriately.

[42] An equation between 'melody' and 'path' or 'road' is found in a number of languages and musical traditions (Roseman 1991: 6–9; Zeranska-Kominek 1994). A tantalising, but speculative, correlation also exists between the Quechua *taki* ('song') and Aymara *thaki* ('path'). (According to Mannheim, these languages share about 20 per cent of their vocabulary [1991: 40]). My Quechua-speaking hosts, who also use the Aymara *thaki* (or Spanish *cinta* 'ribbon') to refer to the footpath in libation sequences, were however careful to differentiate these concepts. Arnold and Yapita explore a number of aspects of the concept of *thaki* and its relationship to song in their evocatively titled 1998 book *Río de vellón, río de canto* (river of fleece, river of song).

individual contemplation – as in a number of philosophical traditions around the world – but rather outwards to dialogue with others or an 'Other'. But it should be stressed that this seems to be more a matter of cultural presentation and a reflection of attitudes concerning appropriate behaviour than any objective commentary on the processes by which people come to know. Hence, despite applying considerable personal energies to the annual creation of new music, Andean rural musicians will often attribute such creations to dialogue with external sources of knowledge. In other cultural traditions, such musical creations might be attributed to the competences or genius of the individual – even when based heavily upon existing models and working within prescribed parameters.

The tendency for my Andean hosts to direct their quest for knowledge outwards is perhaps also reflected in the almost exclusively dynamic nature of their music. The notable absence of gentle meditative musical styles might, at least in part, be attributed to the privileging of dialogue and exchange over and above personal contemplation. But it is crucial that the dual nature at the heart of this dialogue, which is characteristic of so many aspects of musical behaviour in northern Potosí, is not viewed as some kind of essentialised structural duality. Rather this stress on dialogue seems to emphasise that interaction, as a way of knowing and acting, is essential to life in this harsh Andean environment where, as in the interlocking melodies performed between paired *jula jula* panpipes, 'one without the other would die out'.

References

Allen, Catherine. 1988. *The Hold Life Has: Coca and Cultural Identity in an Andean Community*. Washington: Smithsonian Institution.

Academia Mayor de la Lengua Quechua. 1995. *Diccionario quechua–español–quechua. Qheswa–español–qheswa simi taqe*. Cusco: Municipalidad del Qosqo.

Arnold, Denise. 1992. 'At the Heart of the Woven Dance Floor: The Wayñu in Qaqachaka'. *Iberoamericana* 16 (3–4) [47–48]: 21–66.

Arnold, Denise, and J. Yapita. 1998. *Río de vellón, río de canto: cantar a los animales, una poética andina de la creación*. La Paz: Hisbol.

Attali, Jacques. 1985. *Noise: The Political Economy of Music*. Trans. B. Massumi. Manchester: Manchester University Press.

Austern, Linda. 1999. 'The Siren, the Muse and the God of Love: Music and Gender in Seventeenth-Century English Emblem Books'. *Journal of Musicological Research* 18: 95–138.

Bauman, Richard. 1977. *Verbal Art as Performance*. Prospect Heights, IL: Waveland Press.

Baumann, Max Peter. 1996. 'Andean Music, Symbolic Dualism and Cosmology'. In M.P. Baumann (ed.), *Cosmología y música en los Andes*. Frankfurt: Vervuert/Madrid: Iberoamericana: 15–66.

Blacking, John. 1973. *How Musical is Man?* Seattle: University of Washington Press.

——, 1995. *Music, Culture and Experience: Selected Papers of John Blacking*. Ed. R. Byron. Chicago: University of Chicago Press.

Bourdieu, Pierre. 1977. *Outline of a Theory of Practice*. Trans. R. Nice. Cambridge: Cambridge University Press.

Cereceda, Verónica. 1987. 'Aproximaciones a una estética andina: de la belleza al *tinku*'. In J. Medina (ed.), *Tres reflexiones sobre el pensamiento andino*. La Paz: Hisbol: 133–231.

Cooke, Derryk. 1959. *The Language of Music*. London: Oxford University Press.

Diamond, Beverley, M.S. Cronk and F. von Rosen. 1994. *Visions of Sound: Musical Instruments of First Nations Communities in Northeastern America*. Chicago and London: Chicago University Press.

Dransart, Penny. 1997. 'Cultural Transpositions: Writing about Rites in a Llama Corral'. In R. Howard-Malverde (ed.), *Creating Context in Andean Cultures*. Oxford: Oxford University Press: 85–98.

Fardon, Richard. 1995. 'Introduction: Counterworks'. In R. Fardon (ed.), *Counterworks*. London and New York: Routledge: 1–22.

Feld, Steven. 1994. 'Communication, Music and Speech about Music'. In C. Keil and S. Feld, *Music Grooves*. Chicago: University of Chicago Press: 77–95.

——, 1996. 'Waterfalls of Song: An Acoustemology of Place Resounding in Bosavi, Papua New Guinea'. In S. Feld and K. Basso (eds.), *Senses of Place*. Santa Fe: School of American Research Press: 90–135.

Fogel, Alan. 1993. *Developing through Relationships: Origins of Communication, Self and Culture*. Hemel Hempstead: Harvester Wheatsheaf.

Frith, Simon. 1996. *Performing Rites: Evaluating Popular Music*. Oxford: Oxford University Press.

Grebe-Vicuña, María Ester. 1980. 'Generative Models, Symbolic Structures and Acculturation in the Panpipe Music of the Aymara of Tarapaca, Chile'. PhD thesis, Queen's University, Belfast.

Guaman Poma de Ayala, Felipe. 1980 [c. 1615]. *El Primer Nueva Corónica y Buen Gobierno*. Ed.J. Murra and R. Adorno. Mexico: Siglo Veintiuno.

Harris, Olivia. 1982. 'The Dead and Devils among the Bolivian Laymi'. In M. Bloch and J. Parry (eds.), *Death and the Regeneration of Life*. Cambridge: Cambridge University Press: 45–73.

——, 1995. 'Knowing the Past: Plural Identities and the Antinomies of Loss in Highland Bolivia'. In R. Fardon (ed.), *Counterworks*. London and New York: Routledge: 105–23.

Harrison, Regina. 1989. *Signs, Songs and Memory in the Andes: Translating Quechua Language and Culture*. Austin: University of Texas Press.

Hobart, Mark. 1995. 'As I Lay Laughing: Encountering Global Knowledge in Bali'. In R. Fardon (ed.), *Counterworks*. London and New York: Routledge: 49–72.

Hoffman, Stanley B. 1978. 'Epistemology and Music: A Javanese Example'. *Ethnomusicology* 22(1): 69–88.

Huanca, Tomas. 1989. *El yatiri en la comunidad aymara*. La Paz: CADA–Hisbol.

Hulme, Frederick. 1909. *The History, Principles and Practice of Symbolism in Christian Art*. London: Swan, Sonnenschein & Co. (5th edn).

Ingold, Tim. 1993. 'Tool-Use, Sociality and Intelligence'. In K. Gibson and T. Ingold (eds.), *Tools, Language and Cognition in Human Evolution*. Cambridge: Cambridge University Press: 429–45.

Keller, Charles, and Janet Keller. 1996. *Cognition and Tool Use: The Blacksmith at Work*. Cambridge: Cambridge University Press.

Kutscher, Gerdt. 1950. *Eine altindianische Hochkultur*. Berlin: Gebr. Mann.

Leichtman, Ellen. 1987. 'The Bolivian *Huayño*: A Study in Musical Understanding'. PhD thesis, Brown University.

Mannheim, Bruce. 1991. *The Language of the Inka since the European Invasion*. Austin: University of Texas Press.

McAllester, David. 1971. 'Some Thoughts on "Universals" in World Music'. *Ethnomusicology* 15: 379–80.

Mercado, Claudio. 1996. 'Detrás del sonido, el mundo'. *Takiwasi* (Tarapoto, Peru) 4 (año 2): 46–61.

Nettl, Bruno. 1983. *The Study of Ethnomusicology: Twenty-Nine Issues and Concepts*. Urbana, IL, and Chicago: Illinois University Press.

Platt, Tristan. 1986. 'Mirrors and Maize: The concepts of *yanantin* among the Macha of Bolivia'. In J. Murra, N. Wachtel and J. Revel (eds.), *Anthropological History of Andean Polities*. Cambridge: Cambridge University Press: 228–59.

Rice, Timothy. 1994. *May It Fill Your Soul: Experiencing Bulgarian Music*. Chicago and London: University of Chicago Press.

Roseman, Marina. 1991. *Healing Sounds from the Malaysian Rainforest: Temiar Music and Medicine*. Berkeley and Los Angeles: California University Press.

Sanchez, Walter. 1996. 'Algunas consideraciones hipotéticas sobre música y sistema de pensamiento. La flauta de pan en los Andes Bolivianos'. In M. Baumann (ed.), *Cosmología y música en los Andes*. Frankfurt: Vervuert/Madrid: Iberoamericana: 83–106.

Scruton, Roger. 1993. 'Notes on the Meaning of Music'. In M. Krausz (ed.), *The Interpretation of Music*. Oxford: Clarendon Press: 193–202.

Seeger, Anthony. 1987. *Why Suyá Sing: A Musical Anthropology of an Amazonian People*. Cambridge: Cambridge University Press.

——, 1993. 'When Music Makes History'. In S. Blum, P. Bohlman and D. Neuman (eds.), *Ethnomusicology and Modern Music History*. Urbana, IL, and Chicago: University of Illinois Press: 23–34.

Silverblatt, Irene. 1987. *Moon, Sun and Witches: Gender Ideologies and Class in Inca and Colonial Peru*. Princeton: Princeton University Press.

Stobart, Henry. 1994. 'Flourishing Horns and Enchanted Tubers: Music and Potatoes in Highland Bolivia'. *British Journal of Ethnomusicology* 3: 35–48.

——, 1996. '*Tara* and *Q'iwa*: Worlds of Sound and Meaning'. In M. Baumann (ed.), *Cosmología y Música en los Andes*. Frankfurt: Vervuert/Madrid: Iberoamericana: 67–82.

——, 1998. 'Lo recto y lo torcido: La música andina y la espiral de la descendencia'. In D. Arnold (ed.), *Gente de carne y hueso: las tramas de parentesco en los andes*. La Paz: ILCA/CIASE: 581–604.

Stokes, Martin. 1994. 'Introduction'. In M. Stokes (ed.), *Ethnicity, Identity and Music*. Oxford: Berg: 1–27.

Sullivan, Lawrence. 1988. *Icanchu's Drum: An Orientation to Meanings in South American Religions*. New York: Macmillan.

Taylor, Charles. 1991. 'The Dialogical Self'. In D. Hiley, J. Bohman and R. Shusterman (eds.), *The Interpretative Turn: Philosophy, Science, Culture*. Ithaca, NY: Cornell University Press: 304–14.

Torres Rubio, Diego de. 1966. *Arte de la lengua aymava* [1616]. Actualización de

Mario Franco Inojosa. Lima-Peru: LYRSA.

Turino, Thomas. 1983. 'The Charango and the Sirena: Music, Magic and the Power of Love'. *Latin American Music Review* 4 (Spring/Summer): 81–119.

——, 1989. 'The Coherence of Social Style and Musical Creation among the Aymara of Southern Peru'. *Ethnomusicology* 33(1): 1–30.

——, 1993. *Moving Away from Silence: Music of the Peruvian Altiplano and the Experience of Urban Migration*. Chicago and London: University of Chicago Press.

Urban, Greg. 1986. 'Ceremonial Dialogues in South America'. *American Anthropologist* 88(2): 371–86.

Zeranska-Kominek, Slawomira. 1994. 'The *yol* (Road) of Music: An Anthropological Concept of Asian Musical Works'. In I. Deliege (ed.), *Third International Conference for Music Perception and Cognition* (Proceedings): 101–102.

PART II

Knowledge, Power and Authority

CHAPTER FIVE

Coming to Power: Knowledge, Learning and Historic Pathways to Authority in a Bolivian Community

Astvaldur Astvaldsson

The main issue studied in this chapter is the relationship between 'traditional' socio-political powers in a Bolivian community and the ways in which knowledge about and access to these powers were granted. I will first look at the sources of political power and then concentrate on the preparations for the first in a series of 'rites of passage' that show how knowledge about politics was produced and disseminated in such a way as to reveal hierarchical structures and processes that integrated the socio-political and religious spheres of life. In fact, this 'rite of passage' and the process that led up to it are best understood as being part of a learning process that provided young people with comprehensive knowledge not just of politics and religious matters but of the basic principles and practices of the society into which they were being initiated. Although the main rite referred to below is no longer performed, the rationale that underpinned it has not been totally lost. On the contrary, current practices are viewed and often debated in relation to 'how things used to be', especially by the older people

I shall also discuss some of the characteristics of knowledge and learning in the community. These are comparable to those of other societies that, similarly, rather than using alphabetic writing, rely on oral traditions and symbolic landscapes and objects for recording and preserving their knowledge (cf. Astvaldsson forthcoming). It is not being suggested that change is only happening now and that change and 'tradition' belong to separate worlds. On the contrary, as I have argued at length before, tradition is best understood as process and 'true historical continuity is always marked by ongoing transformations' (Astvaldsson 1998a: 204). Yet, while change tends to be legitimised and sacralised through ritual, which allows transformed reality to appear as continuous, radical change often leaves visible ruptures in old practices, which normally means that the knowledge related to them must be reformulated if it is to survive.[1]

---

[1] The knowledge–power theme that this study's title announces evokes Foucault's influential work (e.g. 1990) and some of the basic consequences of his concept of power–knowledge are

The sources of political power

The ethnographic data on which this study draws were gathered, mainly, in the community of Sullka Titi Titiri (hereafter Titiri), Jesús de Machaqa, highland Bolivia, in the early 1990s. The study focuses on the practices of that community, although my own fieldwork and that of others (cf. Albó 1993 and Ticona and Albó 1997) suggest that similar traditions existed elsewhere in Jesús de Machaqa at least.[2] The main body of data was obtained through informal interviews with elderly members of the community (mostly men between 50 and 90 years of age), who had 'walked their path' and knew about 'old' communal traditions that focused mainly on its male deities (*wak'a achachila*) and that existed in the form described below until the late 1970s. Information was also acquired through participation in the fiestas and rituals that the community continued to celebrate at the time and that were normally transformed versions of older traditions.[3]

The socio-political and ritual path (*thakhi*) of the community's authorities, which was much more complex prior to the late 1970s, began with a

---

corroborated by the data discussed below: for example, his idea that power is not best understood as being exercised from the top down (by a dominant upon a dominated class) but rather as something that permeates the whole of society; and his understanding that knowledge cannot be separated from the workings of power, for it is embedded in power relations. Yet while the present study does invite comparison with Foucault's theory, such a discussion poses several intricate questions that cannot be properly debated in the limited space available here. The main problem arises from the disparate kinds of data Foucault's work and the present study deal with. While this study looks at power–knowledge at community level in the Andes, Foucault was mainly preoccupied with the concept in relation to the rise of the modern state and capitalism, roughly from the late seventeenth to the early twentieth century. As Foucault shows, during that time the essence of both knowledge and power and the relations between them changed so radically that a totally new order of things was created. Hence, while the power–knowledge concept may have some basic consequences for different societies, at another level, the meaning of and relationship between its two components seem to be so distinct that a detailed comparison is rendered largely irrelevant, if not impossible. In view of these complications, Foucault's ideas are not extensively developed here, though this might be feasible in a study that looked more closely at the migrant community. Instead, the theoretical framework of the discussion owes more to the work of Foucault's fellow countryman, Pierre Bourdieu, whose 'theory of practice' and criticism of structuralism I have found highly pertinent to the argument.

[2] The first period of fieldwork took place from December 1990 to October 1991 and the second during December 1993 and January 1994. Apart from Titiri, relevant data was collected in some of the other communities of Jesús de Machaqa, from migrants in La Paz and, to a lesser extent, in communities outside Machaqa.

[3] Since I worked almost exclusively with male consultants, and indeed with male assistants, a degree of 'machismo' might be seen to be involved in my work. However, this was almost inevitable, because most of the themes and material treated in my study of the community have a prominent male character (see Astvaldsson 2000b, especially Chapter IV). My main assistant was Don Felix Layme, who is from Titiri. Together we collected numerous testimonies in Aymara, and he helped me with the initial interpretation of them; eventually, they were all transcribed and translated by others.

candidature, denominated *chhiphiña* by local people. It was both a bride-service and a learning process and started several years before a person could be considered for public office: a key purpose of it was to deliver young people into adulthood. The candidature meant that candidates had to fulfil a number of social and ritual obligations before they could 'graduate', i.e. before being allowed to become a 'head' (*p'iqi*), a basic local authority.[4] A second stage in the process was a ritual libation (*ch'alla*) that affirmed the election of the ten men who were to become 'heads' for the next three years. The *ch'alla* was carried out during the fiesta of the Virgen del Rosario, which continues to be celebrated in the *mestizo* town of Jesús de Machaqa at the beginning of October every year. The process culminated with the induction of the 'heads', which took place during a communal ritual in mid-January every three years and involved elaborate sacrifices to the local and regional male deities, the *wak'a achachila*.[5]

The purpose of the ritual was to secure good government, sociocultural continuity, order, harmony, growth, and procreation by reinforcing the reciprocal relationship that the community had entered into with its deities. This relationship was seen to give the community a degree of indirect control over vital natural forces, such as rain, wind, frost and hail, which are known or imagined to influence crop cultivation and the procreation of both animal herds and human beings. These forces were considered to be attributes of the local and regional *wak'a achachila* – in particular of the *marani*, certain high snow-capped mountains, such as Illimani and Sajama, the most powerful regional deities.[6] The deities were also repositories of the political powers that were transferred to the incoming authorities during the initiation ritual. In fact, they were said to have a political system that mirrored that of the human community and to pass on political roles within their ranks in the same way that they were passed from one individual or a group of individuals to another within the communities and the region.[7] Ideally this was so, yet individual deities did not progress through the hierarchy but had a fixed status and continued in office year after year. This does not change the fact that the basic principles of hierarchical authority

---

[4] The terms *mantiri* (incoming) and *machaqa* (new) are used for those about to take office. Those leaving office are referred to as *misturi* (outgoing) and *mirq'i* (old or former), or by an aymarised form of the Spanish term *pasado* (past), indicating someone who has fulfilled his duties. The 'heads' (*p'iqi*) were the community's basic authorities and the *chhiphiña* candidates were called 'junior heads' (*sullka p'iqi*). They were at the bottom of the hierarchy of communal authorities (the hierarchical structure of authority in Titiri is discussed in full detail in Astvaldsson 1996, 1998b, 2000b).

[5] Secondary sacrifices were offered to Pachamama, a collective female entity incorporating all private and communal fields (the soil/earth).

[6] *Marani* literally means 'the owners of the year', but, in this context, translates roughly as 'those in charge of community matters during the year'.

[7] In a similar way, Isbell (1978: 59, 151) says the Wamanis of Chuschi, southern Peru, have an organisational hierarchy likened to various levels of governmental structures.

within their ranks were conceived of in the same way as those within human society.[8]

Socio-political powers, then, while granted to individuals, did not become theirs by right, to keep and use as they pleased, which is still true in Titiri despite the changes that have taken place. Instead, great discretion was required and, essentially, individuals became temporary recipients of powers that were derived from and belonged to the local and regional deities. They could only be used in accordance with certain communal precepts, practices and rules (cf. Astvaldsson 1996, 1998b), which the candidates learned about and learned to respect through the practices covered by the candidature.[9] Moreover, people are well aware of the dangers inherent in the inclination to seek personal power, and the socio-political system and learning process it involved were designed to counter such a tendency in favour of communal welfare.

The learning process emphasised both the ritual/religious and the socio-political aspects of political power. It stressed respect, which had to be shown in practice for the sources from which power was derived, for those to whom it had been granted (reigning local authorities), and for the community in favour of which it was to be employed. Although knowledge was of course partly passed on through word of mouth, it was done as part of a system that emphasised good practice and the fulfilment of social and ritual duties, and always during active participation in the relevant practices. The first part of the process was long and complex (in theory it took three years, though it could take six, nine or even twelve). Only candidates who fulfilled all the requirements involved were allowed to go through the final stages and become local authorities.[10]

As my discussion already indicates, and as my examination of the *chhiphiña* sequence below will further underscore, the way in which the people of Titiri related to and talked about social, political and religious aspects of community life raises key questions about the essence of knowledge and learning in this and similar communities. For example, we have seen that certain 'anomalies' exist between real practices and ideal structures. In fact, while they often recognised complex aspects of society and

---

[8] Practical logic allows for such 'anomalies', for, to use Bourdieu's paradox, it is not the logic of such logic that is important but rather whether it has a practical (workable) application in a given situation; in other words, whether it represents 'an adequate description of things' (Bourdieu 1990: 137–38), i.e. whether it is 'believable'.

[9] As elsewhere in the Andes, taking on community office is a burdensome and costly service to one's community. Office holders are subject to strict public scrutiny and can be fined or impeached if anything goes wrong. The only benefit is the prestige that comes with carrying out one's duties successfully.

[10] As I discuss below, although many aspects of these practices have been discontinued, the ideas still persist. They might serve as a basis for a new approach to modern politics in a social environment where individualism and abuse of power have long been rife at national level and are becoming an increasingly serious problem at the level of native communities.

culture, people rarely framed their awareness in the analytical terms used by academics. The way in which young people learned about socio-political powers and most other things reflected this, and mirrored the essence of learning and knowledge in Titiri.

Drawing on Bourdieu's seminal work, in general terms, it is probably true to say that, in societies that do not use alphabetic writing for recording and preserving information, learning and knowledge have traditionally been 'practical' rather than 'academic', although it is impossible to draw a strict line between the two modes in any kind of society. In the past, children began the learning process at an early age (virtually as soon as they could walk) by accompanying and helping their parents, older brothers and sisters, and relatives with daily duties, such as herding and domestic work. Later, agricultural tasks alongside socio-political and many other skills were learned in a similar way, through active participation and experience rather than through formal schooling.

If learning and knowledge are explained in 'practical' rather than 'academic' terms, correspondingly, the understanding of complex phenomena is best described as 'intuitive' rather than 'analytical' – as is of course true for the majority of people in all societies, and indeed for all of us when it comes to commonplace knowledge generally (cf. Bourdieu 1977; Tyler 1978). This was borne out by the way in which the people of Titiri related to and talked about most aspects of their society and culture. When asked about things such as socio political matters, which involved complex ritual processes and relationships both among people and with and among local and regional deities, their answers tended to be descriptive rather than analytical, or they came in the form of a tale. Although ritual specialists and others who had exceptional knowledge in specific fields were sometimes more analytical and willing to speculate, native exegesis never gave rise to the same degree of abstraction as we expect of the academic knowledge produced by 'Western' analysts. Part of the reason for this is that analytical models, which academics are so used to working with, are most often removed from 'real practices', and it is precisely the practices themselves rather than any analysis of them which are meaningful to the people who carry them out. In other words, basic knowledge of communal practices in Titiri was preserved and disseminated in and through the practices themselves rather than abstractly.[11]

This does not mean that people who live in societies that do not use alphabetic writing for recording and preserving information are somehow less capable of reflective thinking than the people of modern cultures. On the contrary, the people of Titiri reasoned and debated in many contexts; for

---

[11] In a study of Quechua song, Harrison (1989: 30) describes this kind of cognitive process as follows: 'The images which abound in the song text are not causally related; the splashing of the water in the river and the bathing of the snake-women do not explain but *are* the belief system. The plastic image is the very essence of the logic in a society which does not value syllogisms but, instead, intuitive understanding, dream patterns, and the power of song.'

example, about the appropriate ways of performing certain tasks or, as I witnessed at the end of 1993, about how to punish two local officials (*jilaqata*) who had insulted the community by getting into a drunken fight (one of their tasks was to keep the peace; after considerable debate it was decided to fine rather than demote them, as some people had demanded, which would have been a very severe blow to their prestige). Rather, the point is that although we do not analyse everything we do, that does not mean that we don't know what we are doing. Practical knowledge serves a particular purpose: it enables us to cope, in a practical way, with 'the emergency situations of everyday life'. Yet through intuition we also tackle some of the most complex things in life, phenomena that have no rational explanation. Moreover, intuitive knowledge is instant and defies reasoning, an aspect that often seems to have unsettled Western analysts.[12]

The life-span in Titiri

Miracle and Yapita have argued that the Aymara divide the life-span of human beings into six age grades: baby, child, youth, adult, elder and the dead (1981: 39). Although it may be misleading to generalise about the Aymara and about Andean peoples generally, it is true to say that in Titiri the life-span of human beings was divided into grades or stages, but these divisions appear more complex than the examples cited by Miracle and Yapita. Each grade was associated with certain stages in the socio-cultural and biological development of the individual, as an active member of his or her community. Passing from one age category to another was marked by a 'rite of passage', designed to deliver individuals or groups of people into a new stage in their socio-cultural life, a new role within society. These rituals were socio-cultural processes that provided society with a degree of control over its members and served to legitimate the important steps from one socio-cultural category to another, by putting certain obligations – social, political and ritual – on both individual members and groups. These obligations entailed learning about, acknowledging and showing respect for the community heritage and for common 'law'.

As Bourdieu points out, there are very few, if any, strict rules or laws in native societies, but rather 'precepts of custom' that 'have nothing in common with the transcendent rules of a juridical code'. He also notes that 'it is [. . .] not sufficient to say that the rule determines practice when there is more to be gained by obeying it than disobeying it' (Bourdieu 1977: 17, 22). In the community of Titiri local 'law' has traditionally been inscribed in the local and regional deities and the practices related to them and, while things are constantly changing, that continues to be true. Similarly, through the ritual practices surrounding the deities the 'law' has continued to be both

---

[12] In his work on José María Arguedas, Rowe (1996) provides an insightful discussion on the role of intuition in the Andean context.

interpreted and enforced: breaking it is potentially disastrous for individuals and their families (for instance, I heard of a young man who, after taking to stealing, had been left paralysed by the deities). Yet it is important to note that this does not mean the 'law' is set in stone; on the contrary, one of the key purposes of the rituals has been to reinvent tradition. Hence, through the *chhiphiña* sequence, and other rituals, knowledge of communal practices was disseminated and reproduced. The candidates learned to use social skills and to follow socially sanctioned rules. They learned about the limits of their freedom to act and the consequences that transgression might bring. In other words, while the teaching and learning inherent in the *chhiphiña* sequence clearly empowered them, they also learned about the limits of that power.

The *chhiphiña* sequence refers to a set of social and ritual processes that took people from adolescence into adulthood: i.e., the period from reaching puberty to finding partners, marrying and taking on collective socio-political responsibilities. It formed part of a greater series of 'rites of passage' that began shortly after birth and continued until people had fulfilled their obligatory socio-political duties to society and became elders.[13] Although rituals like those involved in the *chhiphiña* sequence have not always been referred to as 'rites of passage' in the anthropological literature on the Andes, I believe they are best understood in that context. Van Gennep's broad theory makes it clear that these kinds of ritual form part of his category of 'rites of passage', even though he does not discuss them directly.[14] This does not mean that Andeanists have failed to work with the idea of progress through a civil religious hierarchy in a way similar to what I describe for *chhiphiña*: although they may not actually use the term 'rites of passage', Van Gennep's model is almost invariably implicit in their work.[15]

However, for various reasons, there are significant differences in the emphasis given to the subject in the present study as compared to earlier

[13] Some of the rituals that took place later in life are discussed at length in Astvaldsson 1995 and 2000b. Also, for an overview of the progressive paths of the 'traditional' authorities in Jesús de Machaqa, see Albó 1993.

[14] Van Gennep writes: 'The life of an individual in any society is a series of passages from one age to another and from one occupation to another. Wherever there are fine distinctions among age or occupational groups, progression from one group to the next is accompanied by special acts [. . .] Among semicivilized [sic] peoples [. . .] every change in a person's life involves actions and reactions [. . .] to be regulated and guarded so that society as a whole will suffer no discomfort or injury [. . .] For every one of these events there are ceremonies whose essential purpose is to enable the individual to pass from one defined position to another' (Van Gennep 1960: 2–3). If it is right that ritual initiations into the different posts of political office are effectively 'rites of passage', then that complicates the question of Aymara age categories referred to earlier, especially the period of adulthood, which Miracle and Yapita seem to consider as one unbroken age category.

[15] For a discussion of the more widely recognised 'rites of passage' in the Andes, see Bastien 1985. Taking a more innovative approach, inspired by Van Gennep's work, Platt (1983: 48–49) has argued that Andean 'devil worship', in particular as part of migrant *campesinos*' transformation to the class of miners, should be considered as a true 'rite of passage'.

ethnographies, especially those produced by anthropologists working in southern Peru in the 1970s and 1980s (e.g., Isbell 1978; Allen 1988). Many of these focused on Quechua-speaking communities near Cuzco, the epi-centre of the Inka state, which differ in notable ways from Quechua- and Aymara-speaking communities in Bolivia. Second, there are often conspic-uous disparities between communities that speak the same language, even neighbouring ones. Third, ethnographies tend to reflect the particular inter-ests of those who write them and the kind of information that is made avail-able to outsiders depends on many often quite unpredictable factors, as well as 'luck' or 'chance' – to use a pan-Andean concept.

Isbell and Allen describe processes through civil religious hierarchies that are comparable, though by no means identical, to those I encountered in Titiri. Abercrombie (1986) does the same for K'ulta, Oruro, Bolivia (see below). In each case the data is different and each author stresses certain aspects of the system with which they deal. For example, for the case of Chuschi, Isbell describes a dual system of authority centred on the basic opposition of *comuneros* versus *vecinos*, which is not nearly as weighty in Titiri. The 'indigenous prestige hierarchy' she discusses is also different in many ways: for instance, class within the community is more pronounced and material wealth has more effect on how and whether men ascend the hierarchy. Most importantly though, Isbell (1978: 138) chooses not to describe the rituals involved (they seem to have been abolished by popular vote in 1970). And, while her outline of 'the ideal ritual steps toward mar-riage' is of intrinsic interest, it does not include a discussion of the kind of social and ritual obligations that are so important to the *chhiphiña* bride-service. Allen does not discuss these rituals either and some basic principles of the system she describes differ from what is found in Titiri: for instance, adulthood is reached later. However, Allen (1988: 115–22) mentions the educational aspects of the hierarchy and provides a piquant examination of the workings of informal powers exerted by both the women and the 'elders' (older men deemed to have led a good life) of Sonqo. This has close par-allels in Titiri (cf. Astvaldsson 1996, 1998b).

One thing that distinguishes Jesús de Machaqa as a whole from many other areas is that it was a free community, rather than a hacienda, during most of the colonial period. Hence, its socio-political and religious struc-tures may have developed differently from those of many other communities and some older elements may have been better preserved. The *chhiphiña* sequence formed part of these structures and seems to have been particu-larly elaborate in this area. At least, my review of the literature suggests that there is more and in some ways unique information forthcoming there.

Chhiphiña

Today it is obligatory for all married male members of the community, accompanied by their wives, to act as 'heads' for one year, although relatives can serve as substitutes. However, before the *chhiphiña* sequence was abandoned in the late 1970s, the 'heads' served for three years running and people did not automatically qualify for office. Instead, within each of the ten zones into which the community is divided, groups of candidates, nominated by the authorities, by community members, or by their families, had to compete for the prestige of being granted real authority.[16] They did this by fulfilling the social and ritual obligations required of them during the three years that the *chhiphiña* period ideally lasted.

When people were asked about the meaning of the term *chhiphiña*, rather than providing a glossarial explanation or a sociological analysis, they usually gave a loose description of their own experience. These descriptions revealed that the *chhiphiña* sequence entailed a combination of social and ritual duties, which in their culture would not normally be divorced from each other. The candidates carried out these duties for the benefit of their zones, the reigning authorities, and the whole community in order to secure their selection to office. This can be discerned from the following words, voiced by one community member.

> Primeroxa . . . kimsa mara, sullka kawisa numrasiña. Sullkanakat. Taqpach sarnaqañapataki ukax. Uma waytaniri, **sirwisiyu lurarapiña**, ukhama. Kimsa mara. Jichhax kimsa marat ukax mistxi . . .

> First . . . [so that they could serve as 'heads' for] three years, the junior 'heads' had to be appointed. From the [group of] young men. So that all would go well [so that all of them would progress to the next stage]. Water had to be fetched, [the reigning 'heads'] had to be rendered a service [offered alcohol and food in fiestas], like that. [This lasted] three years. Now, [after] three years they came out of this [initial service period].

The term *lurarapiña* describes obligatory action carried out by the subject for the benefit of someone else and *sirwisiyu* refers specifically to the serving of alcohol and food to the authorities in the communal fiestas, which was a key element of *chhiphiña*. However, it is also clear from this quotation and from the rest of my data that the *chhiphiña* sequence entailed other kinds of 'service', such as fetching water. On another occasion *chhiphiña* was described to me in Spanish as 'a candidature of a kind, presenting the authorities with gifts in the fiestas' ('una especie de candidatura poniendo presentes ante las autoridades comunales en las fiestas'), which again points to the ritual aspects. The gifts were usually small bottles of pure alcohol, referred to in Aymara as *t'inkha*, something given as a sign of gratitude. By presenting them to those serving as officials, the candidates did honour to them. They also showed respect for the civil institutions of the community and, most importantly, for the power with which the reigning authorities had been invested in the initiation ritual they had gone through. Although,

---

[16] The community seems to have been divided into ten zones since some time after the 1952 Revolution: before that it was divided into four zones and hence there were four 'heads'.

ideally, the candidature took three consecutive years to complete, it could take longer if interrupted or if a candidate failed to fulfil his social and ritual obligations properly (e.g., failure to provide a gift at a fiesta) and thus was not successful that time around.

However, the *chhiphiña* sequence, its overall implications, its historical origin and its more intricate meanings are more complex than might appear from a quick look at its immediate social and ritual aspects, as described by local people. Their utterances are typically marked by an emphasis on the practical aspects. Thus, they are a good example of the native discourse of familiarity that tends to draw attention to the most remarkable 'moves', rather than being comprehensively descriptive or providing a close analysis of the principles that 'govern' the practice (Bourdieu 1977: 19). Unravelling all the implications of the sequence requires taking a closer look at the term *chhiphiña*. Drawing on ethnographic data and both modern and colonial dictionaries, my research shows that the term has an extensive and complex semantic range. These findings have notable implications, not just for the historical significance of the processes in question but also more broadly for political thought and cosmology in Titiri. Also, they give further insight into the essence of 'traditional' knowledge and how society passed it down to its young people, through living practices, so that they could become fully fledged members of the adult world.

It is worth reiterating here that the difference between the information provided by local people's answers to questions on the meaning of *chhiphiña* and the kind of information academic analysis produces does not have to mean that people were unaware of many of the aspects revealed by the latter. Rather, because knowledge of particular practices was preserved and disseminated in and through the practices themselves, native attitudes did not require knowledge of them to be organised in the same way and expressed in the analytical terms used by Western exegesis for the practices to be accurately understood. Each practice produced the knowledge relevant to it and participation provided novices with all the information they needed.

From practice to analysis: the deeper meanings of chhiphiña
Let us now look closer at the overall meaning of *chhiphiña*. The ethnographic information shows that the three-year sequence was carried out by junior members of the community, who were about to marry or had recently married. On the one hand, it involved social duties that included helping out with routine tasks of everyday life, such as fetching water. More specifically, it involved participation in agricultural labour in the communal fields, and it was designed to train young people and prepare them for other tasks and activities, such as building a house, which are better understood as part of basic 'schooling' than as a service. The sequence also entailed participation in communal fiestas, where the candidates had to present their superiors with gifts of alcohol and food, which are key ingredients in all sacrifices and vital to the success of fiestas. Fiestas are geared towards securing commu-

nal welfare by feeding the deities and thereby reproducing the community's reciprocal links with them. All the duties benefited the community and fulfilling them effectively proved one's respect for it and for its people. The candidature was also designed to teach young people respect for the community's reigning officials and the authority with which they had been invested when they were initiated. This authority, in a nutshell the right to speak publicly about community matters and the power to command people via language, was derived from local and regional male deities, who protected the community against outside threats and dangers, both natural and human (cf. Astvaldsson 1996, 1998b, 2000b). Thus, the candidature shows how the community's political and religious systems formed part of an integral whole.

The lexical information, while reflecting communal practices, enriches our understanding of *chhiphiña* and allows us to fill in some of the lacunae left by the native language of familiarity (cf. Bourdieu 1997: 18). The meanings given by the dictionaries (see Astvaldsson 1995, 2000b for detailed analysis) include: to break up clods of earth; to weed, using a stone (some synonyms mean 'to sow'); to care for the plants in various ways; and to make *chuño* and adobes. *Chhiphiña* also means to hit or smash with a stone; to punch and fight with the fists (the face and chest are particular targets for such punches); to hurt and wound; to fight with clubs; to kill *vicuñas*. Moreover, it means to be or to make someone else glad or happy; to whisper; to plan secretly; to thatch. Finally, combined with the term *usu* (illness) and certain suffixes, *chhiphiña* and some of its synonyms take on the meaning of plague and falling ill, and express a situation in which frost attacks a field or part of a field, but not the surrounding area. According to the modern dictionaries (Lucca 1983, 1987; PEEB 1984; Paredes 1971), the only meanings still in use are: to be or make someone else glad or happy; to whisper; to plan secretly.[17] The last two are those that people in Titiri identified immediately, while only the older generations were aware the term's relation to the candidature of the junior 'heads'.

Although it seems, at first, that the lexical information gives diverse and even contradictory meanings for the term, these meanings are nevertheless directly or indirectly related to each other and agree with the principles of communal practices. Agricultural work and fiesta participation formed part of the *chhiphiña* sequence and continue to be part of ongoing processes of socio-political, cultural and economic life, which include ritual fighting.[18] *Vicuña* hunting was also significant to these practices in the past in a region

---

[17] Cotari et al. (1978), Carvajal et al. (1978) and van den Berg (1985) have no entries for the term.

[18] Although things may have been different before, 'ritual fighting' in Jesús de Machaqa does not take the same organised and violent form today, as is the case in parts of Northern Potosí and Peru. However, it can be recognised in a more subtle form in music, dances, and some of the verbal utterances and punch-ups that occur during communal and regional fiestas.

where this animal was part of the local diet: *vicuñas* were found in considerable numbers in the area until recently.

It is crucial that those going through the *chhiphiña* sequence were newly 'wedded' couples and that getting married is a long process.[19] These young couples were in the process of building their own house. They lived in the bridegroom's father's house, where the bride helped her mother-in-law with domestic work and was having to prove her ability to run a household. Meanwhile, the husband carried out his duties outside the house, for the community and his family group, as well as working in the couple's own fields. We know that nobody could become a 'head' without having his own house, and it is interesting to note that, in the case of *ayllu* Qaqachaka, Arnold (1992: 46) reports that newly wedded couples did not generally finish building their houses until three years after marriage. This period coincides with the time that the *chhiphiña* sequence ideally lasted. Thatching a house marks the completion of its construction: in fact, the structure is not considered to be a house until it has been thatched. The most common Aymara term for 'to thatch' is *utachaña*, which literally means 'to make a house'; Bertonio (1984 [1612]) lists the term as a synonym of *chhiphiña*. This shows how the tasks and duties associated with becoming an independent member of society coincided, forming an integrated process, *chhiphiña*, which was a learning process that culminated in the initiation of young people into adulthood.

In the case of *ayllu* K'ulta, Abercrombie (1986: 114) notes that the 'first tasa payment has become a rite of passage into full adulthood, carried out after the completion of a new household and finalizing receipt of inheritance'. And, he adds, 'it is also an initial step on the path towards patriline and ayllu office'. Moreover, this author says that before a man can become an authority 'he must become an adult within his patriline; a brother among brothers. Adult status is achieved through a series of steps in which he is progressively detached from the status of yuqalla (and the feminine productive roles attached to it) and consequently overcomes his subordination, as yuqa (son), to his own father and patriline "fathers"' (1986: 127).[20] Hence, 'the steps involved might profitably be seen as stages in the marriage process'. That is exactly one way in which the various aspects of the *chhiphiña* sequence can be understood.

Thus, to summarise, the term *chhiphiña* describes a prolonged trial and transitory period for newly 'wedded' couples. During this time they as individuals and their relationship as a social unit had to undergo the scrutiny of their families and community, and they had to prove themselves as responsible community members. They built their own house, broke in their fields,

---

[19] Rather than being formally married, it is just as likely that these couples were cohabiting. Cohabitation in Titiri can last for many years, during which several children may be born.

[20] The terms *yuqalla*, *wayna* and *sullka*, which all denote youth, were also used in Jesús de Machaqa to describe the young men before they became 'heads'.

harvested their first crops and most probably had their first children, and so on. They also served their families, authorities and community by helping out with the tasks of everyday life and participating in the all-important fiestas. In the process, they learned to show commitment to the interests of their community and respect for the deities who influenced and protected its welfare, and from whom the men received their right to govern when they were initiated into office at the end of the *chhiphiña* sequence.[21] Thus, the term *chhiphiña* does not literally have to be taken to have all the diverse meanings given by the dictionaries. Equally, although this might be tempting, it would be naïve to propose an 'original' meaning for such a complex term: for example, if we narrowed its meaning down to the act of breaking down some form/matter into a new, more malleable form, including young people who are being 'moulded' into responsible members of the community (which is certainly one of its key connotations), then how would we account for the meanings 'to be or make someone else glad or happy'; 'to whisper'; 'to plan secretly', which seem to be the only ones to have survived into the present? Rather, *chhiphiña* evokes a wide semantic field: one of its functions in Titiri was to describe a socio-cultural process of which the activities it designated formed an integrated part. Practical logic allows a set of values that would otherwise be considered as opposites (agricultural work, fighting, pleasure, etc.) to be brought together and expressed collectively through both language and living practices.

What is known, how it is learned, how things change

When discussing the traditions surrounding the preparation and initiation of the 'heads', people often expressed the worry that today candidates were young and inexperienced when they took on the responsibilities of communal authority. This was especially well reflected in the comments of the elders, who had experienced different times and worried about divisions in the community, which were often linked, directly or indirectly, to the discontinuation of the old rituals. They frequently referred to the acting 'heads' as 'youngsters' (either *wayna* or *menores de edad*) and their concerns were related to the fact that the community no longer showed the same commitment as before to the *wak'a achachila*. The new situation, in which many of the younger generation knew little about and were no longer interested in the old traditions and ancestral knowledge, was seen as a direct consequence of the discontinuity in the learning processes in which those wanting to become authorities were earlier required to take part. Also, it was felt that

---

[21] As I discuss elsewhere (Astvaldsson 1996, 1998a), the *wak'a achachila* Turiturini, around whom the initiation ceremony of the 'heads' was centred, is considered to be a *wak'a* of married couples. This becomes particularly fascinating and more easily comprehensible in the context of the *chhiphiña*, where we encounter young couples who are about to establish themselves as legitimate families and who, at the same time, are preparing for becoming local authorities.

this had created an atmosphere in which the 'heads' no longer commanded the same degree of respect as before, for they were not imbued with ancestral powers and authority in the same intense way as they had been through the former January initiation ritual.[22]

Many of the people from Titiri with whom I spoke, not just the young but serving 'heads' and *jilaqata* (higher ranked community leaders), knew very little about 'how things used to be' and many did not even know the names or locations of the community's most powerful local deities. The fact that they had not participated in the old rituals is not, of course, the only reason for this lack of knowledge but it is a decisive factor. Even my friend and assistant, Felix Layme, who is relatively well educated and has a keen interest in the history and traditions of his community, which had led him to interview some elders long before I arrived there, knew next to nothing specific about the old traditions. Although he knew some of the names, he had never seen some of the community's most powerful local deities and had no idea where they were located. Part of the reason for this, of which he was well aware, was that since he moved to La Paz as a young man he had never served as a 'head' and hence not participated in the ritual initiation. Another reason for his lack of this knowledge, of which he may not have been aware but which I gradually came to realise, was that those living in the community may have been reluctant to give him access to the communal deities and power. From their perspective, he – like many others – not only lived in the city but had also acquired ambiguous powers concomitant with the 'high' status he enjoyed within the culture to which he had moved. Furthermore, there may have been certain personal and family issues at play in this particular case. Nevertheless, the fact that the rituals no longer take place means that the knowledge related to them is no longer reproduced and disseminated systematically, and older people are keenly aware of this. In fact, this is related to 'traditional' attitudes to knowledge and to what is actually knowable, and to how knowledge is both produced and disseminated.

As indicated above, native knowledge of working practices and religious ceremonies is largely contained in their execution. This means that only those who have taken part in a given practice can really claim to have meaningful knowledge of it. Yet their knowledge is seldom more than partial, for most practices require the participation of a number of individuals, who have to come together to *make the practice complete*, each playing a special role or lending particular expertise to the occasion. In fact, the people of Titiri were often very aware of the limitations of their personal knowledge. For example, when I asked one of the men I worked with to elaborate on a key aspect of the January initiation ritual, he declined, saying he could not because he might lie. Although he had participated in the ceremony he was

---

[22] The 'heads' used to receive these ancestral powers at the end of the initiation ritual in what was described as a warring attack on them by the *wak'a achachila*, who were literally seen to enter into their minds and bodies (cf. Astvaldsson 2000b, Chapter VII).

uncertain about this particular aspect and did not feel that his limited knowledge gave him the right to speculate about the meaning of the ritual. Instead, he pointed to his elderly father, who, he said, knew much more about the traditions of the community, for he was older and had more participant experience. This attitude reflects a society in which a clear distinction is made between first-hand knowledge and hearsay and in which those who think they know everything are usually ridiculed and scorned. When I later spoke to the father, who was an elder and one of the most experienced and knowledgeable people I met, he was able to provide a much broader perspective on the ritual; however, his knowledge was also limited.

In fact, full knowledge of complex socio-political processes and ritual practices belonged to the community rather than to individuals and is perhaps best described as 'shared knowledge', which again reflects how, in essence, socio-political and ceremonial knowledge and powers were conceived of: they resided with the community and ultimately with the deities. Moreover, the social and ritual practices were learning processes that produced and reproduced knowledge, not just for those who took part in them for the first time but equally for those who participated in them again and again. I noted that those who had the most complete knowledge of the ritual practices were normally either those who had taken part in them most often or those who had played particularly important roles (e.g., ritual specialists), or both. Yet theirs was practical knowledge, whereas my role has been to pull it all together and come up with analytical models and tools that have hopefully allowed me to produce a comprehensive and readable account – although of course a partial one.

The material presented above raises questions about why the old customs of the community were discontinued. While it is clear that a combination of factors contributed to it, it is difficult to pinpoint the particular reasons behind these radical changes. However, we can address this issue from a more general perspective. As Bourdieu asserts, ritual practices are logical, but only up to a certain point, since their logic is practical logic, that is, good in practice (Bourdieu 1990: 65). It is the logic of practices that have emerged in response to particular situations and that have proved adequate for those situations. However, such practices are liable to incur negative sanctions when the environment with which they are actually confronted becomes too distant from that to which they were first objectively fitted (Bourdieu 1977: 78). This is what has happened in Titiri as a consequence of radical modernisation. It is clear that the old practices no longer 'make sense' to many people, especially those of the younger generation. The logic underpinning them no longer provides 'an adequate description of things', since the 'reality' on which it was based has been called into question by the modern world and by the new knowledge it has brought with it. In summary, in the last 40–50 years radical change has taken place and is still increasing in pace: thus, the socio-political and economic context that provided the backdrop for the *chhiphiña* sequence and the initiation ritual has slowly been disintegrating.

Yet this does not mean that the knowledge related to the old traditions has been totally lost, and the option of reviving the initiation ritual was even discussed in the meetings of community leaders in late 1993. For several reasons, though, it is unlikely that this will happen. Nevertheless, the destructuration is only partial.[23] For example, authority is still seen to be derived from the male deities and, although the community no longer oversees the ritual initiation, individuals can (and some do, as I witnessed in 1994) make their own offerings to the deities when they enter political office. Other community rituals, more directly associated with animal rearing and agriculture than with political authority, are still celebrated every year, such as Carnival and Santa Bárbara. During the latter, which takes place at the beginning of December, offerings are made simultaneously to the communal fields (*aynuqa*) planted at this time and to Thä Achila, a collective male entity that represents the *wak'a achachila* who influence climatic conditions. The purpose of this ritual is in many ways comparable to that of the discontinued January ritual. It serves to reinforce both the community's links with its deities and the communicative links between the complementary powers of male and female deities, which have to be brought together so that life and growth are regenerated. Although this ritual has been simplified (e.g., live llamas are no longer sacrificed), ritual offerings are still crucial. It should also be noted that changes in agriculture have not been nearly as dramatic as recent socio-political changes, which may help to explain why this ritual has survived, albeit resemanticised, while others have not.

There is also another way in which the old knowledge is being put to use, although radically reformulated. The essence of learning and knowledge in places like Titiri has changed greatly in the last few decades, with most children now receiving basic education and more and more young people going on to study at college and university. The effects of formal education have often been drastic, transforming attitudes to most aspects of native culture and leading to widespread rejection of the old ancestral ways, in particular by those who have gone to the cities and received formal education (e.g., rural schoolteachers). Yet native people are increasingly undertaking positive re-evaluation of their practices, ideas and knowledge, as compared to Western attitudes, and the work of foreign, and increasingly also native, academics has probably helped to make this re-evaluation possible. In fact, often led by their formally educated sons and daughters, people have begun to re-examine their roots and are rapidly realising that many aspects of their culture have intrinsic values and may be worth reviving, albeit in a radically transformed cultural and socio-political context, in the face of increased disillusionment with many aspects of the modern world. My conversations with young Titiri intellectuals, both in La Paz and when they visited the commu-

---

[23] Wachtel (1977: 85) coins the word 'destructuration', which he uses 'to signify the survival of ancient structures, or parts of them, no longer contained within the relatively coherent context in which they had previously existed'.

nity, made me realise that they are putting what is mainly academic knowledge about the past to new use. For example, they view the values, principles and ideals of native communality as overwhelmingly favourable in comparison with the corrupt system of government that for so long has blighted the country. In fact, they raised serious questions about whether the kind of communality that has traditionally characterised places like Titiri, where the authorities have served and been accountable to the community, could not be used to inform future government. Such views point to a new awareness that might influence political and social processes in years to come: the *chhiphiña* may have been abandoned but aspects of its inheritance may yet have a role to play in the future.

References

Abercrombie, Thomas. 1986. 'The Politics of Sacrifice: An Aymara Cosmology in Action'. PhD thesis, University of Chicago.

Albó, Xavier. 1993. 'El Thakhi o "camino" en Jesús de Machaca'. In R. Thiercelin (ed.), *Cultures et sociétés Andes et Méso-Amérique. Mélanges en hommage à Pierre Duviols*. Aix-en-Provence: Publications de l'Université de Provence: I, 51–65.

Allen, Catherine. 1988. *The Hold Life Has: Coca and Cultural Identity in an Andean Community*. Washington: Smithsonian Institution Press.

Arnold, Denise. 1992. 'La casa de adobes y piedras del Inka: Género, memoria y cosmos en Qaqachaka'. In Arnold, Jímenez and Yapita: 31–108.

Arnold, Denise, D. Jímenez A. and J. de D. Yapita. 1992. *Hacia un orden andino de las cosas*. La Paz: Hisbol/ICLA.

Astvaldsson, Astvaldur. 1995. 'Wak'a: An Andean Religious Concept in the Context of Aymara Social and Political Life'. PhD thesis, University of London.

——, 1996. *Sociopolitical Organization, Authority, Gender and Kinship in the Bolivian Andes*. Research Paper 19. Liverpool: Institute of Latin American Studies, University of Liverpool.

——, 1998a. 'The Powers of Hard Rock: Meaning, Continuity and Transformation in Cultural Symbols in the Andes'. *Journal of Latin American Cultural Studies* 7(2): 203–23.

——, 1998b. 'Las cabezas que hablan: autoridad, parentesco y género en una comunidad andina'. In D. Arnold (ed.), *Gente de carne y hueso: las tramas de parentesco en los Andes*. La Paz: CIASE/ILCA: 227–61.

——, 2000a. 'The Dynamics of Aymara Duality: Change and Continuity in Sociopolitical Structures in the Bolivian Andes'. *Journal of Latin American Studies* 32: 145–74.

——, 2000b. *Jesús de Machaqa: La marka rebelde. Vol. IV: Las voces de los wak'a: fuentes principales del poder político aymara*. La Paz: CIPCA.

——, forthcoming. 'Reading without Words: Landscapes and Symbolic Objects as Repositories of Knowledge and Meaning'. In a special issue of the series *British Archaeological Reports*. Ed. P. Dransart. London: Archaeopress.

Bastien, Joseph. 1985. *Mountain of the Condor*. New York: Waveland Press.

Berg, Hans van den. 1985. *Diccionario religioso aymara*. Iquitos: Ceta and Idea.

Bertonio, Ludovico de. 1984 [1612]. *Vocabulario de la lengua aymara*. Cochabamba: CERES, IFEA and MUSEF.

Bourdieu, Pierre. 1977. *Outline of a Theory of Practice*. Cambridge: Cambridge University Press.

——, 1990. *In Other Words: Essays Towards a Reflexive Sociology*. Cambridge: Polity Press (in association with Basil Blackwell, Oxford).

Bourdieu, Pierre, and L.J.D. Wacquant. 1992. *An Invitation to Reflexive Sociology*. Cambridge: Polity Press (in association with Basil Blackwell, Oxford).

Carvajal, Juan, Vitaliano Huanca, Juana Vásquez and Pedro Plaza. 1978. *Diccionario aymara–castellano*. La Paz: Instituto Nacional de Estudios Lingüísticos.

Cotari, Daniel, Jaime Mejía and Víctor Carrasco. 1978. *Diccionario aymara– castellano, castellano–aymara*. Cochabamba: Instituto de Idiomas, Padres de Maryknoll.

Foucault, Michel. 1990. *Archaeology of Knowledge*. London: Routledge.

Harrison, Regina. 1989. *Signs, Songs and Memory in the Andes: Translating Quechua Language and Culture*. Austin: Texas University Press.

Isbell, Billie Jean. 1978. *To Defend Ourselves: Ecology and Ritual in an Andean Village*. Prospect Heights, IL: Waveland Press.

Lucca, Manuel de. 1983. *Diccionario aymara–castellano, castellano–aymara*. La Paz: CALA. (Abbreviated version, La Paz: Los Amigos del Libro, 1987).

Miracle, Andrew, Jr, and J. de Dios Yapita Moya. 1981. 'Time and Space in Aymara'. In M. Hardman (ed.), *The Aymara Language in its Social and Cultural Context*. Gainesville, FL: Florida University Press: 33–56.

Paredes, Manuel Rigoberto. 1971. *Vocabulario de la lengua aymara*. La Paz: Isla.

Platt, Tristan. 1983. 'Conciencia andina y conciencia proletaria: Qhuyaruna y ayllu en el norte de Potosí'. *HISLA: Revista Latinoamericana de Historia Económica y Social* 2: 47–73.

——, 1986. 'Mirrors and Maize: The Concept of *Yanantin* among the Macha of Bolivia'. In J.V. Murra, N. Wachtel and J. Revel (eds.), *Anthropological History of Andean Polities*. Cambridge: Cambridge University Press: 228–59.

Proyecto Experimental de Educación Bilingüe, Puno. 1984. *Diccionario aymara–castellano. Arunakan liwru: aymara–kastillanu*. Lima and Puno: PEEB.

Rowe, William. 1996. *Ensayos Arguedianos*. Lima: Sur.

Ticona, Esteban, and X. Albó. 1997. *Jesús de Machaqa: La marka rebelde. Vol. III: La lucha por el poder communal*. La Paz: CIPCA.

Tyler, Stephen. 1978. *The Said and Unsaid: Mind, Meaning, and Culture*. New York: Academic Press.

Van Gennep, Arnold. 1960. *Rites of Passage*. London: Routledge & Kegan Paul.

Wachtel, Nachel. 1977. *The Vision of the Vanquished: The Spanish Conquest of Peru through Indian Eyes: 1530–1570*. Hassocks, Sussex: The Harvester Press.

Wacquant, Loïc. 1992. 'Toward a Social Praxeology: The Structure and Logic of Bourdieu's Sociology'. In Bourdieu and Wacquant: 1–59.

CHAPTER SIX

Juggling Knowledge, Juggling Power: The Role of the Professional Indigenous Activist in San Pablo, Ecuador

Janet Lloyd

In the last decade, the indigenous movement in Ecuador has gained substantial new ground. This success can be partly attributed to the skills of the professional indigenous activists who form the subject of this chapter. At the forefront of the movement, professional activists form a bridge over the immense socio-economic and cultural gulf between the domain of local indigenous concerns and the arenas of national and, increasingly, international politics. In a multi-layered movement, their role is complex: locally, they seek to meet the needs of a vast array of grassroots organisations that exercise growing control over rural political spaces. Nationally, as parliamentarians, they were active in the drafting of the 1998 Constitution, proposing nothing less than a total restructuring of Ecuadorian society and a radical redefinition of the relationship between the state and its people (IWGIA 1998: 107). Internationally, leaders of CONAIE (the Confederation of Indigenous Nationalities of Ecuador) lobby the powerful in Washington, Geneva and Brussels, funded by an expanding network of influential Western allies (Selverston 1994: 140).

In this chapter, I explore how the professional activist moves between the seemingly irreconcilable worlds of the illustrious conference rooms of international institutions and the more humble earth floors of community meeting houses, by skilfully juggling different ways of knowing the world and distinctive understandings of politics. Walking a tightrope between conflicting, culturally specific, historically derived bodies of knowledge, they must reconcile local indigenous political customs with the norms of national and international political structures. Drawing on my work with the indigenous NGO, CEPCU (the Centre for Pluricultural Studies), in the San Pablo region of northern Ecuador in 1996 and 1997, I look at how the relationship between *profesionales indígenas* (indigenous professionals), as they call themselves, and *comuneros* (community members) is affected by this need to balance community ways of knowing and practising politics with the priorities of national and international actors.[1] Given the obvious tensions

---

[1] CEPCU is an urban-based organisation founded in 1991 by a group of *profesionales*

and conflicts inherent in their work, it is not surprising that the *profesional indígena* emerges as an ambiguous character who meets with a combination of grudging respect and hostility.

I wish to link my analysis of the professional activist to the theme of power and knowledge. Due to the inextricable links between power and knowledge, documented by authors such as Foucault (1980) and Said (1978, 1994), the knowledge of the powerful is assumed to be superior to that of the less powerful. In his discussion of 'the colonisation of reality' by the discourse of development, Escobar shows how dominant ways of knowing become the yardstick against which alternatives are measured and positioned (1995: 5). These totalising forms of knowledge ignore and suppress multiple other ways of knowing. In the eyes of many powerful national and international actors, indigenous knowledge, indigenous ways of conceiving reality and indigenous solutions to indigenous people's problems are devalued and 'parochialized' (Moore 1996: 2). Furthermore, as Hobart concludes, 'as systematic knowledge grows, so does the possibility of ignorance. Ignorance, however, is not a simple antithesis of knowledge. It is a state which people attribute to others and is laden with moral judgement' (Hobart [ed.] 1993: 1).

Through various political projects, indigenous intellectuals have attempted to reverse this process of devaluation and parochialisation by defending and promoting indigenous knowledge. The professional activist's defence of indigenous knowledge is vital because knowing differently is central to the construction of indigenous identity and the production of indigenous culture. Through their beliefs, values and customs and their everyday physical and moral practices, indigenous peoples produce and reproduce their own 'ways of knowing' the world (Weismantel 1988: 8; Escobar 1992: 70).[2] The indigenous cause is a struggle over land and resources, yet it is also a struggle for the right to a different knowledge and culture. Hence, organisations such as CONAIE stress the importance of protecting intellectual property rights, of practising historically derived

---

indígenas from the Otavalo and Cayambe communities (the two Quichua cultural groups of the region). CEPCU mainly worked in the valley of San Pablo, an area of the canton of Otavalo. It was originally intended to function as a centre for indigenous political debate, education and mobilisation, with the long-term aim of setting up and running an independent structure of local indigenous government in the canton of Otavalo. However, after two years, CEPCU almost disintegrated. Prominent local, national and international activist Luis Maldonado took over and refocused CEPCU's official agenda towards socio-economic and environmental matters. This change in direction had much to do with the funding agenda of a small German NGO named Hanns Seidel, which approved CEPCU's projects and provided sufficient funds to pay five professional activists and four *promotores* (promoters) to carry them out.

[2] I use the term 'ways of knowing' not to indicate an objective, abstract or fixed exercise, rather to refer to knowledge created and enacted through a range of situated practices. As Hobart argues, although knowledge is often assumed to exist independently of the knower, knowing is a subjective process that occurs in historically and culturally specific contexts (1995: 51).

farming techniques, of retelling history from an indigenous perspective and of incorporating indigenous values and aspirations into the range of economic and social programmes targeted at indigenous communities. The affirmation of indigenous knowledge is vital to the process of political empowerment. Yet the scenario that is evoked, often by activists themselves, of local indigenous kinds of knowledge struggling against non-indigenous master narratives can be misleading. The hierarchy of knowledge that I outlined above is real, but the workings of that hierarchy are complex.

Firstly, structures of power in any society undergo a constant process of fragmentation and redefinition around what Tiffin and Lawson refer to as 'multiple systems of difference and interpellation' (1994: 231). The power of non-indigenous groups is limited by grey areas of ambivalence and contradiction which emerge as seemingly established boundaries dissolve and distinctions cloud. Dixon illustrates this point in his discussion of the 'boundaries of civility' in colonial Australia, in which he explores the breakdown of discursive boundaries of race and gender as women and indigenous peoples challenge the centre by criss-crossing borders (Dixon 1994: 140). Similarly, in his investigation of the interaction between so-called 'local' and 'global' knowledge in beauty contests in Belize, Wilk challenges the assumed polarities of global hegemony and local appropriation. He argues that, although Western standards of beauty have been incorporated into Belizean ideals, other local concepts of beauty emerge and flourish alongside, both in contradiction and in relation to global white images (Wilk 1995: 111).

Secondly, indigenous ways of knowing do not comprise a singular, uniform, fixed entity. Rather, indigenous experiences and definitions of identity and knowledge can be inconsistent, ambivalent and conflictive (Archetti 1997: 129). Indigenous identity clearly occupies a range of shifting positions, reproduced through and not despite difference (Hall 1990: 402). Thus, indigenous ways of knowing are contested not only between different highland indigenous groups and communities, but equally within communities. Disagreements do not exist at the level of abstract debate, but focus on pressing issues such as the definition of indigenous identity, the meaning and function of community and the place indigenous peoples occupy in wider society. Such disputes form part of the essence of local indigenous politics, which is characterised as much by factionalism as by solidarity (Sánchez Parga [ed.] 1990).[3]

Indigenous politics thus emerges out of the interface between diverse local, national and global kinds of knowledge. Consequently, the indigenous movement can appear riven by contradiction. Not all sectors have evolved

[3] Sánchez Parga states that, in the highland communities of Ecuador, factionalism is as strong a force as reciprocity and solidarity. He argues that factionalism and reciprocity play complementary roles by ensuring the maximisation of scarce resources within groups, reinforcing social networks and preventing the concentration of power within any one sector of the community (Sánchez Parga [ed.] 1990: 47).

in the same way or at the same speed. For example, although CONAIE now communicates around the globe through its homepage on the Internet, many grassroots organisations find communication hindered by an inability to pay local bus fares. Diversity and division intertwine with nationally coordinated displays of unity and solidarity. Perhaps it is not surprising that the individuals at the head of such a movement are often themselves ambiguous characters. The professional activist is usually an educated, well-travelled urban dweller seeking to build a career as a politician or spokesperson within the indigenous movement. As Warren (1998) and Watanabe (1995) have observed in Guatemala, so I have noted that in Ecuador the professional activists at the fore of indigenous politics have a different perspective on indigenous culture and identity than that of indigenous peoples at a grassroots level. Activists fulfil the role of spokespeople, yet they speak for indigenous peoples whose experiences in life are often very different to their own. Many activists do visit communities and are obviously well versed in community issues, yet, as I now discuss, their relationship with community peoples remains far from clear-cut. While professional activists have provided leadership and direction to the indigenous movement in Ecuador, their presence has also been a source of antagonism and division. The relationship between *comuneros* and the *profesionales indígenas* of CEPCU provides insight into the ambivalence of their role and the sometimes precarious nature of their authority.

Before discussing CEPCU's involvement in the communities, I want to comment on their troubled relationship with their funding organisation Hanns Seidel. This power/knowledge dynamic is clearly demonstrated in the criteria for funding imposed by Hanns Seidel. The expanding role of NGOs in civil society in the last decade has been justified partly by their perceived ability to 'reach the poor' and their recognition of the value of local knowledge and the usefulness of input from local people (Edwards and Hulme 1995: 4). However, my own research (Lloyd 1998) and the work of others, such as Clark (1992) and Rivera Cusicanqui (1990), indicates that in many cases the underlying assumption of a unidirectional flow of knowledge between Western 'experts' and indigenous peoples is still in evidence. Hanns Seidel attempted to impose European ideas about formality, professionalism and good management onto CEPCU. In order to gain recognition as 'responsible' leaders of a 'serious' organisation, CEPCU's professional activists were obliged to respect non-indigenous norms of communicating, organising and practising politics. In accordance with German definitions of efficiency and order, Hanns Seidel expected to receive regular records of punctuality and attendance, progress reports, minutes of meetings, inventories of goods and so forth. Money was docked from the wages of those who arrived late, or who had not carried out their required tasks. These criteria for funding made no allowances for indigenous concepts of oral tradition, time, work and organisation and, therefore, had a damaging impact on CEPCU's work. However, again, the reality of the relationship between

CEPCU and Hanns Seidel defies the imposition/appropriation dichotomy. Hanns Seidel's conditions undoubtedly made the professionals' job more complicated, yet, as I will show, they themselves could visibly warm to non-indigenous values and practices.

I illustrate my point with a discussion of CEPCU's leader, Luis Maldonado. I feel it is important to mention that Luis imparted much of the following information about himself during lunch breaks at community workshops when he seemed to prefer to talk to me about himself than mix with *comuneros*. First of all, he described himself as someone who has always been different – even as a teenager in his native Otavalo community of Peguche of the early 1970s he took to vegetarianism, Buddhism and wearing black clothes. In his early political career with FICI (the Federation of Indigenous and Farming People of Imbabura) and the former Ecuarunari (Awakening of the Ecuadorian Indian) he was ridiculed by his colleagues, whom he described as hard-line activists with rigid ideas about indigenous identity who forced him to eat meat and wear indigenous sandals.[4] Like many indigenous activists of the 1980s, Maldonado went on to gain his university education in Cuba, where he developed an understanding of social-ist revolutionary discourse which influenced him during his time at CONAIE working as coordinator of the Ecuadorian 'Five Hundred Years of Indigenous and Popular Resistance' campaign. He then spent some time living on a houseboat in Amsterdam working with the NCIV (the Netherlands Centre for Indigenous Peoples) to assist the several hundred Otavalos illegally stranded in Holland. In the early 1990s he returned to Otavalo to found CEPCU and, now being divorced, to live with his parents in the town of Otavalo.

Although community born and bred, Luis Maldonado, like most *profesionales indígenas*, was very much an urban Otavalo in his dress, speech and atti-tudes. Older Otavalo men prefer to have their hair tightly braided, and wear a hat, poncho, sandals, and loose white trousers hanging just below the knee. Most younger men have their hair loosely tied, and wear trainers, jeans and T-shirts. Maldonado took a middle road, having his hair braided, wearing a hat, trainers and white jeans, rather than white trousers. Perhaps influenced by his time in Europe, or perhaps in response to the prevalent racist stereo-type of the *longo sucio* ('dirty Indian'), Maldonado was always immaculately clean, and carried his own plate and cutlery when eating in communities. Otavalos are considered 'model Indians' by wider society, because of their perceived wealth, and also because of their clean, neat appearance and polite manners (Salomon 1981). Wealthier Otavalos are keen to live up this image for various reasons, such as to placate Protestant missionaries, to aid business,

---

[4] Interestingly, the former Ecuarunari, now called the Confederation of Peoples of Quichua Nationality, has recently responded to some of the leadership dilemmas raised in this chapter by restructuring its organisation with the aim of giving back the roles of representation and policy-making to grassroots groups (IWGIA 1998: 113).

or, in the case of Maldonado, to be accepted by prominent *blanco-mestizos*. However, Maldonado appeared to assume that all indigenous peoples should meet these criteria, for the need for personal hygiene was a favourite theme of his workshop speeches. His irritation over the *comuneros'* hygiene standards was only eclipsed by his annoyance at what he saw as their stubbornness and inflexibility. He could not understand why many *comuneros* found his 9.00 am to 5.00 pm workshop timetable inconvenient, and became impatient at what he saw as their lack of punctuality and intermittent attendance. Again, perhaps this is a response to the racist stereotype of the unreliable, lazy Indian, which he has partly internalised himself.

Maldonado's unwillingness to take into account community norms was also reflected in his non-indigenous style of speech.[5] The workshops took place in the usually cramped community *casas comunales* (community meeting rooms), with the participants sitting on small chairs or wooden planks and Luis Maldonado standing at the front of the room. Luis would commence his 90-minute speech with an explanation about CEPCU and the aims of the workshop. He would move on to a political message about his plans for an independent government in the San Pablo region and a call for all indigenous peoples to unite and to organise. Although speaking in Quichua, his style was didactic and he spoke firmly and concisely, employing an authoritative, assertive tone and displaying his knowledge and understanding of both national and local municipal politics. He looked directly at his listeners and moved about at the front of the room. In contrast, community speakers spoke in low voices using a subtle tone and tended to look at the floor and shuffle. They tended to talk more indirectly, spending time talking around a subject before clearly stating their point. I never witnessed any attempt to draw attention to themselves or inflate the importance of their commentaries. In the community meetings I witnessed, nobody distinguished themselves from the group by standing on their own at the front of a room.

It is obvious that Maldonado's ability to use non-indigenous styles of speech is a vital skill when dealing with influential *blanco-mestizos*. However, he appeared unaware that his method of communication was inappropriate among community peoples. *Comuneros* resented what they perceived as a high-handed approach and were only too aware that, as one Huaycopungo *comunero* declared, 'nos tratan como huahuas' ('they treat us like kids'). In some communities *comuneros* made scant effort to conceal their disillusionment with the workshop or their mixed feelings towards Maldonado. Many individuals complained loudly about the inadequate food offered by CEPCU and I am sure that Maldonado's efforts to keep

---

[5] Alcida Ramos' study of the speeches by different Brazilian indigenous leaders is equally applicable to Ecuador. She affirms that leaders of indigenous organisations must use Western styles and channels of communication as a means of achieving visibility and legitimacy in a country that refuses to recognise indigenous genres of communication (1988: 228–31).

his jeans and trainers dust-free were the subject of ridicule after his departure. Equally, his marital status must have caused comment, since, when outlining a profile of potential candidates for the municipal elections, *comuneros* stated that only married individuals should be considered, as being single, separated or divorced cast doubt over one's moral character.

Maldonado usually rounded off the workshops with an invitation to the participants to visit him at CEPCU's office if they had any further queries. However, the urban setting, the office environment, and arranged appointments completely discouraged community peoples from visiting CEPCU. On the rare occasions when a *comunero* did show up, they were reluctant to enter the office and preferred to conduct their business on the landing outside, or shout their messages from the corridor. Obviously, as with the workshop schedules, the office opening hours took no account of daily work schedules in communities.

The ambiguous position of CEPCU's professionals becomes particularly obvious when compared to the characteristics and role of the 'traditional' community leader.[6] In his study of community politics in Cayambe, Ramón makes a comment applicable to San Pablo. He states that the role of a community leader is ideally that of 'an unpaid community official' serving the people who elected him (Ramón 1994: 47). His authority and legitimacy were measured in accordance with his ability to protect the community's interests. As Walter observes, traditionally, the ritual cycle known as the *fiesta-cargo* system was a mechanism of serving the community as its wealthier members impoverished themselves by sponsoring community religious festivals. In return, they won prestige and respect from the community (Walter 1981: 173). In order to fund a festival a leader needed many allies to assist him and his wife. Necessarily, a leader was a man able to engage in reciprocal relations with a wide network of community members and in godparent relations with local *mestizos*. A good leader was a generous individual with a wide social network who was ready to share his assets with the community.

To maintain many social allies a leader needed not only financial resources and competent social skills, but also a good reputation and moral

---

[6] My discussion of so-called 'traditional' indigenous understandings of leadership must be placed in the current context of the ongoing process of the fragmentation of authority occurring, to varying degrees, within almost all communities in the San Pablo area and beyond. The authority of the *cabildo* (community government) has diminished as community cohesion is threatened by a number of factors, such as religious differences, generation divides, increased socio-economic differentiation, and migration, which leaves many men, and more and more women, absent from the community for long periods. In most communities, power has never been held by any one individual or organisation, rather it has tended to be spread between different sectors and families. However, recently, this situation has become exaggerated to the point where, in some communities, it is hard to identify any one organisation that can be said to lead the community. Consequently, an authority vacuum has opened up which various actors and sectors within the community are attempting to fill.

character to recommend him to potential allies. Rasnake, referring to the community of Yura, in Bolivia, commented that 'the *kuraka* (leader) couple is in many respects the moral leader of the *ayllu*' (1988: 81). Similarly, I found that in the San Pablo region, moral strength is vital to any leader. A good leader is an *alli runa* ('good person'), meaning a married man who is hard-working, responsible, mild-tempered, modest, honest, able to be gentle and assertive and able to speak persuasively but with integrity. These observations are affirmed by Allen's work in the community of Sonqo in Peru, where, she states, a good leader is held to be 'morally upstanding, level-headed, moderate, and well-spoken' (1988: 118). Stein's research in Hualcán, Peru indicates that an *alli nuna* (sic. 'good person') is a 'man who knows how to protect himself in a way not socially disruptive [. . .] who has successfully resolved his conflicts from a social point of view, one who rarely allows his temper to flare up, one who does things for other people and inspires confidence in the community' (1961: 181). Good moral character is based on knowledge of community life, rituals, norms and values. Thus, a good leader is a man able to practise community ways of living, to uphold community values and morality, and to reproduce indigenous ways of knowing.

In more recent times, knowledge of the outside world has become a vital characteristic of any effective leader. Community leaders are still responsible for maintaining relations with a range of outside actors such as governmental development workers, national and international NGOs, political parties, and Protestant missionaries. The ability to negotiate with outsiders is of critical importance. 'New' skills, such as literacy and numeracy, administration, and knowledge of the legal system, the national political system and the foreign aid system, are vital. Time spent as a health or literacy worker, or as a cooperative manager, is beneficial to a successful community leadership. However, it is not possible to argue that traditional community leaders in the San Pablo region, or in the Ecuadorian Andes as a whole, have been entirely pushed aside by these newer authority figures. Although the above-mentioned 'new' skills are desirable, they have by no means devalued 'older' attributes, such as in-depth knowledge of the community, a sound moral character and a wide social network. As encounters between San Pablo *comuneros* and Luis Maldonado show, these new and old styles of leadership sit together in an uneasy dynamic of mutual contempt and grudging respect.

I illustrate these different understandings of leadership with an account of an episode that occurred in Angla, a Cayambe community. On leaving this remote community the truck carrying CEPCU workers and myself became stuck in a deep pothole. The *mestizo* driver attempted to extricate the truck but failed, so we had to call on the *comuneros* for help. They instantly set to filling the hole with stones and branches, working smoothly and efficiently as a team, without seeming to need to discuss or debate what to do. Maldonado, on the other hand, leapt into the mud and started issuing orders, obviously keen to demonstrate authority. He did not seem to notice that the *comuneros* were politely ignoring him, leaving him to become increasingly frustrated and completely encrusted in mud, while they calmly worked on, exchanging banter and jokes. The *mestizo* driver did not help matters by stubbornly refusing to listen to indigenous instructions and driving the truck ever deeper into the hole. Two hours later, in almost total darkness, with Maldonado in a daze and the *comuneros* ferrying stones and cracking jokes about where I would sleep if we had to stay the night, the driver decided to cooperate and the truck came out of the hole. It is interesting that while Luis was eager to show authority by leading from the front, the *comuneros* quietly demonstrated his superfluousness by working together as a team.

Yet, whatever the reaction of community peoples, figures such as Maldonado are indispensable to indigenous politics because the same skills and knowledge that appear out of place in community meetings are well received by non-indigenous authorities. In the company of *blanco-mestizos* Luis Maldonado came into his own. I attended a programme of forums in Otavalo proposed by Maldonado to discuss and build understanding about different points of conflict between *mestizos* and indigenous peoples. The forum was composed of a leading academic, two local authority representatives, a local anthropologist, a local politician and Maldonado as the only indigenous spokesperson. Despite being vastly outnumbered, Maldonado eloquently and authoritatively articulated his arguments in defence of indigenous opinion. He commanded respect and his opinions were taken seriously. He cleverly and diplomatically out-manoeuvred and out-talked all present, and exposed the deep-rooted prejudice and ignorance of most of the *mestizos*. Similarly, any *mestizos* visiting the CEPCU office automatically asked for and were dealt with by Maldonado. Even when the *promotores* evidently knew more about the matter at hand, *mestizos* seemed uncomfortable in their presence, reluctant to listen to their halting Spanish and unable to fathom the meaning of either their muttered one-word answers or their seemingly long-winded and vague commentaries.

Thus, for 'chameleon-like' leaders such as Maldonado, literacy and eloquence become weapons in their struggle for political survival, enabling them, as Brown states, to 'successfully walk in two worlds' (1993: 312). The indigenous movement in Ecuador is not a singular, homogeneous entity; rather, it operates on many different levels and encompasses a range of socio-economic realities, cultural values and political agendas. Professional activists have flourished in Ecuador because they have been able to negotiate widely different political arenas. In the past, community peoples often rejected indigenous political figures who entered local office. Now, in Ecuador, however ambiguous their relations with professional activists, indigenous peoples are increasingly willing to mobilise behind indigenous candidates not just for local office but for national government. This willingness stems from the understanding that, although they mistrust figures such as Maldonado, it is precisely such people who can make the indigenous voice heard in *blanco-mestizo* and Western political circles.

To conclude this chapter, it is interesting to compare briefly the figure of the contemporary *profesional indígena* with that of the *kuraka* or *cacique* (indigenous colonial elite), as they were known in Otavalo. In his study of the powerful Otavalo *caciques* of the nineteenth century, Guerrero observes that their political survival depended on their 'doble ropaje de legitimidades' (1989: 327). This 'double legitimacy' rested in their dual knowledge both of the workings of indigenous community life and of the functioning of the state. Guerrero concludes that the *cacique* was indispensable to both the indigenous and non-indigenous peoples because nobody else could do his job. Without searching for misleading historical continuities, the figure of the Otavalo *cacique*, and of the Andean *kuraka* in general, sheds light on the role of the professional indigenous activist today.

Perhaps the authority of the *profesionales indígenas* is more tenuous as they often have neither official *mestizo* approval, nor an intimate knowledge of *comuneros* and their ways, let alone a position of cosmological significance within community life, as was enjoyed by the *caciques*. Furthermore, the professionals must struggle not only for political survival, but also for economic survival. Warren states that the poor pay and constant job insecurity of Guatemala's Pan-Mayan activists often hampers their ability to consolidate politically (1998: 182). It is no wonder that Ecuadorian professional activists such as Maldonado have such a keen ability to read the non-indigenous mind: their livelihoods depend on it. A professional career in indigenous politics is doomed to failure without the skill of winning international funding.

Yet, in other ways, just like the *caciques*, the *profesionales indígenas*, with their groomed appearance, their eloquent Spanish, their formal education, and their ability to adhere to *blanco-mestizo* norms of communication and behaviour, present, for *blanco-mestizos*, the acceptable face of the indigenous world. Juggling distinctive kinds of knowledge and juggling different forms of legitimacy, they must, as Brown states, 'master the arts of persuasion appropriate both to native society and to the nation-states in which they reside, taking up one and dropping the other like a change of clothing' (1993: 312). These qualities have enabled them to negotiate the complex local, national and international forces that run through indigenous politics. It is this ability that wins them grudging respect from most indigenous peoples and a foot in the door to *blanco-mestizo* institutions of power.

References

Allen, Catherine. 1988. *The Hold Life Has: Coca and Cultural Identity in an Andean Community*. Washington, DC: Smithsonian Institution Press.

Archetti, Eduardo. 1997. *Food, Symbol and Conflict of Knowledge in Ecuador*. Oxford: Berg.

Brown, Michael. 1993. 'Facing the State, Facing the World: Amazonia's Native Leaders and the New Politics of Identity'. *L'Homme* 33(2–4): 307–26.

Clark, John. 1992. 'Policy Influence, Lobbying and Advocacy'. In M. Edwards and D. Hulme (eds.), *Making a difference: NGOs and Development in a Changing World*. London: Earthscan: 191–202.

Dixon, Robert. 1994. 'The Unfinished Commonwealth: Boundaries of Civility in Popular Australian Fiction of the First Commonwealth Decade'. In C. Tiffin and A. Lawson (eds.), *De-Scribing Empire: Post-Colonialism and Textuality*. London: Routledge: 131–40.

Edwards, Michael, and David Hulme. 1995. *Non-Governmental Organisations – Performance and Accountability Beyond the Magic Bullet*. London: Save the Children/Earthscan.

Escobar, Arturo. 1992. 'Culture, Economics, and Politics in Latin American Social Movements Theory and Research'. In A. Escobar and S.E. Alvarez (eds.), *The Making of Social Movements in Latin America: Identity, Strategy and Democracy*. Boulder, CO: Westview Press: 62–88.

——, 1995. *Encountering Development: The Making and Unmaking of the Third World*. Boulder, CO: Westview Press.

Foucault, Michel. 1980. *Power/Knowledge: Selected Interviews and Other Writings, 1972–1977*. Brighton: The Harvester Press.

Guerrero, Andrés. 1989. 'Curagas y tenientes políticos: La ley de la costumbre y la ley del estado (Otavalo 1830–1875)'. *Revista Andina* 7(2): 321–66.

Hall, Stuart. 1990. 'Cultural Identity and Diaspora'. In J. Rutherford (ed.), *Identity: Community, Culture, Difference*. London: Lawrence & Wishart: 222–37.

Hobart, Mark. 1995. 'As I Lay Laughing: Encountering Global Knowledge in Bali'. In R. Fardon (ed.), *Counterworks: Managing the Diversity of Knowledge*. London: Routledge: 49–72.

Hobart, Mark (ed.). 1993. *An Anthropological Critique of Development: The Growth of Ignorance*. London: Routledge.

IWGIA (International Work Group for Indigenous Affairs). 1998. *The Indigenous World*. Copenhagen: IWGIA.

Lloyd, Janet. 1998. 'The Politics of Indigenous Identity in Ecuador and the Emergence of Transnational Discourses of Power and Subversion'. PhD thesis, University of Liverpool.

Moore, Henrietta. 1996. 'The Changing Nature of Anthropological Knowledge: An Introduction'. In H.L. Moore (ed.), *The Future of Anthropological Knowledge*. London: Routledge: 1–15.

Ramón, Galo. 1994. *Comunidades andinas desde dentro: dinámicas organizativas y asistencia técnica*. Quito: CECI/Ediciones Abya-Yala.

Ramos, Alcida. 1988. 'Indian Voices: Contact Experienced and Expressed'. In J. Hill (ed.), *Rethinking History and Myth: Indigenous South American Perspectives on the Past*. Urbana, IL, and Chicago: University of Illinois Press: 214–34.

Rasnake, Roger. 1988. *Domination and Cultural Resistance: Authority and Power among an Andean People*. Durham, NC, and London: Duke University Press.

Rivera Cusicanqui, Silvia. 1990. 'Liberal Democracy and Ayllu Democracy: The Case of Northern Potosí, Bolivia'. In J. Fox (ed.), *The Challenge of Rural Democratization: Perspectives from Latin America and the Philippines*. London: Frank Cass: 97–121.

Said, Edward. 1978. *Orientalism*. London: Penguin Books.

——, 1994. *Culture and Imperialism*. London: Vintage.

Salomon, Frank. 1981. 'Weavers of Otavalo'. In N. Whitten (ed.), *Cultural Transformations and Ethnicity in Modern Ecuador*. Urbana, IL: University of Illinois Press: 420–46.

Sánchez Parga, José (ed.). 1990. *Etnia, poder y diferencia en los Andes septentrionales*. Quito: Ediciones Abya-Yala.

Selverston, Melina. 1994. 'The Politics of Culture: Indigenous Peoples and the State in Ecuador'. In D. Van Cott (ed.), *Indigenous Peoples and Democracy in Latin America*. Basingstoke: Macmillan: 131–54.

Stein, William. 1961. *Hualcán: Life in the Highlands of Peru*. New York: Cornell University Press.

Tiffin, Chris, and Alan Lawson. 1994. 'Introduction: The Textuality of Empire'. In C. Tiffin and A. Lawson (eds.), *De-Scribing Empire: Post-Colonialism and Textuality*. London: Routledge: 1–11.

Walter, Lynn. 1981. 'Social Strategies and the Fiesta Complex in an Otavaleño Community'. *American Ethnologist* 8(1): 172–85.

Warren, Kay. 1998. 'Indigenous Movements as a Challenge to the Unified Social Movement Paradigm for Guatemala'. In S. Alvarez, E. Dagnino and A. Escobar (eds.), *Culture of Politics, Politics of Culture: Re-Visioning Latin American Social Movements*. Oxford: Westview Press: 165–95.

Watanabe, John. 1995. 'Unimagining the Maya: Anthropologists, Others, and the Inescapable Hubris of Authorship. *Bulletin of Latin American Research* 14(1): 25–41.

Weismantel, Mary. 1988. *Food, Gender and Poverty in the Ecuadorian Andes*. Philadelphia: University of Pennsylvania Press.

Wilk, Richard. 1995. 'Learning to be Local in Belize: Global Systems of Common Difference'. In D. Miller (ed.), *Worlds Apart: Modernity Through the Prism of the Local*. London: Routledge: 110–31.

PART III

Conflicting Paradigms of Knowledge

CHAPTER SEVEN

Why Nazario is Leaving School: Community Perspectives on Formal Schooling in Rural Bolivia

Pedro Plaza Martínez

Formal schooling for mother-tongue Quechua-, Aymara- and Guaraní-speaking children in rural Bolivia has undergone a major revolution since 1994, with the introduction of Intercultural Bilingual Education (EIB) as a central axis of the Education Reform Law (Ley 1565 of 7 July 1994). The Reform began to be implemented in 1995, building on the Intercultural Bilingual Education Project (PEIB) which had been piloted in a limited number of schools in the five preceding years.[1] The changes were also due to the trend of growing recognition of indigenous linguistic and cultural rights in the region, which in turn determined the implementation of education reforms (López 2000: 15); and the availability of economic resources through the intervention of economic agencies such as the Inter-American Development Bank, which on 16 November 1994 approved a total cost of US$ 204.2 million for the *Programa de Reforma Educativa*, which is projected to last 20 years (I-ADB n.d.). Among the central pedagogical tenets of the Reform, in addition to the official use and study of Quechua, Aymara or Guaraní in the classroom, are the principles of constructivist, pupil-centred learning, and the design of more culturally relevant curricula.

In this chapter I shall discuss some of the results of fieldwork which I conducted in the *núcleo* school of El Paredón, district of Tarabuco, department of Chuquisaca, during 1995 and 1996, at a time when the school was just entering its transition to the Reform model.[2] Due to its previous participation in the PEIB, El Paredón had been selected to take part in the Reform from the outset. As shall be seen, during that early phase, the pedagogical ideals referred to above had not yet been fully adopted. Moreover, between school authorities on the one hand, and community members (*comunarios*) on the other, very differing perceptions of what formal schooling in the rural

---

[1] The PEIB was a pilot bilingual education programme implemented by the Ministry of Education of Bolivia and UNICEF in three linguistic regions, Aymara, Quechua and Guaraní, from 1990 to 1994.

[2] The full account of this experience is the basis of my PhD thesis (Plaza 1998).

community stands for, and is good for, were in evidence. Their conflicting discourses about the function of formal education make up the central theme of this chapter.[3]

In his plea against formal schooling in the West, Illich (1991) has noted that children dedicate many thousands of hours to their school careers. Indeed, in accordance with the Bolivian Code of Education, rural schools must provide five hours of classes per day, for 200 days per year (Bolivian government 1955: 41). Theoretically, this would mean exactly one thousand classroom hours per year, although this is usually reduced due to, for example, strikes, demonstrations, staff meetings, training sessions, and teacher and pupil absences. Furthermore, as the peasants of the Bolivian highlands usually live in scattered rather than concentrated settlements, many children are obliged to spend at least two hours walking to and from school each day, and in some cases as many as four. In short, in spite of disruptions during the school year and early dropout, rural children dedicate a large amount of their time to schooling. However, to what degree is this investment of time considered to be adequately compensated by the learning experience? Is acquisition of knowledge the principal reason for attending school? How do pupils and parents conceive of the school experience? And is the knowledge pupils acquire deemed relevant or beneficial to their long-term needs as rural peasants and productive members of society?

In this chapter I shall address some of these questions by examining pupil and parent perspectives on the school of El Paredón. I shall also consider some of the community attitudes to schooling which emerged when Nazario, a twelve-year-old boy, dropped out of school to take up community responsibilities in place of his deceased father. A number of writers have noted how the rural school appears like 'a foreign body' (Ansión 1988: 61), 'a strange organism' or 'an island within the community' (Soto 1996: 141), or as 'an alien cultural institution at the heart of the indigenous community' (Howard-Malverde and Canessa 1995). The point I would like to stress is that the community and school belong to different worlds, with distinct values, cultural identities, and spheres of knowledge. Thus, as Yraola has noted, teachers have 'few dealings with the community members' and these relationships are always established 'in terms of inequality' (1995: 21), such that both teachers and *comunarios* seem to be insulated in their own cultural ways.

---

[3] Vast numbers of works on education have been produced in Bolivia, covering many themes, such as the history of education (Suárez 1986; Arias 1992, 1994; Pérez 1962); its relation to the rural community and the 'Indian' question (Arias S. 1924; Barrera 1985; Choque Canqui 1992; Claure 1989); criticisms, diagnostics, proposals, policies and plans (CONMERB 1984; CSUTCB 1991; Donoso 1940; ETARE 1993); textbook analysis, the curriculum, methodologies (Apala et al. 1990; Bolivian government 1997; Cárdenas 1992); literacy, languages and cultures, bilingual education (Briggs 1980, 1983; Choque 1996; Luna 1971; SENALEP 1983, 1984). Most surveys have been conducted focusing on parents and teachers, and achievement tests on pupils; however, in this chapter I shall consider the views of pupils, which I shall complement with parents' perspectives.

While teachers' lack of enthusiasm for mingling with the locals has often been seen as another cause of the failure of school (Baptista 1974: 10), from another perspective the school has been described as 'an instrument of acculturation' (Barrera 1985: 15), such that teachers are viewed as agents (or even instruments) of the dominant society. But how do community members view the school and its teachers? Is the school considered a valuable service and source of knowledge, skills and opportunies, or, for example, an unwelcome instrument of the state and a grudgingly accepted obligation? I shall begin by exploring children's views of their school experience, and then consider absenteeism and what this tells us about community priorities and attitudes.

Children's perspectives on formal schooling

To find out about children's perceptions of their school and classroom experience, I conducted a series of interviews with pupils of El Paredón's central school,[4] recorded on tape and video, where they talked about their teachers and the things they learned, but also of their experience in the community as cultural participants. In general I just asked them to tell me about things they remembered of their school careers, from the first grade to the present.[5]

From the start it became clear that the children's assessment of teachers and the learning they acquired in school was closely linked to punishments and to language use. The personality of the teacher, and the corresponding quality of teacher–pupil interaction, also emerged as one of the most critical dimensions of the children's school experience.

Bernaco Vela Condori (third grade) reminisces about his pre-school year:

(1)   With Miss Consuelo, she was nice, [but] sometimes she used to hit us, when we could not read. Some of us used to shed a tear. [. . .] she used to teach us *a i o*, those things. [. . .] little drawings, houses, little cows, everything, little sheep. That was all.

---

[4] Rural primary schools in Bolivia are designated 'sectional' (*seccional*) schools, located in the more remote communities and usually covering only two grades, and 'central' (*núcleo*) schools where children go to study up to fifth grade. Although I observed and talked with children of other schools, I concentrated my work with these children because they got to know me quite well due to my constant presence in the school of El Paredón, where I was living at the time. The task was made easier because, as I had a jeep, they were harassing me constantly to have a ride. So I traded words for rides. El Paredón is a predominantly Quechua-speaking community.

[5] Except where immediately relevant to the analysis, the Quechua originals of the interview transcriptions are presented in the Appendix. During the interviews, pupils persistently addressed me as *profesorniy* ('my teacher'), apparently assuming that, although I did not teach any classes, I was another teacher at the school. This vocative, roughly equivalent to the English schoolchild's use of the term 'sir' or 'miss', occurs at the end of almost every sentence as a sign of respect, the pupils constantly reminding themselves of our respective status, and the power relations between us. However, to avoid overburdening the reader, the term is not always represented in the translations.

Telmo Tardío Vargas (fourth grade) talks about his first-grade class:

(2)   In the first grade we had teacher Edgar [. . .] He was not too mean, but he
       made us read well. We learned well. Sometimes when we could not [do
       something] he did hit us. [. . .] he used to hit us with a stick.

In most accounts these themes appear again and again, but for Juan Vela
Flores (sixth grade) the use of languages in the classroom (Quechua and
Spanish, or exclusively Spanish) was an important ingredient of the school
experience:

(3)   In the first grade the teacher was Carmela. [. . .] She was all right. In the
       first grade I was just learning for the first time there, in Spanish and also in
       Quechua [. . .] how to read and to write . . . There was a book entitled
       Margara . . . it was . . . it was in Quechua. [. . .] Then the following years
       there were other books. [. . .] In the third grade [the teacher] was José. José
       . . . (María or Vargas) [whispering to himself]. That one taught us exclu-
       sively in Spanish. He was more or less, no . . . he used to punish us, he would
       hit hard.

Juan went on to talk about punishment and I questioned him further on this
matter:

(4)   J: Because they used to play. We too used to play, he used to hit us [with
       a stick] because of that. 'You play too much', he used to tell us.
       P: 'Did he hit you for no reason?
       J: Ah, no, my teacher. We ourselves bring punishment upon us, by
       playing. He had a little stick, it was this thick. He would hit us on our backs,
       on our hands. (Tape 2, 951120)

From these accounts it would appear that corporal punishment in the
classroom was a common occurrence; or at least, an experience that left
strong marks in the minds of the pupils. The denunciation of this 'punish-
ing' aspect of rural schools is widespread in the Andes (see, for instance,
Caiza 1989: 309–10; De La Torre 1997, for Ecuador; Ansión 1988: 88–95,
for Perú). But what is striking from my interviewees' accounts is the
common view that punishment is all right. Many considered that it was only
inflicted upon those who played too much, and that through their actions
the pupils brought punishment upon themselves. Furthermore, the instrument of punishment was sometimes even described as *k'achitu* ('beautiful').

Accordingly, punishment was presented by pupils themselves as an
effective means of restraining them from playing when they should have
been working. For example, Eduardo Vela Flores, a fourth grade student,
mentioned that his 'mean' (*saqra*) kindergarten teacher used to hit them
with a stick (*warrutewan*), punch them (*saqmawaq*), or box their ears,
causing some to cry (*wakinqa waqarpayaq kayku*); and 'after that, at the next
opportunity, we stopped playing' (*Chantaqa, jukpaqwanqa, manaña pukllaq-
chu kayku*). From the second grade on, Eduardo has had his current fourth-

grade teacher.[6] At no point does he brand her as 'mean', but he has no qualms about disclosing her use of corporal punishment, while affirming that she has taught them well:

(5)   P: And how was she?
      E: Sometimes . . . she smacked us. She grabbed us by the hair, hit us, pinched our ears.
      P: And then?
      E: She taught us acceptably well.

The following, more extended description by Gabino Tardío (sixth grade) provides us with a particularly insightful account of one of his teachers and her teaching methods:

(6)   I then came back to the third grade [after the vacation]. There the teacher was Mrs. DD. [. . .] She taught us in the Spanish tongue, she didn't know Quechua, she spoke only in Spanish. In that third grade she taught us . . . we spoke in Spanish. Then speaking to us so, she taught us more. Then . . . she was so so, she would be busy cooking, because of that she didn't use to look after us well. No . . . she used to cook with wood, that kept her occupied until twelve o'clock, then . . . she used to go out, when she went out we played. Then when she came back in she would give us an exercise, at the top of the page, and leave us telling us to do that, but when she was not inside we didn't do it either. Sometimes she would hit us because of that, she would whip us, with a cane . . . she would bring in a branch of *molle* for that purpose. We just had to suffer it but she did that to us because we didn't do our work. After twelve o'clock she would come back in. She had a little boy, that Dioni [. . .] she would bring in knitting to make a jumper for him, she used to do that. Meanwhile she would make us go to the blackboard, telling us to draw, we used to draw there all kinds of little things, we drew what we could. After that she taught us well, addition . . . she would make us count from one hundred . . . to one thousand. We couldn't do that, but with patience we could do it, then we used to do it. Then we did additions, doing additions . . . mm [but] when we couldn't do them she would whip us with a belt again. Then . . . she would scream in Spanish . . . She would go out, coming back in she would scream like that, coming back in, 'Fools why don't you do it?' she would scold us . . . 'Mud heads,' she would blurt out. We just stood there, then she would whip us, speaking like that. Then she would make us stand in a corner when we couldn't do it, some of us could do it, some could not, because of that she used to tell us so.

This saga continued for two more years in a similar fashion. Gabino confided that the teacher continued to teach them in her special way. She

---

[6] The practice of a teacher remaining with the same class as it is promoted grade by grade is common in the rural schools of this region; it is also found in Bahrain (Al-Mannai 1996).

would, for example, bring in a thick notebook and dictate from there, always teaching in Spanish (and this taking place in the bilingual classroom then under the PEIB's jurisdiction), and she would write examples on the blackboard for the pupils to copy. Although all the subjects – language, social sciences, biology, and mathematics – were covered, Gabino was dissatisfied.

Mario Vargas Condori had a different experience. While Gabino was considered a good student, it seems that Mario had to struggle to pass the grades, especially during his early years. In spite of the fact that many pupils in the rural areas leave school after a couple of years, passing a grade is always crucial for the pupil.

(7)   My name is Mario Vargas Condori [. . .] I did not pass for two years, I did not pass the grades, [but] I just didn't pass the first grade. Then again [the teacher] would separate those of us who could not do it and place us at the back, and those who could were placed at the front. [. . .] Then there was no way I could do it, I used to get tired of it. Umm. Being tired of it I used to tell my father 'I will not go in [to school]' . . . He would oblige me by force to come to school . . . Then I entered another class, I couldn't cope with that either . . . I failed again. Then teacher NN arrived, with him I read.[. . .] Teacher NN was also the same, he would give us some work and then we would do it, but some of us did not do it, some of us did not do it. He would make us stand on our heads, all those of us who did not do the work.

Then Mario demonstrated standing on his head. These punishments (being made to stand on hands, raise hands in the air, walk like ducks, and so on), he explained, caused many to cry and made them unable to walk properly the next day due to the muscular pain. Eventually, in spite of his difficulties coping with schoolwork and his many absences he was promoted to the next grade, a feat he had not believed he would achieve:

(8)   Then I missed and missed school, and then entered in June, but fortunately I passed. I didn't believe I would pass [. . .] I was so happy, I walked around happily saying that 'now I have passed'.[7]

Mario's happiness, in my view, illustrates that children care about school, and that passing the grade is an important ingredient of the process.

To sum up, the repertoire of corporal punishments included: the 'pig', whereby the victim has to support his body on his hands while his feet are placed horizontally on some elevation (a variation was having to stand upside down); kicking; hitting with the hand, the knuckles, or a stick; and whipping, sometimes on bare bottoms for better effect, as one child disclosed. The effects were undoubtedly painful; some children cried and, later on in the playground, complained about the mean teacher. In the classroom

---

[7] Since the school year generally begins in March, to enter in June is a little bit late.

it also had the effect of reducing the children to silence, and, according to the pupils' own accounts, it served as a deterrent to bad behaviour and as an incentive to dedicate oneself to schoolwork. In other words, in the terms of Michel Foucault (1991), punishment had the effect of obtaining 'docile bodies'.

Although it has been seriously contested in recent years in Bolivia, and is proscribed under the terms of the Reform, from the pupils' accounts given above, it seems that corporal punishment has not yet disappeared from the classroom. However, I must add that with the exception of the use of sticks, used more symbolically than physically to control pupils during line-ups, I personally saw no serious misdemeanour in this respect.

Although corporal punishment might be considered ephemeral, it lingers in the mind, as the narratives reviewed above have shown, hence conferring on it a lasting effect. The notion of symbolic violence is useful here, as a way of conceptualising the exercise of authority in the rural school. As Ansión states, the exercise of authority in the rural school is a form of symbolic violence, 'applied to children, with the complicity of parents and even the children themselves, in the hope that schooling will help them in the long term' (1988: 88).

Absenteeism

While corporal punishment, and sometimes bullying where younger children are concerned, might deter some pupils from attending school (Ansión 1988: 88–91), these cannot be taken as the principal reasons for non-attendance. Two community activities, in particular, periodically cause children to miss school. Firstly, as children are closely integrated into the productive apparatus of the family, they have to help their parents to work the fields or care for animals. This causes the children to miss school, sometimes for a day, a few days, or even weeks.

While the obligation of parents and children towards school attendance is often resolved by requesting a leave of absence, teachers complain that such permission is not always sought and that parents expect even very young children to participate in agricultural work. For example, the pre-school teacher in El Paredón stressed that absenteeism was high just before All Saints (2 November 1996), because many pupils had to participate in the agricultural work of the planting season. 'They even come to ask for leave of absence for these tiny tots. And they are so little,' she said, referring to her six-year-old pupils. When I asked what tasks they performed in the fields, she explained that 'They say that they help with spreading manure' as fertiliser in the fields (Tape 87, 961030).

The other community activity which leads to large-scale absenteeism is the celebration of ritual festivities, such as Mama Guadalupe, Pukllay, and especially All Saints. During the latter I witnessed less than 15 per cent attendance. These festive occasions are important for adults, but also for children, for whom they might be compared, for instance, to a visit to an entertainment park for their urban counterparts. With the implicit consent of their parents, children simply do not attend school at these times. With such reduced numbers of pupils, teachers spend lesson time on revision, or, more usually, return to their homes, leaving the *comunarios* to concentrate on their festivities.

Absenteeism resulting from clashes between the school calendar and the community's agricultural-ritual calendar has been widely indentified in the literature on rural education in the Andes (Barrera 1985:17; Choque 1996: 82; Yraola 1995: 94; Ansión 1988: 70–71).[8] In many respects this highlights conflicting cultural attitudes to the knowledge acquired in school and how this relates to community activities and obligations, a theme which I will now develop.

The boy who wanted to become a *comunario*

In this section I shall consider the discourse surrounding the case of Nazario, a twelve-year-old boy who, following the death of his father, became head of the family and dropped out of school in order to take up his responsibilities as a *comunario* – a full and active member of the community. This example brings out the central importance of public obligations for the organisation of the community, and the respective values ascribed to school knowledge and practical community-based knowledge.

I will analyse excerpts from the tape-recorded meeting with the purpose of showing (1) the community's point of view with respect to Nazario's dropping out, and (2) the contrast between the discourses of the education system, represented here by the headmaster (H) and the teacher (G), and those of the *comunarios*, including Nazario (N) himself. Italics indicate the use of Spanish or loanwords from Spanish.

(9)   H: . . . and the case of the dropout, what is the matter with him? His name
      is Flores . . . Nazario Flores . . .
      G: He is over there.
      N: I also am no longer able to [come] . . .

These three interventions at the start of the discussion already illustrate the main line of confrontation: the perspective of the headmaster and the teacher, vis-à-vis that of the community. The headmaster, assuming his authority, not only purports to find out what is happening with respect to the 'retiree', but also to solve the problem by bringing about Nazario's return to school. He and the teacher are keen to retain as many students as possible, in the interests of school statistics. In addition, the teacher's inter-

---

[8] Despite the observed facts, the school statistics available at the *Dirección Distrital* of Tarabuco paint a more optimistic picture. According to these figures, the average attendance of all grades in the *núcleo* of El Paredón in 1995 was a healthy 94.33 per cent.

vention, a volunteered interruption, has the effect both of affirming her knowledge of the situation (i.e. identifying the 'retiree') and of recognising and submitting to the authority of the headmaster, for whose information she comes out with her accusation ('Allá está'). At the same time, her use of Spanish has the effect of reminding everybody of their linguistic and cultural affiliation: the Spanish-speaking teachers versus the Quechua-speaking community. The headmaster, however, ignores her codeswitch and proceeds in Quechua with the meeting.

On the other hand, Nazario's point of view is embodied in just three words: 'Ñuqapis ma atiniñachu . . .', 'I also am no longer able [to come to school]', whereby he succinctly asserts that he is no longer able to attend school. This implies that he was trying to do so but had to give up, and that there are also others in the same situation. The interchange continues:

(10) H: Are you Nazario?
       N: Yes, my father has died.
       H: Have you been left by yourself?
       N: Um . . .
       H: Is he becoming an orphan?' [asking others present]
       N: Yes.

While the headmaster attempts to identify the pupil, Nazario comes straight to the point: his father has died. Afterwards, a *comunario* explains that nobody in the community would either 'pull' or 'push' anyone in or out of school deliberately; that it was perhaps due to the fact that the boy's father had died, meaning he had to take his place in the organisation (i.e. the peasants' union, *sindicato*), having no older brothers to do so for him. This explanation, however, is not enough for the headmaster. The same *comunario* adds that they had suggested that Nazario could come once or twice a week to school, but since there was no one else to assume his responsibilities (as an affiliate and head of his family), he had to quit altogether.

The headmaster then uses all his persuasive powers to try to convince the *comunarios* that they should help the orphan boy: saying that the union leaders are there to give advice, not only to tout for contributions (for example, labour quotas). Teenagers need orientation, he argues: forcing Nazario to be a man at the age of twelve would lead him into drinking, or to being led astray by a nubile female. Also, leaving school now would mean losing all he had learned and failure to get his *libreta* (certificate).

The *comunario* spokesperson (C) tries again to clarify the boy's circumstances. He explains that the conflicting pressures of trying to go to school while simultaneously attending meetings and fulfilling his labour quotas had, in the end, determined Nazario's decision to quit school, a situation they had had to accept:

(11)   . . . then we also require that he speaks [in meetings], therefore we have already taken he him to our works, meetings, but then we are also thinking about his schooling, where is he going to attend, where is he going to belong, to the meetings or to work, to which one of them? Only the words are missing, because his father happened to die, therefore we request his labour quotas, he does his work, therefore what can we do?

The headmaster responds by insisting that the community should help the boy, that he should be allowed to attend school, and that he should be released from his obligations as an 'affiliate', at least for the time being. The *comunario* in turn explains that the system of quotas is vital for the survival of the community and that in the absence of monetary resources their manual work is the only way to sustain their lives.

In spite of the apparent *fait accompli* described by the *comunario*, the headmaster, changing his tactics slightly, lays things on the line:

(12)   H: Very well. Could I . . . can't we still solve the problem so that he returns [to school]? Let's see, what do you say? The majority has the word.
C: It would be possible, Mr Headmaster, now that you are here Mr Headmaster you can solve it. You know, when in a meeting like this we impose a fine, he is not going to be able [to pay], Mr Headmaster.
H: But what do the majority of you say? Because what the majority decides, that must be done, whether there is the goodwill or not. If you come to an agreement with me, as soon as I turn my back you will start pressurising him again.
C: That's right.
G: That's what'll happen.

The headmaster tells the *comunarios* that he does not want that to happen and, given their assurances, it seems that he is finally able to steer the community into accepting that the boy should return to school. Apparently, the *comunarios* find it difficult to say a straight 'no' to the choice laid before them by the headmaster. Some people even refer to the need to help each other, although doubts and ambiguities remain. When the teacher expresses her doubts about their commitment to help the orphan boy, some reassert that they will help. The headmaster tries to take advantage of the new mood, pressing the audience into a commitment to help the boy:

(13)   H: . . . thus we have heard *compañeros*, could we lend a hand, this does not mean that we would work [for him] . . . that we hand over money for him to live with . . .
C: No, no, no . . .
H: . . . we are not advocating that extreme, we are only discussing how we could help him to finish school, because it has already been established that he is prepared [to continue his schooling]. He may not be able [to fulfil his responsibilities as a *comunario*] . . . we would have to take care of that but

all of us, not just the leaders, nor only the *secretario general*. Could we help
in that way?

C: We could, Mr Headmaster, we will help.

The headmaster genuinely thinks he has solved the problem. Now he just
wants to obtain the community's reassurance, to seal the commitment. But
then Nazario, who has remained silent all of this time, interrupts the headmaster's grand plans:

(14)   N: I did not come to school then . . . [child cries]
       P: What did he say? [I ask Ms G, the teacher]
       G: He said he would not like to attend school, that he'd rather attend the
       literacy programme.

While some *comunarios* immediately accept the idea that Nazario should
attend the literacy classes, both the headmaster and the teacher dismiss it,
saying that the boy already knows more than they can teach him in the literacy classes. Thus, all the headmaster's efforts to secure the community's
help start to crumble. Some *comunarios* agree that Nazario could continue
his education in the literacy programme. But then it becomes clear that
although they would accept Nazario's return to school, he would still have
to fulfil all his 'affiliated' obligations. One *comunario* says:

(15)   The quota *compañeros* is for everybody, everywhere . . . whatever we do, we
       have to contribute *compañeros*, that cannot be overlooked. Would he not
       contribute if he returns [to school]? That would not be acceptable if he
       returns.

Another adds:

(16)   . . . *compañeros*, this is OK to a certain degree . . . of course we are capable
       of helping *compañeros*, it is not no; this is something that should be pondered
       further, the only problem, *compañeros*, is that we are not able to speak the
       same language . . . all of us *compañeros* . . . we have to find an answer *com-
       pañeros*, we would have to make amends to what has been said *compañeros*,
       that we could do, *compañeros*; at least from my perspective this would have
       to be done: we will not be able, *compañeros*, to go down on his quotas, we
       will not be able to reduce his turns, perhaps I would be able to do so on a
       personal basis, but no, *compañeros*, reiterating, he may not attend the meet-
       ings, and he would have to be willing to do his homework, that would be it
       compañeros . . . that I would want . . . whenever he gets [school] homework,
       he can do it *compañeros*, at least one day a week, at least he can remain in
       school, that is all. That is it, Mr Headmaster.

The community position is clear: Nazario can attend school if he wishes, but
there is no way of lessening his obligations, except that he would be relieved
of his duty to attend meetings. Notice the Spanish loanwords that pepper
the *comunario*'s language in Excerpt 16 (e.g. *claro, por lo menos, compañeros*;

see Appendix); a code-mixing which gives the impression of investing his speech with authority and prestige. It is clear that school is viewed as a rival drain on human resources, rather than an investment which could increase Nazario's productive potential. The headmaster tries once more to convince Nazario to commit himself to the school, asking him directly whether he would come back if his obligations to the community were relaxed. Nazario answers:

(17) N: Not one day in the week.
      H: Nazario, if they do not oblige you to give quotas, if they don't require
         that you work for the school, or the roads or any other work of the commu-
         nity, if they do not oblige you [to fulfil these obligations], if they do not
         demand that you do these things, would you remain in school, would you
         finish or not? . . . You still don't want to? that depends on you.
      N: [Nazario remains silent]
      H: What?
      G: No, he says he doesn't want to . . .

One last time, the headmaster asks Nazario whether he would come back to school if he were exempted from community duties, to which Nazario simply responds 'No' (*mana*). The episode ends with the headmaster turning his frustration on the boy, suggesting that he does not want to return to school because he must have already tasted the worldly things of adult-hood. He also reminds the community that the decision to introduce the fifth grade into the sectional school that the boy was attending had been made in an effort to get the most out of the teaching posts assigned to the community and to counter the practice of leaving school after three or four grades, asserting that today everybody should know how to read and write. While the *comunarios* insist that Nazario can still go to school and be given the required homework, the headmaster once more urges the community to help the boy to remain in school, freeing him from his affiliated obligations. But a *comunario* retorts:

(18) . . . that we would still demand . . . as from any 'affiliated' *comunario*. We
      just want him to attend school once a week and for the teacher to give him
      homework . . . that is what we expect.

Thus, in spite of the *comunarios'* apparent willingness to help the boy, there are certain obligations that he would have to fulfil in any case, especially in view of the paucity of their numbers. At this point, a little more than an hour has already elapsed, but both the headmaster and the *comunarios* maintain their perspectives intact: the headmaster trying to convince the *comunarios* to change their point of view in favour of education (an abstraction); the *comunarios* skilfully manoeuvring around the headmaster's suggestions and pushing for the acceptance of their cultural reality (concrete participation from the boy). Finally, the headmaster gives up. There seems nothing else to be said, except for him to air his frustration against the resilient *comunarios*.

As has been shown, sending children to school has become a community affair, something that can be, and is, decided in a community meeting. But sending children to school seems to be conceived of by the *comunarios* more as a burden, or imposed obligation, than as a blessing or service to the community.[9] It is also evident from this example that there is a time to go to school, and a time to become a *comunario*. The *comunarios* clearly do not hold the educationalist conception of school as a preparation for life, with the idea that a child should only accept adult responsibilities on completion of schooling, having acquired specific forms of knowledge and skills. Rather, in this case at least, it would seem that the forms of knowledge obtained in school are considered a low priority, if not irrelevant, to the child's long-term needs and productive role in society. The discussion between school authorities and *comunarios* suggests that the child's 'needs' are in fact subordinated to those of the community as a whole.[10] This now leads us to an exploration of parents' attitudes to the school, which they both support and distrust, in their midst of their community.

Parents' perspectives on school

I have advanced the idea that parents and the wider community contribute to school dropout rates. I shall now focus on their ways of thinking with respect to the school. The case of the boy-*comunario* suggests a paradox here: on the one hand, the community strives to have its own school; on the other hand, *comunarios* take their children out of school for reasons relating to the demands of internal community organisation. D'Emilio, discussing the introduction of school among the Guaraní, observes that 'for the peasant, the relation with the school is conflictual and ambivalent, and characterised by a tension between repulsion and attraction' (in Mejía 1991: 38). Both sides of this paradox have been noted in the literature, but there seems to be no disagreement with respect to the interest of the community in securing a school. For instance, Sanginés Uriarte notes that in Bolivia the expansion of

[9] This was stressed when one of the *comunarios* suggested that Nazario's younger brother attend school without incurring absences.

[10] This incident suggests that the fulfilment of the obligations of each head of family 'affiliate' is collectively enforced; each individual knows what his agreed-upon obligations are, he is willing to fulfil them but at the same time is on the watch so all other members of the 'affiliate' structure also keep their side of the bargain. I have the impression that the community is effectively 'glued together' by discourse and practice. The relationship between the members of the organisation does not have the purpose of extracting knowledge or energy for the benefit of the individual; rather it is horizontal and egalitarian, thus all contributions (in labour, for instance) are for the benefit of all. The interesting thing is that the implementation of this system does not need a written law, or enforcement agencies, because none of the 'affiliates', in their quest for equity, shun their contribution, nor are they willing to give more than necessary. Thus, every 'affiliate' is a contributor, but also a watchdog.

the school system to the countryside after the 1952 Revolution was made possible by the contribution of the peasants themselves: in the construction of school buildings, often as a symbol of prestige, in maintaining private teachers in the absence of state provision of teachers, and so on (1968: 97).[11]

Although one parent was very positive about El Paredón's new bilingual education programme, a more typical view was that school in the past was good, because there was much work and little play, whereas nowadays it is characterised by too much play – a perception that has been heightened by the Education Reform. Although acceptable for pre-school children, play was considered by parents to be bad for for those in the first year or above (cf. Ansión 1988). This was a common complaint and highlights parents' distrust and hesitating commitment to send children to school. Recent attempts to introduce games into modules as part of the Education Reform have been understood by parents as yet more proof of the school's breakdown. In contrast to today, the school of yore was deemed good because it emphasised working activities, principally reading and writing. As Lorenzo, a former literacy promoter from Churikana, put it:

(19)   . . . in the past we were made to write a lot; then when it was not well [written] we were made to do it again; then . . . we were made to read . . . so that we could remember; but now . . . some say, because we were in school [we know] . . . but now it is no longer the case. (Tape 118, 961222).

However, such views must be interpreted with caution, as adults' and children's perceptions of the amounts of time dedicated to work and play at school are undoubtedly different. A child is likely to view play as lasting a short time, and classroom activities as taking longer due to their inherent difficulties and the stress of the situation. Adults, on the other hand, who look at the school from the fields where they are working, can only see pupils when they are outside playing, thereby giving them the impression that while they work, teachers are taking it easy and allowing the children to play. At any rate, the idea that pupils play too much in school nowadays is perceived as negative on two counts: firstly, as detrimental to the main objective of school, that of imparting the knowledge of how to read and write; and secondly because it encourages unacceptable behaviour: 'in school children['s behavior] break[s] down' (*escuelapi pierdekun wawa*).

A further aspect of the Education Reform criticised by parents was the official prohibition of corporal punishment. Like the pupils themselves, parents viewed punishment positively and as a necessary aspect of the learning process. As Lorenzo (L) explained to me:

(20)   L: . . . with that [punishment] he does it carefully. If it is not like that, they do it crooked . . . they do all kinds of things . . .

[11] In 1966, according to statistics given by Sanginés, there were 1,424 'private schools' in the countryside serving 65,336 pupils, that is, about a quarter of the total rural student population (1968: 98,101).

P: Is it OK to punish them?

L: It is good with that, with that punishment. With the fear of being punished we do it carefully, they say. Now am I going to be punished if I do not do it well? therefore I will do it carefully, I myself would say so, that is what they say.

As well as its proscription of corporal punishment, the Education Reform's innovations were criticised for making schools teach types of knowledge and skills readily available in the community. For example, when one teacher introduced tasks to develop manual skills using clay and other materials in accordance with the Reform, and children were asked to bring in flour and salt from home to make geometric objects, parents were incensed. Firstly, the idea of making inedible objects from foodstuffs was incomprehensible and, secondly, the moulding of materials to make objects such as cooking pots was already common knowledge in the community. As one man put it:

(21) What is the point of moulding mud [clay], the making of . . . those cooking pots. Well we already know [how to make those things], we ourselves can teach those things.

Another ubiquitous complaint concerned the use of Quechua in bilingual education, as it was felt that this led to inadequacies in the teaching of Spanish (Choque 1996: 43, 47, 73). The perception of parents seemed to be that an excessive or exclusive attention was being given to the mother tongue, which 'they already know', thus reducing the time and resources available for teaching Spanish as a second language. This point was stressed by Benigno, an elder from a community of El Paredón:

(22) What do they teach Quechua for? Saying, 'We all know Quechua', those who have children simply say 'We want Spanish, they should teach [our children] more Spanish.'

Certain other people made it clear that parents felt cheated in their aspiration for their children to learn Spanish in school. However, according to Lorenzo, most parents do not reflect on why they send their children to school, doing so out of a sense of obligation, and viewing school as a waste of time and a pointless routine.

(23) Most people keep on saying because 'we just go to school as part of a routine', both in the past and today, it is just the same, without thinking seriously, they say. Thereby, just as we would say 'get out' to a dog, OK? in the same way they tell their children to go to school, the children just go, probably without asking themselves why they are going. Parents likewise do not think, about their children's education, hoping that they will get some profession, 'we do not think about these things'.

In spite of all the efforts of the community to construct and maintain a school building, it would seem that sending the children to school was viewed as an imposition, rather than an act of free will. If this is the case, the idea that *comunarios* see schooling as a long-term investment (Ansión 1988: 77) must be reconsidered, at least in the case of El Paredón. In many ways schooling emerges almost as a rite of passage involving children for a minimum number of years, terminated as soon as they can be productively integrated into community life. Attempting to learn to read and write appears more as an esoteric ritual from which most are excluded, or of which they acquire minimal understanding, rather than as a practical preparation for living and working in rural communities.[12] As Lorenzo put it:

(24)   Because, some say, because are we going to be urbanites? to be there just looking at paper, they say; therefore in the countryside we eat working the fields, with that we buy everything . . . (Tape 118, 961222)

I do not know the extent of this rejection of literacy in El Paredón, but similar ideas about the relative value of symbolic objects, such as letters, identification cards, and even money, in relation to foodstuffs, are voiced in other areas.[13] As one *comunario* commented: 'Am I going to eat letters?' ('letratachu mikhusaq?').[14] On the one hand there is a tendency to appropriate urban values, (even to the point of internalising an anti-'Indian' ideology (Abercrombie 1992: 96), while on the other hand, there is resistance and even rejection sustained by the exigencies of the vernacular mode of production and modes of thought (concrete and pragmatic, rather than ideal and abstract).

To reinforce my point, an evident paradox exists whereby, on the one hand, rural communities strive to have a school in which they sometimes invest heavily, and on the other hand, they take their children out of school, temporarily to migrate to labour centres, help in the fields and participate in fiestas, or permanently, when the pupils have come of age. I suggest that this paradox[15] is due to the fact that the rural school is the point of encounter (or conflict) between the Western-urban and the local vernacular community, and their respective systems of knowledge and values. But although community life is self-contained in many respects, as a 'vernacular mode of production' (Illich 1981, 1991) it is by no means isolated from the outside world. Indeed, 'faced with colonial and state domination, [indigenous communities] are inevitably altered by their relationship to dominant forces' (Abercrombie 1992: 95), such that the White-Creole and 'Indian' sectors, as differing sources of knowledge, are 'interpenetrating' (Abercrombie 1992: 95–130).

[12]   Functional illiteracy rates will undoubtedly continue to remain high: 20 per cent in Bolivia nationally, 39.3 per cent in Chuquisaca department (INE 1997). The figures for rural illiteracy are likely to be very much higher.

[13]   For example, in San Pedro de Buena Vista, Northern Potosí, I witnessed complaints about the issue of identification cards.

[14]   In Guaman Poma de Ayala's *Nueva Coronica y Buen Gobierno* a similarly phrased question is asked by the natives to the Spaniards: 'Kay quritachu mikhunki?', 'Do you eat this gold?' or 'Are you going to eat this gold?'

[15]   See also Ansión for Peru (1988: 79–82).

Peasant people come into contact with the urban world not only through the school in their midst but also through the widespread experience of urban migration.[16] People make temporary visits to urban areas for a number of reasons: to work, to sell crops and handicrafts, to visit relatives, to hear mass and get married, and sometimes just for the fun of it. Yet paradoxically, as a local literacy promoter stressed to me, entering urban space as temporary migrants threatens rather than promotes the acquisition of reading and writing skills. These migrations seem to foster the idea that literacy is useless, because the *comunarios* sell their manual labour and never their literacy skills. This reinforces the local perception among them that concrete manual work is effective, whereas abstract literacy and most other forms of school-based knowledge are useless. According to this line of thinking, it is also a valid alternative to get the children out of school when they are of age to work, for instance as peons, and therefore raise some money for the family.

Another interpretation of this phenomenon is that long-term investment in education is sacrificed to short-term exigencies, as Ansión has argued for the case of Peru (1988: 82). But, although parents express the desire for their children to become 'professionals', in practice, community behaviour, values, identity, and ways of knowing tend to inhibit the social rupture this would entail. Indeed it is to be questioned whether parents, or pupils, actually think of school as a form of long-term investment and practical planning for the future.

In summary, parents dedicate considerable energies and resources to building and maintaining schools and ensuring their children attend classes, sometimes even paying the teachers from their own pocket,[17] but they take their children out of school as soon as they are 'strong enough' to become workers, peons, or to participate in migrant labour. Also, while they seem to recognise the benefits of literacy, Spanish, and mathematics 'to defend ourselves' (Ventiades and Plaza 1996), they think that 'letters' are of no use in the real world: 'one is not going to eat letters'. In addition to expressing the desire that their children become 'professional', community members despise those who adopt urban fashions. Finally, while at times they reassert their 'peasant' (*kampu runa*) identity, they also buy manufactured clothing.[18] In brief, while communal practices are geared to reproducing the vernacular mode of production, aspirations of some *comunarios* are geared towards Castilianisation and modernisation.[19] Following Fairclough (1996:

[16] According to recent statistics it appears that Bolivia now is more urban than rural: in 1992, 57.55 per cent of the population lived in urban areas, 42.45 per cent in rural ones (INE 1997).

[17] In the *núcleo* of El Paredón the schools of Michkhamayu and Pisili maintain some private teachers, even today (1999), albeit in combination with private and religious interests, respectively.

[18] In the town of Tarabuco, many peasants from surrounding communities buy cheap used clothing, 'any piece for one boliviano' (some 15 pence at the time).

[19] Similar aspirations are expressed in Southern Peru (Ansión 1988).

88), it must be emphasised that the nature of discourse is conflict between opposing views, like a tug of war, and this seems to be attested by discourses about education in the rural communities of Chuquisaca.

Conclusions

Both school and community are producers of ideas and culture. With regard to the cultural products of formal education, this account of the discourses and practices surrounding the rural school in Bolivia suggests that perceptions and expectations radically diverge between the two groups. The impasse reached during the meeting over Nazario is an evocative illustration of this. That my field observations were conducted at a moment in El Paredón's history when the school was entering a phase of transformation to a new pedagogical model was opportune, in that it brought these differences of perception into particularly stark relief: what is understood as reformed pedagogy by educational planners is seen as play, breakdown of values and behavioural codes, and 'teaching things we already know' in the community's eyes. And paradoxes persist at other levels: literacy, from the average *comunario*'s perspective, offers uncertain economic returns; corporal punishment cannot be uprooted from disciplinary practices overnight, by simple edict from outside;[20] and in a precarious, largely subsistence economy, where children constitute an essential part of the labour force at certain times of year or in certain family circumstances, a rigid schooling regime simply does not fit. Nonetheless, despite the paradoxes, the two sets of perspectives affect each other; the two sources of knowledge – that of the outside and that of the inside – are interpenetrating.

Two points need to be stressed: the place of school in the rural community and the paradox of the community that struggles to have a school in its midst but restricts the length of schooling for its children. In the first case, although Bolivian society is diverse and the encounter between the 'European invaders' and the 'Indians' has determined all kinds of mixing (in races, languages, cultures, social organisations, and so on), the polarisation of the 'urban-occidental' and the 'Indian' nonetheless remains. In this

---

[20] The matter of the place of corporal punishment in the community, as opposed to the school, needs to be investigated further. From my own observations, I would judge that corporal punishment as a means of correcting children is perhaps not the norm in the community. To take two instances: (1) In the home of Domingo Vargas, the *comunario* from Qullakamani, I observed that mistakes are corrected verbally rather than by physical punishment; (2) In Niño Corín in the north of La Paz region, in interviews I conducted some years ago, talking about the education of the children, Feliciano Patzi, my Quechua collaborator, found that physical punishment was not favoured by the *comunarios*. Rather, they would resort to enticement or promises, such as 'if you do or do not do this or that, I will buy you a jumper, or I will take you to town'. In sum, in spite of the talk about the need for physical punishment as an ingredient for effective teaching, which I encountered among the *comunarios* in relation to the school, I have not been able to observe actual physical punishment in the community.

context, the school is an institution designed, maintained and controlled by the urban pole, while the rural community is an entity that harbours knowledges, and teaching and learning practices, different from those brought in by the school. Thus, in spite of the present intentions of the education reform, and in spite of the new role conferred on the *Juntas Escolares* ('School Councils') that allows them to intervene in various educational and administrative matters, the school continues to be an institution imposed from without. And since the rural community belongs to the Indian pole and the school to the urban one, with different languages, cultures and even different mentalities, the possibility of conflict is always latent. The paradox emerges because in this contact/conflict between the urban and the Indian, the need for education through schooling appears as a means of social mobility or as means to defend oneself. Thus the *comunarios* display all kinds of efforts to have a school in their community, but, having one in their midst, find all kinds of justifications to impede the attendance of pupils.

Appendix: interview transcriptions

(1) *Señorita Consuelo*wan, k'achalla, *awis*nin maqawaq kayku, mana *liyi*y atiptiyku. Wakinqa waqarpaq kayku. [. . .] yachachiwaq kayku *a i o* chayta. [. . .] *ribujitus*ta, wasi*s*ta wakita*s*ta tukuy ima *ovejitas*ta. Chayllata.

(2) *Primero*pi *profesora Idegar*wan karqayku [. . .] Payqa ma allin saqrachu karqa, *pero* sumaqta *leye*chiwarqayku. Allillanta yachakurqayku. *Awis*nin mana atiptiykuqa maqawaqpunitaq kayku. [. . .] k'aspiwan *warruti*waq kayku.

(3) *Primero curso*manta pacha *Carmela* karqa. [. . .] Allillan karqa. *Primer curso*pi *reciella*nraqpuni yacharqani chaypiqa, *kastillanu*pi qhichwapipis. [. . .] *leyi*yta *escribi*yta . . . *Libro* karqa *Margara* sutin karqa . . . karqa . . . qhichwa*s*manta karqa chay, *prufisur*. [. . .] Chaymanta chay qhipan watas juk *libros*ñataq karqa. [. . .] *Tercero*piqa karqa *José* karqa. *José* . . . (*Maríachus/Vargas*chus karqa) *Puro kastillanu*manta chayqa yachachiwarqayku. *Regular*lla karqa, mana . . . *kastiga*kuq, sumaqta *garrote*kuq, *prufsr*.

(4) J: Pukllaq kanku chaymanta. Ñuqaykupis pukllallaqtaq kayku chaymanta *garruti*waq kayku. 'Ancha pukllankichik' niwaq kayku.
     P: Qhasillamantachu *garroti*kuq?
     J: Ah, mana *profs*. Ñuqallanchiktaq pukllaspa *garroti*chikunchik. Juk *barretita*n karqa, chaywan; ah . . . k'aspimanta ruwasqitapuni karqa, k'achitu . . . *garrote*napaq jina rakhitu karqa. Wasapi *garrote*kuq, makisninchikpi. (Tape 2, 951120)

(5) P: Chayri imayna karqa.
     E: *Awes*nin . . . saqmallawaykupuni, *prufsny*. Chay chukcha*s*niykumanta jap'iwayku, saqmawayku, [lingri]*s*niykuman jap'iwayku.
     P: Chantarí?
     E: Allillanta ñuqaykuta yachachiwayku, *prufsny*.

(6)   *Escuela*man ñuqa *tercero curso*man kutiyamuni. Chaypi *profesora* Mrs. DD
karqa, prufisuray [. . .] Pay yachachiwarqayku kastilla qallupi, [qhichwata]
mana yachaqchu, *puro kastillanu*manta parlan. Chay *tercer curso*pi yachachiwayku kastilla simimanta parlayku. Chanta jina parlawaspa yachachiwayku
pay astawan ña ruwayta. Chaymanta . . . as tumpa *regular*lla karqa, mikhu-
nallata wayk'ukapuq, chaymanta mana allinta qhawawaqchu kayku. Ma . .
. llamt'awan *cocina*kuq chayllata *atiende*muq *doce*kama, chaymanta . . . lluq-
sipuq jawaman, ñuqayku chay lluqsipuptinqa pukllaykutaq chaykama.
Chay kutiyyamun *muestra*ta qurpuwayku laphi *hoja*pi pata *kantu*npi ruwar-
papuwayku, chayta ruwankichik ñispa saqiwayku, chay mana chay ukhupi
kaptin ni ruwaykupistaqchu. *A veces* chaymanta maqawaq kayku, siq'uwaq
kayku, juk warata . . . mollemanta waritata apaykamuq chaywan. Jina awan-
tallayku *pero* chaytapis chay mana ruwasqaykurayku jinawaq kayku.
Chaymanta *doce*manta kutiyyamun. Chay wawitayuq karqa chay Dioni [. .
.] chaypaq chumpa ruwanata ima apaykamun chayta ruwaq. Chaykama
ñuqaykuqa *pizarron*man lluqsichkayku, dibujaychik ñiwayku, dibujayku
chaypi imaymanitasta, atisqaykuta dibujakuyku. Chaymanta *suma*ta
yachachiwaq kayku, *suma*ta . . . pachakmanta . . . waranqakama yachachiwaq kayku. Chayta mana atiriqchu kayku, allinmanta atiq kayku *pero*,
atispaña ruwaq kayku. Chaymanta jina suma*s* ruwayku, suma*s* ruwaspa mm
chayta mana atiptiyku siq'ullawaqtaq kayku. Chaymanta . . . *kastillanu*-
manta qhapariq . . . Jawata lluqsirpaspa, chaymanta kutiyyamuspa chay
jinata qhapariq, kutiyyamuspa *'Tontos por qué no hácen?'* ñispa niwaq kayku
. . . *'Cabeza de barros'* ñirpawaq kayku. Jina kakuchkayku ñuqaykuqa, chaymanta siq'urpariwayku chay jina ñispa. Chanta juk *ladu* k'uchituman mana
atiptiyku sayarpachiwayku, wakin atiq kayku wakin mana, chaymanta jinata
ñiwaq kayku. (Tape 2, 951120)

(7)   Ñuqaq sutiy kachkan *Mario Vargas Condori* [. . .] iskay watata mana *pasa*rqanichu, *curso*sta ma *pasa*rqanichu, *primer curso*llapi ma *pasa*rqanichu.
Chantaqa wakmanta ñuqaykuta mana atiqta rak'irquwaq kayku qhipa *kantu*-
man, atiqkunarí ñanpaqpi karqanku. [. . .] Chaymantaqa nipuni atiqpunichu
kani, qhillakuq llimphu kani. umm. Qhillakuspaqa ma yaykuymanchu ñiq
kani ñuqa, tataytaqa . . . *Fersa* kachamuwaq payqa . . . Chanta chantaqa watiq
jukmanñataq yaykuni, chaytapis niñapuni niña . . . ma *pasa*llaniñataqchu.
Chanta chaymantaqa *profesor NN* chamurqa chaywan paywan *leye*rqani. [. .
.] *profesor NN-pis* jinallataq karqa, jukta *tariya*ta qurpawaq kayku chanta chay
ruwaq kayku, wakin ma ruwaykuchu, wakin ma ruwaykuchu. Uma chaki-
mantapuni mana ruwaqta sayachiwaq kayku. (Tape 2, 951120)

(8)   Chantaqa *falta*kullarqani *falta*kullarqani, chantaqa *junio* yaykurqani, *antis*
*pasa*ni. Mana *pasa*nayta *creye*kurqanichu [. . .] kusikurqani kusisqa purir-
qani *pasa*ni kunan ñispa.

(9)   H: . . . *y* juk kay *retirado*manta, imataq *pasa*n paywan? sutin *Flores* . . .
Nazario Flores . . .

G: *Allá está.*
N: Ñuqapis ma atiniñachu . . .

(10) H: Qam kanki Nazarió?
N: Arí, tatay wañupun.
H: Qam sapayki *queda*kapunki?
N: Um . . .
H: Wakchitu kapuchkanchu?
N: Arí.

(11) . . . *entonces* paymantapis parlakunanpaq *falta*llantaq, *intuns* pay payta ñuqayku aysaykuna *trabaju*man, *asambleas*man, *intus*qa *escuela*man ñichkallaykutaq, mayqinmantaq pay asunamunqa, mayqinmantaq pay *pertenece*munqa, *asamblea*manchu, *trabajo*manchu o mayqinman? *solamente palabras faltan, entoncs* paypa tatan wañupun, *entons*qa ñuqayku *kotas trabajuman* mañayku, *trabaja*pun, *entos* imanasuntaq?

(12) H: Ya *bueno.* Atiymanraq . . . atisunmanraqchu *solucio*nayta pay kutiykunanpaq o manañachu? Ima ñinkichik qamkuna *a ver? Mayoríapi palabra.*
C: Atikunman *señor director,* kunan kaypi kachkaptiyki *señor director solucio*nay. *Sabes* ñuqayku ajina *reunion*pi ñuqayku jinata *multa*ptiyku, ma atinqachu, *señor director.*
H: *Pero* qamkuna *mayoría* ima ñinkichiktaq? *Porque mayoría decidi*sqa chay junt'akunan tiyan, *si* kan *voluntad* o mana kan *voluntad. Si* ñuqawan *arregla*sunchik, ñuqa kutiripusqaytawan watiq mat'iyta qallaripuwankichik.
C: Y claro.
G: Eso va ser.

(13) H: . . . ajina uyarinchik *compañeros,* atisunmanchu juk makita yanapayta, mana ñisunmanchu *de que trabajo*wan . . . qullqita jaywaykuyta chaywan kawsakunanta . . .
C: Mana mana mana . . .
H: . . . mana chaymanchu chayasanchik, *sino* imaynatataq yanapasunman *escuela*ta tukunanpaq, *porque ya* ñiwanchikña ña chay *prepara*sqetaña kachkan. Kunanchá ma atinqa [. . .] qhawarisunman chayta *pero entero*manta, ma *dirigente*llachu, nitaq *secretario general*llachu, atisunmanchu chayta yanapariyta?
C: Atisunman *señor director,* yanapasun.

(14) N: Ñuqa ma *escuela*man yaykurqanichu chanta . . .
P: Ima ñin?
G: *Yo no entraría a la escuela dice, más bien a alfabetización entraré.*

(15) *Kota*ta *compañeros* maypipis tukuy . . . maytapis rinayaspa churanchikpuni *compañeros,* chayqa mana chinkananpaq, mana chaytaqa churanqachu ñispachu . . . kutiykunman, mana atiykumanchu kutirinanta.

(16) . . . *compañeros,* jukchhikanta allillan . . . *claro* atisunchik atiyta *compañeros,*

ma manachu; qhawanapaq kachkan *pinsa*na kachkan, *solamente, compañeros*, ma atichkanchikchu jukllawan qhayqeayta . . . tukuyninchik *compañeros* . . . ima yuyaytapis *trata*rinanchik kachkan *compañeros*, kay pataman *compañeros* junturinanchik kachkanman, chayqa atikun a *compañeros; por lo menos* qhawasqaymanqa kachkamanchá kay: mana atisunchu *compañeros kotas*ninmanta *rebaja*riyta, mana atisunchu *turnus*ninmanta *ribaja*riyta, *por lo menos personal* atiymanchá, mana *compañeros reitera*spa, ama *wasis*man [bases] yaykunqachu, *pero tareas*nintataq qunman jurqhunman *y* chaytataq ruwamunman *voluntad*ninpi, chay kanman *compañeros* . . . ñuqa chayta munayman . . . maypichus kanman *tareas* chaytaqa atin *compañeros, por lo menos* kanmanchá juk *semana*pi juk *diya*llapis, *por lo menos* mantinikunan *nada más*. Chay *señor director*.

(17) N: Juk *semana*pi *ni* juk *diya*ta mana.
H: Nazario, mana churachisuptinku *kotas*, mana junt'achisuptinku *jornales escuela*pi, ñankunaspi o imas *trabaju*chus kachkan *comunidad*pi, mana junt'achisuptinku, mana *exigi*suptinku, qam *sigui*waqchu *escuela*pi, tukuchawaqchu manachu? . . . Manapuni munankichu? chay qhanmanta.
N: [Nazario ch'inlla]
H: Ja?
G: *No, no quiere dice* . . .

(18) . . . chaytaqa *sigui* mañaykuman . . . *filiado*manta jina. *Solo* munayku ñuqaykuqa *simana*pi juktapis jamunanta *y tareas*tataq *profesora* qunan . . . chayta ñuqayku qhawayku.

(19) . . . ñawpaqta sumaq qhillqachiwaq kayku; chanta mana allin kaptintaq watiqmanta ruwachiwaq kayku; chanta . . . *leye*chiwaq kayku . . . yuyanaykupaq jinata; *pero* kunanqa . . . ñinkutaq wakinqa, *porque* ñuqayku ñawpaqpi *escuela*pi karqayku . . . kunan manaña

(20) L: . . . chaywanqa allinsituta ruwayparin. Mana jinas kaptinqa wist'uta . . . tukuy imaymanasta ruwanku . . .
P: Allinchu *kastiga*nanku?
L: Chaywan allin, chay *kastiga*nawan. *kastiga*nawaykuta manchaywanqa allinta ruwayku ñinku, jina ñinku. Kunan *kastiga*wanqachu mana allin ruwaptiyqa? *entonces* allinsituta ruwasaq ñiymanpuni ñuqallapis, jinata ñinku.

(21) Imapaqtaq chay t'uru q'allpiy, chay mankas . . . ruwakun. *Bueno* ñuqanchik yachallanchikña, yachachinallanchik kachkan.

(22) Imapaq yachachinku qhichwata? Ñuqanchikpis yachallanchik qhichwata ñispa *castellanu*ta munanchik, *castellanu* astawan yachachipuwasunman ñillanku wawasniyuqkunaqa. (Tape 46, 950805)

(23) *Mayor parte* ñillankupuni *porque* riyllata riyku *escuela*manqa ñawpaqpipis kunanpis jinallapuni mana *normale*ayta *piensa*spachu ñinku. *Entonces* imaynatachá allqutapis lluqsiy ñirpasunman i? *entonces* ajinallata *escuela*man riy

ñirpanku, wawaqa rillan, nichá t'ukurinchu imapaq rini ñispa. *Ni* tatan mamanpis *ni*llataq mana t'ukurinkuchu, kay wawayqa yachachun ñispa, ima *profesion*niyuqllapis lluqsinanpaq ñispa, mana t'ukuykuchu a.

(24) *Porque* mana, ñinku wakin, *porque* llaqta runachu kasunman? ajinata *papel* qhawaspalla kanapaq, ñin; *entos campo*piqa *labranza*pi trabajaspa, chaywan mikhunchik, chaywan imatapis rantikunchik . . . (Tape 118, 961222)

Acknowledgments

I would like to express my appreciation to Henry Stobart and Rosaleen Howard for their editorial revisions to my chapter.

References

Abercrombie, Thomas A. 1992. 'To be Indian, to be Bolivian: Ethnic and National Discourses of Identity'. In G. Urban, and Joel Sherzer (eds.), *Nation-States and Indians in Latin America*. Austin: University of Texas Press: 95–130.

Al-Mannai, Latifa Ali. 1996. 'Questioning Assessment: Policy and Classroom Practices in Bahrain Primary Schools'. PhD thesis, University of Liverpool.

Ansión, Juan. 1988. *La escuela en la comunidad campesina*. Lima: Proyecto Escuela Ecología y Comunidad Campesina.

Apala, Pedro, Carmen Rosa Huanca, and Celestino Choque, with L.E. López. 1990. 'Currículo para la modalidad intercultural bilingüe para el ciclo básico del area rural'. Paper presented to the Seminario-Taller Internacional: Hacia un Currículo Intercultural Bilingüe, November 1990. La Paz: MEC, UNICEF and UNESCO-OREALC.

Arias S., José. 1924. *La Educación del indio y las bases para su organización. (Estudios socio-pedagógicos)*. La Paz: Escuela Tipográfica Salesiana.

Arias, Juan Félix. 1992. 'Milenarismo y resistencia anticolonial: los apoderados-espiritualistas en Icla-Tarwita, Chuquisaca, 1936–1964'. PhD thesis, Universidad Mayor de San Andrés.

——, 1994. *Historia de una esperanza. Los apoderados espiritualistas de Chuquisaca 1936–1964*. La Paz: Aruwiyiri.

Baptista Gumucio, Mariano. 1974. *Analfabetos en dos culturas*. La Paz: Los Amigos del Libro.

Barrera de Martínez, Susana. 1985. *La educación campesina. Testimonio de un conflicto cultural*. La Paz: UNICEF.

Bolivian government. 1955. *Código de la Educación Boliviana. Decreto Supremo No. 03937, 20 de Enero de 1955*. La Paz: Ministerio de Educación Pública y Bellas Artes. (Editorial Fénix.)

——, 1997. *Guía didáctica de segundas lenguas*. La Paz: MEC, Viceministerio de educación inicial, primaria y secundaria, UNST.

Briggs, Lucy T. 1980. *Análisis técnico del Programa de Educación Bilingüe del PEIA 1979*. La Paz (mimeo).

——, 1983. 'Bilingual Education in Bolivia'. In A. Miracle (ed.), *Bilingualism: Social Issues and Policy Implications*. Athens, GA: The University of Georgia Press: 84–95.

Caiza, José 1989. 'Hacia un modelo de educación bilingüe autogestionario'. In L.E.

López and R. Moya (eds.), *Pueblos indios, estados y educación*. Lima and Quito: PEB-P, EBI, ERA: 309–25.

Cárdenas, Víctor Hugo. 1992a. 'La multiculturalidad en la escuela boliviana actual'. In *Los aymaras. Nuestros pueblos en la escuela*. Cuaderno de Trabajo No. 2. La Paz: Instituto Interamericano de Derecho Humanos, Fundación Friedrich-Naumann: 9–22.

Choque Canqui, Roberto. 1992. 'La escuela indigenal: La Paz (1905–1938)'. In R. Choque Canqui and Tomasa Sinana, *Educación indígena: ¿ciudadanía o colonización?* La Paz: Ediciones Aruwiyiri, THOA: 19–40.

Choque, Celestino. 1996. 'Musuq Yachachiy. Aplicación de La EIB en la Región Quechua de Bolivia. Quinquenio 1990–1994'. Dissertation, Universidad Nacional del Altiplano, Puno.

Claure, Karen. 1989. *Las escuelas indigenales: otra forma de resistencia comunaria*. La Paz: HISBOL.

CONMERB (Confederación de Maestros de Educación Rural de Bolivia). 1984. *Plan Global de Reestructuración del Sistema de Educación Rural. 'De una educación opresora hacia una educación liberadora'*. La Paz: CONMERB.

CSUTCB (Confederación Sindical Unica de Trabajadores Campesinos de Bolivia). 1991. *Propuesta: Hacia una Educación Intercultural Bilingüe*. La Paz.

De la Torre, Carlos. 1997. '"La letra con sangre entra": racismo, escuela y vida cotidiana en Ecuador'. Paper presented to the Latin American Studies Association Conference, Guadalajara, 19 April 1997.

Donoso Torres, Vicente. 1940. *El estado actual de la educación indigenal en Bolivia. Informe del Vice-Presidente del Consejo Nacional de Educación*. La Paz: Consejo Nacional de Educación.

ETARE (Equipo Técnico de Apoyo a la Reforma Educativa) 1993. *Reforma Educativa: Propuesta*. Cuadernos de la Reforma. La Paz: Papiro.

Fairclough, Norman. 1996. *Discourse and Social Change*. Polity Press.

Foucault, Michel. 1991 [1975]. *Discipline and Punish: The Birth of the Prison*. Penguin Books.

Howard-Malverde, Rosaleen, and Andrew Canessa. 1995. 'The School in the Quechua and Aymara Communities of Highland Bolivia'. *International Journal of Educational Development* 15(3): 231–43.

I-ADB (Inter-American Development Bank). n.d. Programa de Reforma Educativa. www.iadb.org/exr/doc98/apr/b093s.htm.

Illich, Ivan. 1981. *Shadow Work*. Open Forum. Boston, MA, and London: Boyars.

——, 1991. *La guerra contra la subsistencia*. Cochabamba: Ediciones Runa.

INE (Instituto Nacional de Estadísticas). 1997. Estadísticas Sociales. www.ine.gov.bo 24–6–97.

López, Luis Enrique. 2000. 'La educación intercultural bilingüe: ¿respuesta frente a la multietnicidad, pluriculturalidad y multilingüismo latinoamericanos?' Cochabamba: Programa de Formación en Educación Intercultural Bilingüe para los Países Andinos (PROEIB Andes Universidad Mayor de San Simón–Cooperación Técnica Alemana [GTZ]).

Luna, Nazario. 1971. *Alfabetización funcional*. La Paz.

Mejía, María Cristina. 1991. *Etnias, educación y cultura. Defendamos lo nuestro*. La Paz: ILDIS.

Pérez, Elizardo. 1962. *Warisata: La escuela-ayllu*. Prólogos de Carlos Salazar Mostajo. La Paz: Empresa Industrial Gráfica E. Burillo.

Plaza Martínez, Pedro. 1998. 'Language, Education and Power in Bolivia: Bilingual Education Classroom Practices'. PhD thesis, University of Liverpool.

Sanginés Uriarte, Marcelo. 1968. *Educación rural y desarrollo en Bolivia*. La Paz: Don Bosco.

SENALEP (Servicio Nacional de Alfabetización y Educación Popular). 1983. *Hacia una Educación Intercultural y Bilingüe*. La Paz: SENALEP.

——, 1984. *Plan nacional de alfabetización y educación popular, Prof. Elizardo Pérez*. Propuesta Técnica. La Paz: MEC.

Soto, Ileana. 1996. 'La interculturalidad en la educación básica ecuatoriana'. In J.C. Godenzzi (ed.), *Educación e interculturalidad en los Andes y la Amazonía*. Cusco: CERA BC: 139–48.

Suárez Arnez, Cristobal. 1986. *Historia de la educación boliviana*. 2nd edn. La Paz: Editorial Don Bosco.

Talavera, María Luisa. 1989. *La deserción escolar del ciclo básico en Bolivia: estudio realizado en cinco departamentos durante 1987*. La Paz: CEBIAE.

Ventiades, Nancy, and Pedro Plaza Martínez. 1996. 'Evaluación de los proyectos de alfabetización en el Departamento de Chuquisaca'. La Paz: UNICEF (mimeo).

Yraola Burgos, Ana. 1995. 'The Language of Quechua Rural Teachers in Bolivia: A Study of Bilingualism-Interlingualism among Rural Quechua Native Speakers'. PhD thesis, University of St Andrews.

CHAPTER EIGHT

Local Knowledge in Health: The Case of Andean Midwifery

Barbara Bradby

Taking local health knowledge seriously

Agriculture and health in development thinking

The term 'local knowledge' is one that resonates around much academic and NGO thinking on development. It has been activated under the politics which promote the move towards 'bottom-up' development practices, and which criticise the 'top-down' nature of much development thinking around science and technology. Yet it is striking to note the extent to which its use is confined to agriculture and farming practices, perhaps more broadly to the field of production, while the field of health and of human reproduction remains dominated by the belief system of Western, 'scientific' medicine.

Norman and Ann Long's *Battlefields of Knowledge* (1992) is perhaps a key text here, one that, through a series of agricultural case studies, demonstrates the agency of subjects who are supposedly the recipients of technological assistance, and the permeability of the knowledge frontier. The authors argue against a dualist distinction between 'insider' and 'outsider' knowledges, instead proposing that knowledge continually criss-crosses this interface, and is generated dialogically in interactions. They are also opposed to the elaboration of ideal types of 'traditional' and 'modern' knowledge, stressing the value of looking at variations from types and norms, and at what is often seen as the 'disorder' of everyday life from the viewpoint of structural functionalism or of development interventions. This theoretical perspective interacts with a methodology which starts from the lifeworlds of actors, and tries to show how they make sense of particular situations through organisational and discursive practices.

This work builds on the economic anthropology of two previous decades which documented, in the case of the Andes, patterns of land-holding, production and exchange among local peoples, as well as the depth of botanical and ecological knowledge underlying them (Alberti and Mayer [eds.] 1974; Lehmann [ed.] 1982). However, it shifts the focus, away from anthropological description of 'authentic' cultures, such as the 'Andean' one, towards a more dialogical view. Recently, this shift has taken a further turn in the work of PRATEC, the Andean Project for Peasant Technologies

(Apffel-Marglin with PRATEC [eds.] 1998). This group of ex-agronomists in Peru advocates 'de-professionalisation' and is opposed to Western notions of 'development' which depend on the divorce of scientific knowledge from values, instead embracing an Andean ethic of 'willingness to nurture and be nurtured' in which social relations and relations with nature merge. The understanding of Andean knowledge must proceed within this ethic of the regeneration of the whole of life through the 'conversation' of people, deities and nature, in the *chacra* (literally, 'the [cultivated] field').

This idyllic picture of Andean culture has, not surprisingly, been taken to task for its emptiness of social content in a decade when the central Andean region was convulsed in the violent, social conflict sparked by Shining Path (Mayer 1994, cited in Apffel-Marglin 1998: 22–23). However, from a different point of view, PRATEC does not go far enough – to take account of women's experience and of the world of the gendered body in the Andes. This would include understandings of sexuality and childbirth, which are absent, even from their description of the phases of the moon in relation to the fertility of the land (Valladolid Rivera 1998:59–61). In this way, the group exposes its roots in agricultural science, with its masculine bias, and like many other attempts to promote local knowledge as an alternative to Western notions of development, stops short of the female body.[1] In taking its paradigm and its examples mainly from agriculture, it remains on a terrain which, though certainly 'contested', still seems relatively safe by comparison with that of the 'women's sphere' of birth, health, and mortality.[2]

[1] The PRATEC volume does, in fact, contain a chapter told from a woman's perspective (Jimenez Sardon 1998). This chapter is also the only one in the volume which uses the words and 'voice' of an Aymara woman directly. It deals in detail with the violence of her first consensual marriage, and explicitly blames the violence on her having gone against the wishes of her aunt and uncle who brought her up as parents, and more generally, on her failure to 'converse' with neighbours and kin. After a particularly bad episode which provoked miscarriage, the parents of both partners arrived with community authorities, and the whole matter was talked through, with the older generation deciding on a separation. Several years later, her parents arranged a marriage for her which has fulfilled the Andean ethic of mutual nurturance. The narrator projects a clear morality of obedience to the older generation, and blames many community ills on young women provoking abortions. My point here is that this interesting piece goes untheorised and almost unnoticed in the rest of the volume. My conclusion from this silence is that the authors' theory can accommodate violence as ultimately reconcilable with the Andean ethic of nurturance because that ethic is utilised socially in the control of deviant behaviour.

[2] Of course it is possible to argue that in the Andean cosmovision, the separation that I am making here between agriculture and health makes no sense. The work of Denise Arnold and her collaborators in ILCA could be seen as filling out the PRATEC vision, from this Andean point of view, where the fertility of the land and of the female body are intimately connected, and where understandings of childbirth are linked to those of cultivation and of mining (Arnold, Yapita et al. 1995; Arnold and Yapita 1996, 1998). The movement for birthing rights among the Inuit of Northern Canada grew out of women's perception that the fight for cultural survival was dominated by men's concerns over the environment (O'Neil and Kaufert 1995: 68).

Turning to development *policy*, there is a sense in which agriculture was again the dominant strand throughout the 1960s and 1970s, rural poverty being seen as a problem of production and of the unequal distribution of resources, a material base from which other problems stemmed. This dominance shifted in the 1980s and 1990s to a more plural conception of development problems, within which, however, health seemed to assume almost the same importance as agriculture did in the 1960s. This parallels the shift in development thinking from seeing men, and particularly male producers, as the recipients of aid and potential agents of development, to a focus on women, mainly seen as reproducers and educators of children.

If this is the case in Latin America, it is not just because the visibility of land reform and agricultural extension agents of previous decades has diminished, as the reforms are reversed and these functions handed over to market forces. It is also because the certainty of the scientific and technical fix of the Green Revolution has run its course, and given way to the criticism and doubting of a subsequent generation. Academic studies have shown how ignoring the knowledge of local people in planning aid projects has led to limited benefits for those people, and at worst, the destruction of their environment (Porter et al. 1991). Countless books have been written which advocate using local knowledge as the basis for development planning, on both ethical and environmental grounds (Dankelman and Davidson 1988; Berkes [ed.] 1989; Taylor and MacKenzie [eds.] 1991; Berkes et al. 1998). But all of this work relates to agriculture, fisheries, common resources, the environment. In the field of health, by contrast, we see a conjuncture rather like that of agriculture in the 1960s, where immutable science meets incontrovertible statistics, and a 'knowledge gap' appears into which Western agencies pour solutions, in a flood restrained only by the availability of resources.

Childbirth, maternal mortality and development

Within this new wave of development practice, one searches in vain for any serious evaluation or use of local knowledges as part of the solution to health problems. Instead, local knowledges and practices are construed in terms of 'cultural barriers' to the implantation of Western science. Medical anthropology has either been ignored by policy-makers, or enlisted in the attempt to find acceptable ways of packaging Western medicine for local peoples. In the field of childbirth these processes are particularly striking. International statistics on maternal mortality are constantly presented as an overwhelming indictment of traditional practices of midwifery and birth, with no questioning of the leap in reasoning from one to the other. The statistics are, indeed, such that they present a hard task for those who would argue with them. In the Bolivian case, with which I am familiar, rates of maternal mortality are very high by international standards. The average national rate is put at 390 per 100,000 live births (equivalent to 0.4 per cent, or 1 death in

251 live births), which compares with rates of 4 per 100,000 in Ireland, or 1 death in 25,000 births. And within Bolivia itself one finds regional disparities, the highest rates being in the rural areas of the *altiplano*, at 929 per 100,000, and the lowest ones in the lowland region (*llanos*) at 166 per 100,000 live births (Bolivia, INE 1994).

Although there is much work remaining to be done to understand better the factors making up these statistics, at one level the figures are indisputable. What *can* be argued with is the frequent deduction from the figures that what is necessary is to introduce Western obstetrics and hospitals on a massive scale. Despite some counteracting tendencies, this has been the thrust of recent Bolivian planning to meet international funders' pressure to lower the maternal mortality rates.[3] Currently, the pressure is being stepped up by the international agencies, as they link debt reduction to achieving quantitative targets in health, one of which, for Bolivia, is a sizeable increase in hospital births.[4]

Of course, common sense tells us that maternal mortality rates in the industrialised countries have come down over the past century in tandem with the growth of hospitalisation and modern obstetrics. Yet closer analysis reveals this 'common sense' to be deeply flawed. Marjorie Tew's work on the UK statistics shows that hospital birth remained more dangerous than home birth during the 1920s and 1930s, resulting in the paradox that middle-class women (who were giving birth in hospital) had *higher* rates of maternal mortality than working-class women (who gave birth at home) (1995: 282). The same paradox is evident in the statistics on maternal mortality in the USA, where the rates for urban women were considerably worse than those for rural women in the 1920s and 1930s (Leavitt 1986: 184). The largest survey of the comparative risks of home and hospital birth at the present, the Dutch survey, shows the risk of the baby dying to be 19 times greater for those delivered by an obstetrician in hospital than for those delivered by a midwife at home (Tew 1995: 348–54).

Tew argues that the general historical trend of a decline in the maternal mortality rate over the last century must be attributed to three principal factors: the lowering of the overall fertility rate, the gradual increase in women's general state of health, and the improvement in nutrition. This general trend was arrested and even reversed among the urban and middle classes who first took on hospital birth in a big way in the 1920s and 1930s. The defeat of what had become an intractable problem for the medical authorities came at a very precise time, in the years following 1936, when the precursor of antibiotics was discovered and first dramatically lowered the

[3] See, for instance, *Plan Vida* ('Plan Life'), which ran from 1994 to 1997 (Bolivia, SNS 1994).

[4] I am grateful to Susanna Rance for her personal communication to me of her notes on a speech given by the Bolivian Minister of Health to this effect in September 1999. The target given was an increase to 65 per cent of all births to be attended by 'institutional personnel' by the year 2002.

rates of post-partum infection in hospital, at that time the highest cause of mortality. The rate of maternal mortality was halved in the UK by 1945, and halved again by 1950 (Tew 1995: 284–85). The pharmacological development of ergometrine, which can prevent post-partum haemorrhage, also played a part at this time.

Given these debates about the historical causes of the decline in maternal mortality in the North, we must be wary of leaping to conclusions about the causes of persistently high rates of maternal mortality in areas of the South. The equation that is often made between high rates of maternal mortality and traditional childbirth practices is highly questionable. A more plausible argument is that local childbirth practices make the best use of the resources available in rural areas, and death rates would be higher without them. As in the historical denunciations of midwives in the North, parteras (local midwives)[5] in Bolivia nowadays are blamed both for intervening too much and for not intervening. They are also blamed for not referring to hospital, yet hospitals are reluctant to pick up problematic cases when they do appear, for fear of worsening their own statistics. The medical authorities steer an ambiguous line between an outright policy of extermination of local midwifery,[6] and a policy of medium-term tolerance, such that parteras are seen as a bridge to reach pregnant women, useful only so long as that bridge is needed.[7]

However, in this process, medical interactions with parteras have been all one-way. In the campaigns that have a long history in developing countries to train 'traditional birth attendants', there has been remarkably little attention paid to their knowledge. Unlike the 'extirpation of idolatries' in seventeenth-century Andean society, there has been no systematic recording of local practices and beliefs accompanying the ongoing, rather naked attempt at cultural destruction. In a field of knowledge that can certainly be likened to a battleground, the first step in any attempt to 'decolonise' knowledge must be to listen carefully to what local practitioners have to say (Apffel-Marglin and Marglin [eds.] 1996). This paper tries to do this by analysing the testimony of one practising partera in present-day Bolivia.

---

[5] In line with the overall argument of this paper, I have translated partera as 'local midwife' rather than 'traditional midwife'. I have also avoided the term 'traditional birth attendant' used in official medical circles. In Bolivia, birth attendants would include husbands and other relatives who are not considered to be parteras. Because the partera has a specialised status closely parallel to the historical status of the 'midwife' in Europe, and because the term 'traditional birth attendant' denies parteras knowledge and status, I have deliberately tried to make the terms partera and 'midwife' interchangeable in this paper.

[6] The situation among the Inuit of Northern Canada is that a policy of total removal of childbirth from local midwives has been effective since the mid-1980s (O'Neil and Kaufert 1995: 60).

[7] See the official international statement of policy on traditional birth attendants, which states: 'Because of the current shortage of professional midwives and institutional facilities [. . .] the WHO, UNICEF and UNFPA promote the training of TBAs in order to bridge the gap until all women and children have access to acceptable, professional, modern health care services' (WHO/UNICEF/UNFPA 1992: 2)

Locating Andean health knowledge

Before turning to this case study, I return to the theme of local knowledge and what it might mean in the area of health and medicine in the Andes. Although 'local' is often used to avoid the connotations of 'traditional', it is all too easy to slip into thinking of local knowledge as that which has been handed down in a particular place – as knowledge that belongs there because it originates there, in that place. However, the historical and ethnographic work of George Foster (1994) has made a persuasive case for the Old World origin of the humoral beliefs that underlie much current medical thinking at local level in Latin America. Although his thesis has been contested (Austin Alchon 1995; Bastien 1989; López Austin 1988), it does deter us from simply assuming that local Andean childbirth practices are in any straightforward way the descendants of ancient practices of these Andean places.

Foster (1994: 150–58) has also shown that the mode of transmission of European medical knowledge in Latin America was through the Spanish elites – through missionaries, hospitals, pharmacies, and written *recetarios*, or home medical guides. Within Spain itself, humoral theory permeated the formal teaching and practice of medicine, but was *not* apparently part of popular belief and practice (Foster: 150–51). Foster therefore argues, less convincingly, that the disruptions of the Conquest period in Latin America account for the rapid spread and easy acceptance of humoral theory at the popular level there (1984: 185). More plausibly, his critics have argued both that there is evidence from some parts of pre-Hispanic America that the 'hot–cold' symbolic distinction already existed, and that even if it did not, the binary system of thought *did*, making its assimilation easy and logical (Austin Alchon 1995).

Humoral theory continued to be the dominant medical theory in Europe through the seventeenth and into the eighteenth centuries. It died out in Spain later than in northern Europe, and was still being taught in Chilean medical schools in 1838 (Foster 1994: 152). The display shelves of old bottles and jars in some Latin American pharmacies testify to its relatively recent practice as orthodox medicine (Foster 1994: 158). The 'filtering down' model argues that popular, folk medicine represents the vestiges of scientific thought of a past era. In the adage of Grattan and Singer, 'the science of one age becomes the superstition of the next' (1956: 6, quoted in Foster 1994: 153). The simplicity of the humoral system as an organising theory of disease causation and cure meant that it could be widely practised and deployed as a theoretical system.

Although the therapeutic resources of medical and popular curers presumably differed, there would have been some continuity between their explanatory systems. But as medical knowledge became more specialised with the rise of modern science, and as cures became regulated and monopolised by medical experts, a discontinuity of both theory and practice must have set in. Hence those who still adhered to the theoretical explanations of humoral theory would be labelled as backward and superstitious by the new experts. And as the formal written basis underlying the practices disappeared, the practices themselves could then be labelled 'empiricist', a term applied pejoratively, for instance, to many contemporary *parteras* in the Bolivian context.

In the case study that follows, the testimony of one practising *partera* is read alongside two other kinds of text. On the one hand, the details of her practices are compared with those of early modern Europe, mainly using the work of Jacques Gélis (1991). In this way, we test Foster's theory on humoral medicine, and more broadly, the extent to which one tradition of Andean midwifery has interacted with and incorporated elements of European, or 'Old World', thought and practice. On the other hand, the testimony of this midwife is compared with those of midwives from a different area of rural Bolivia, as recorded by Arnold, Yapita et al. (1995) as part of the same research project. The aim here is to question how far the testimony of one midwife, and the practices of one locality, can stand in for a 'whole', such as 'rural Bolivia' or 'the Andes'.

The knowledge of a local midwife in Bolivia

Extract 1: A double conversation

Key to participants
B = Barbara Bradby
H = *Partera*'s daughter
M = Mary Aguilar
P = Partera Lidia

Key to transcription symbols

underlined words	= spoken with emphasis
CAPITALS	= spoken loudly
:::::	= prolongation of syllable or letter
[.]	= short pause
[2]	= pause of 2 seconds, etc.
[words]	= words uncertain in the transcription
[[indications]]	= indications of gestures, or explanations added by the author
wor–	= word cut short
// (in the middle of a turn)	= this turn interrupted here by the following turn
// (at the beginning of a turn)	= this turn interrupts the preceding turn
{words} {words}	= words pronounced simultaneously by different speakers

Original (Spanish and Quechua)	English
3301	
B Sí, [.] sí [.] sí Y, una mujer aquí cuando está embarazada este cómo, cómo sabes que estás embarazada?	B Yes, [.] yes [.] yes And, a woman, when she's pregnant, ehh, how, how do you know that you're pregnant?
3302	
H [.] nn Así mirando de su mano nomás sabella.	H [.] nn Like this, just looking at her hand, she [[the *partera*]] knows
3303	
B Así?	B Really?
3304	
H {Así nomás sabe}	H {Just like that she knows}
3305	
M {mm, makillanpi}, [[a la *partera*]] ¿Yachanki?	M {mm, in the hand}, [[to the *partera*]] Do you know [[how to do]] that?
3306	
P nh [[afirmativo]], nh	P aha [[affirmative]], aha
3307	
H Sí, en su mano nomás sabe, como está embarazada, no, o no está embarazada.	H Yes, just in the hand she knows, whether she's pregnant, you know? Or that she's not pregnant.
3308	
B {El pulso?}	B {The pulse?}
3309	
M [[a la *partera*]] {Imaynataq maki a pero}	M [[to the *partera*]] {But how is that? the hand?}
3310	
H [2] In sus vinas nomas//sabe	H [2] In the veins, just from that// she knows
3311	
P //mmm Sus winas onqunampaq p'itikun [.] kay makisitumpis [.] uñawañita p'itikun [.] // onqukunampaq i?	P //mmm Her veins, when she's about to give birth they burst [.] Here in her hand,[.] the little tiny ones burst [.]// When she's just going to give birth, you see?
3312	
M //aaa. y may laditopi jap'in//a?	M //aaa. And which side [[of the hand]] do you feel// then?

3313
P //Kay, kay laditomantá kaysitota,
   kaycha winito ñan aisitunpi a
   winita apagarukun.
   Unqunampaqpuni,
   'chikarababum' kay //
   kayman 'taqq!' samamun [2]

   [[semi-cantado]]
   Ruuu! pha! janpir jamun

   Juj, Juj, Juj, Juj, Juj [[sonido medio
   soplando imitando el pulso de la
   vena]]

P //Here, from this side, just here,
   See this little vein, just there where
   the vein expires.
   When she's just about to give birth,
   this one goes, 'chikarababum!'//
   And over here 'taqq!' it sighs [2]

   [[half-singing]]
   Ho::t, ho::t, the cure comes
   [[flowing]]
   Hoohh, hoohh, hoohh, hoohh,
   hoohh, [[sound half blown,
   imitating the pulse]]

3314
M //aah! Onqunampaq?

M //aah! When she's just about to
   give birth?

3315
P 'Chay unqullanqaña,' ninchis
   'pacha,' //[.]
   'manaña unaytañachu,' nini.

P 'She's going to give birth right
   now,' we say, // [.]
   'It won't be long now,' I say.

3316
M //aa aaya

M //aah ah, I see

3317
B mhm

B mhm

3318
M Qhaway tukuy chay allinllan a?
   porque uspital ukhupiqa makin
   //puni sat'isanku

M Look, all this is so good, don't you
   see? Because in hospital, their
   hands// they're always sticking
   them up

3319
H //NU MIRA pues,
   ni UN // rato no miran!

H //THEY DON'T LOOK, do they.
   Not ONE//moment do they look!

3320
P //Yaykuy MAKI AN! JAH!
   [[de enojada]]

P IN goes the HAND! HUHH!
   [[very angrily]]

3401
M Icharí?

M Right?

3402
H no NO ME gusta hacer
   mirar, poreso yo no, no puedo,
   oye // Nunca me voy, no?

H no, I DON'T like having myself
   looked at, that's why I can't,
   I can't, Here, mum// I never go, do
   I?

3403

M //Ni una vez, has ido al hospital, no?

M //Not once, you haven't been to hospital, no?

3404

H No, no no mi gusta.

H No, no, I don't like it.

3405

B Si // {[has ido o no has ido?]}

B Yes// {[have you been there or not?]}

3406

H //{La infirmira también} ngl me ha dicho,

'Vas a venir, estás enl control,' midice,

'Ya,' le digo nomás, no// ¿para quí?
'para quí al, encuandostoyahí mi woy morer,'
digo yo,

H //{The nurse, too} mm, she told me,

'You're to come, you're down for the check-up,' she told me.

'OK,' says I. No// What for?
'So that to, when I'm in there I'm going to die,'
I say.

3407

B //pero no vas ya

B //so you don't go ok

3408

H para qui me meten mano todo,

no puedo yo! [[se ríe un poco]]

H so they can stick their hands up me and all that,

not me, I can't do it! [[laughs a little]]

The above is an extract from the transcription of an interview with a *partera* in Sucre, Bolivia, which took place in January 1995. This was one of a series of in-depth interviews carried out between October 1994 and February 1995 in a *barrio*[8] of Sucre. The interviews were all carried out by myself together with Mary Aguilar, a trained nurse with experience in public health work, and also a Quechua speaker. The interview with the *partera* came after we had completed nine interviews with members of the 'Mothers' Club', organised by a Bolivian NGO around its medical post in the barrio (Bradby 1999). While several women had described giving birth at home, only one had been attended by a *partera*. As we got to know this woman better, it emerged that the *partera* was her *comadre*[9] and neighbour

---

[8] The use of *barrio*, meaning 'neighbourhood' or 'area', is fairly neutral in Latin America, being applied to any urban area that has a name, outside 'the centre' of a town or city. It is also sometimes used to indicate an informal or squatter settlement on the outskirts of a town. The *barrio* in which Doña Lidia lived, though lacking in several basic amenities, was relatively well established, and was far from squalid or overcrowded, as land sites were large enough to incorporate gardens used to grow crops and raise animals.

[9] Literally, 'co-mother', a widespread relationship of 'fictive kin' in Latin America. For example, I can become 'co-mother' to a woman by being godmother to her child at baptism. This forms a relationship of mutual obligation that lasts for life between the two adults concerned.

in the *barrio*, being from the same rural community, a few hours' journey by road from Sucre. The interview was therefore intended to complement women's accounts of giving birth, particularly of giving birth at home, by documenting the practices of a rural migrant midwife in the same urban context.

Doña Lidia, the *partera*, was a monolingual Quechua speaker from a rural community in North Potosí Department. She had lived in Sucre for about five years, was about 40 years old, and was a grandmother, as well as having a three-year-old child of her own. Mary Aguilar conducted the first part of the interview entirely in Quechua, with occasional interjections and pleas for explanation from myself. Just when the interview with Doña Lidia was drawing to a close, her two teenage daughters came panting in after racing each other up the hill, returning from school. It turned out that one of them was pregnant with her second child, and I started talking to her about this in Spanish, so there followed a second part to the interview, where this daughter talked in particular about her experience of pregnancy and about the family's attitude to the mother practising as a *partera*. The passage reproduced at Extract 1 occurred quite soon into this second part of the interview.

In order to make sense of the pattern of turn-taking and of interruptions in Extract 1, it will help to bear in mind that I myself (B) did not understand much of the Quechua being spoken at the time, and the *partera* (P) did not understand much of the Spanish. The daughter (H) is clearly bilingual between Spanish and Quechua, though she only speaks to us in Spanish in this passage, and her Spanish is highly Quechua-inflected. Mary (M) is also bilingual between Spanish and Quechua, but she speaks only in Quechua here, apart from one question to the daughter in Spanish (3403), and her Quechua includes many Spanish roots. What is going on initially in this passage, therefore, has a lot to do with the linguistic competences of the participants, with translation, and with misunderstanding leading to repair and understanding. (For Mary, the latter came at the time; for me, weeks later, after working on the transcription and translation of the tape with a bilingual, native speaker of Quechua, Jacinta Andrade.) Because this rather complex 'conversation' implies the whole social structure of the encounter between the four of us, including the history and presence of colonial relationships, it is important briefly to analyse it *as* conversation,[10] before going on to look at its content, both as discourse and description.

At the start of this double conversation, I am questioning the daughter in Spanish about her mother's practices, while Mary picks up points from what the daughter is saying and tries to relay them to the *partera* in Quechua. The

---

[10] I do not claim to be doing formal 'conversation analysis' here in the tradition of Harvey Sacks, though I acknowledge the inspiration of this tradition relayed to me by my colleague, Brian Torode.

first two times that Mary does this (3305, 3309), the questions are responded to in Spanish by the daughter. However, before the daughter gets far with her second turn (3310), the *partera* interrupts her, picking up on the Spanish word *venas* (veins) she has heard her use and taking it over into Quechua (3311). Her intervention takes the form of a performative 'lesson' for us, rather than a simple, conversational 'reply'. Shortly into her turn, Mary realises that the midwife is talking at cross-purposes, nevertheless she does not interrupt her flow, but listens, and repairs the misunderstanding on our behalf (in Quechua) at 3314. Quechua discourse dominates while Doña Lidia holds forth, but fails to generate conversation. Mary's evaluative comment at 3318 aligns us clearly with our hosts, and is crucial in generating the angry denunciations that follow. But despite the fact that her comment is made in Quechua, and does generate the *partera*'s outburst at 3320, the daughter drowns out her mother and returns the conversation to Spanish (3319–3408).

'She knows in the hand': the partera's skills

Moving on to look at the content of the passage: during the first few turns of the extract the daughter answers my question about the signs of pregnancy by answering that her mother knows by looking at or 'in' the hand (3301–7). Both Mary (3305) and myself (3308) show interest in whether this means that the midwife uses the pulse in assessing pregnancy. Mary then asks the *partera* to explain how she uses the hand (3309). Her daughter replies on her mother's behalf, saying that she knows from the veins (3310), still referring to determining pregnancy. The Spanish word *venas* is then taken up in Quechua by Doña Lidia at 3311, in a very rich and performative description of the appearance of the veins just before the actual birth (3311–5). It is not immediately apparent to Mary as listener/understander that the *partera* is not talking about the pulse in *pregnancy*, but Mary's interjection at 3314 registers her own realisation of the new sense.[11]

Doña Lidia can tell that the woman is about to give birth, both by the appearance, seemingly, of little split veins in the hands (3311), and also by the feel of the pulse on the wrist (3313). The midwife 'performs' for us first an apparent irregularity of the pulse, as it races (the onomatopoeic 'chikarababum'), 'sighs' ('samamun'), and appears to stop ('taqq!'). She then herself pauses, dramatically representing the apparent halt in the blood flow, before launching into a half-sung representation of the 'heat'

---

[11] The words *onquy* and *onqukuy* in Quechua reproduce all of the ambiguities of the words *enfermar* and *enfermarse* in Spanish. Both sets of words mean literally to 'be ill' and to 'become ill', and are used fairly interchangeably to indicate pregnancy and giving birth. They are words from the popular vernacular, however, and there is an apocryphal story of a nursing student being failed an oral for using the word *enfermarse* instead of the 'correct' term for pregnancy, so neatly reversing the critique current in English-speaking feminist circles of the 'medicalisation' of pregnancy and birth.

of her remedy coming through, followed by her sonic imitation of the quicker, steady beat of the pulse just before birth ('hoohh, hoohh, hoohh . . .'). Modern midwifery texts, also, describe a physiological process of raising of the temperature and the pulse just before birth (Silverton 1993: 300). Humoral theory, of course, sees the 'hot' remedy as having aided the body in achieving this 'warmth', which it was otherwise in danger of losing.

'In goes their hand!': opposing doctors' practices

It is immediately following this rather beautiful and benign description of the process of birth, with the midwife using her expert knowledge to reassure the woman and give her confidence (3315) that the interviewer, Mary, makes a qualitative comment on what has just been said (3318). She expresses approval and compares the midwife's practice favourably with that which she knows well from hospital – repeated vaginal examinations during the process of labour. In so aligning herself, she makes explicit our position of genuine interest in the midwife's practice. As a professional nurse, she is clearly excited by the possibility of non-invasive practices taking the place of the manual penetration[12] that can be so traumatic to women giving birth (Bradby 1998a).

However, Mary's comment also serves as an invitation to Doña Lidia and her daughter to align themselves with us against hospital practice. This they both do extremely forcefully, the daughter by contrasting the 'looking' (mirar) that her mother does, with 'having oneself looked at' (hacerse mirar), and with 'sticking their hands up'[13] (meter mano), which they do in hospital. Her exclaimed, 'They don't look! Not one minute do they look', implies not only that in hospital they do not know how to perform the delicate assessment of the veins and the pulse that her mother does, but also that they are too rushed to have the patience. This assessment by the daughter comes as a forceful interjection while Mary is still speaking, immediately she mentions the word 'hand' (makin) in association with hospital personnel, and before she has even pronounced sat'isanku, a forceful Quechua expression that is used for stuffing a hole or a sausage, for raping a woman, and for anal sex between men (Perroud and Chouvenc 1970). Her mother's angry outburst, 'In goes their hand! Huh!' (3320), occurs after Mary has pronounced this latter word, and interrupts and reinforces her daughter's response.

The subsequent turns by the daughter provide invaluable insight into how the official, public health campaign known as the captación de embarazadas ('securing of pregnant women')[14] is experienced by those who are its targets

---

[12] This is my own phrase, which tries to capture the sexual connotations of the words used in both Quechua and Spanish, and the accompanying sentiments in their use.

[13] The phrase meter mano in Spanish has the sexual connotations of the word 'interfere' in English, as well as the literal sense of 'inserting' the hand.

[14] This campaign, and the effect of 'targets', are explored further in Bradby 1999.

(3402–8). The nurse in the medical post tells her firmly that she is 'in the control', i.e. that her name is registered as a pregnant woman requiring ante-natal check-ups. But for the young woman, going 'there' (implying now the 'hospital' mentioned in Mary's question at 3403) signifies possible death, and certain violation by the process of *meter mano* ('sticking their hands up').

Her emphatic, rhetorical 'why?' (*¿para qué?* – literally, 'for what?', 'to what purpose?') needs listening to, rather than answering, by those who promote such programmes.

Humoral theory, 'old science' and midwifery
In Extract 1, then, we see both the legacy of humoral theory, and its cross-cutting with an 'us–them' ethnic and cultural division. Humoral theory sees the woman's body as at risk from 'cold' during birth, since the body must be in a 'hot' state in order to accomplish the birth. 'Cold' is also caused by loss of blood during the birth process (Foster 1994: 39, 66–67, 70–72). Consistent with this, the *partera* describes the remedy she gives as 'heat' coursing through the veins. Its basis is a sweet, herbal tea of orange-flower (*flor de azahar*, widespread as a drink in labour), heated with wine and *singani*[15] and with egg added. This recipe is similar to that used by Doña Lidia for the poultices she uses on the woman during pregnancy, as part of the process of massage which 'straightens out' the baby and puts it into the correct position. In exploring the text of the *partera*'s testimony further, we find once again that the details of her process are represented through their difference from hospital practices. The description in Extract 2 is preceded by her emphatic statement that, unlike what they do in hospital, she does *not* operate, nor does she 'put her hand inside':

Extract 2

P	Wañusqastapis ma iskapachikunichu. Uspitalmantaqaa [2] upirankuqa a i?	P	Even with a dead child, I don't run away. In hospital [2] they operate for that, don't they?
M	Arí a	M	Yes
P	Nuqá <u>mana</u> upirachí- nitaq makisniywanpis yachanichu jaywaykuyta a, nallani:: [.] qhaqullani,	P	I do <u>not</u> operat- nor would I put my hand inside, you see, that's all I do [.] I do my massage,
	laq'ani runtuwan nnn nawan:::,		I smear on a poultice of egg with ehh,

[15] *Singani* is a white grape liquor, produced in Bolivia, and a favourite national drink of the urban elites. Bolivians on the project team, familiar with its consumption in such settings, expressed scepticism at this *partera*'s naming of *singani* in her recipes. However, Susanna Rance has clarified to me that there are several classes of *singani* sold on market stalls, ranging from cheap varieties sold in large plastic flagons to finer bottled ones (personal communication).

pilirjitawan kutarquspa   with parsley, ground up,
chanta sinkaniwan ch'aqchuykuspa,   then sprinkled with singani,
chán tiliyani   with that I do my cloth-massage
chayllamanta   and that's how
cheqanman churani   I put the baby straight,
uman kaysitupichá, arí?   its little head just here, you see?

Doña Lidia went on to describe how she feels for the baby's head, face and feet, massaging through the poultice, in the process known as *tiliay*. (Neither Mary nor any of the other researchers on the project team were familiar with this word.) After some puzzled questioning, Mary ascertained that the word is derived from the Spanish *tela*, the 'cloth' in question being made from sheep or goatskin. (Hence *tiliay* is here translated as 'cloth-massage'.) In a second description, Doña Lidia said that she sprinkles sugar and *singani* on the goatskin. So we have egg, ground parsley, alcohol and sugar as the ingredients. Later on again (see Extract 3), the midwife describes how she uses her hands to work the baby gradually into position through the poultice, using metaphors that invoke using the hands to scrape earth together into a little pile or mound:[16]

Extract 3

P   Laq'ani runtuwan,   P   I smear on a poultice of egg, and
    chayrayku a   through this, you see,
    asukarkunasmanta qhaqoni,   and with sugar,
    cheqanman churani wisanman, a i,   I straighten the baby out in her
                                        belly, you see,

    kaymanta kashtumanta   From here, and from over here,
    tantaspa ajinamanta,   like pulling something together
                                        into a pile,

    ajinamanta churani kastuman   I put it into position just here, as if
    thawispa laq'ani a.   I were scratching the earth, I smear
                                        it on.

I cannot resist putting Doña Lidia's recipes alongside that of the famous seventeenth-century French midwife Louise Bourgeois, who here describes how she treated a woman who had fallen, lost blood and threatened miscarriage:

I made her take the germs of seven or eight eggs in a fresh egg, with red cramoisie silk, cut up small, about sixty grains, then I had a poultice made for her of white cypress, marjoram and rosemary, as much of one as of the other, pounded on a hot scoop, sprinkled with warm wine, put between two linen cloths on the abdomen above the navel, and had it reheated two or three times

---

[16] The Quechua *tantay* is a very general word meaning to collect something together, while *thawiy* is used for scratching the earth, both of chickens, as they scratch for food, and of people, when they look for root crops left over after the harvest.

a day. I can assure you that she bore her child two months later, this being the full nine months. (Quoted in Gélis 1991: 221)

Pregnancy is seen in humoral theory as a hot state, so that is appropriate to bathe, and take cold foods. Loss of blood, however, as in menstruation or the period after birth, puts the body into a cold state, which therefore has to be warmed – in this case in order to return it to its proper balance during pregnancy, preparing for the great heat of birth. Marjoram in its related form of oregano, and rosemary (both 'hot' herbs) are extensively used in present-day Bolivia, oregano for providing heat in labour, and rosemary for bathing after birth, when cold is a great danger as blood is again being lost.[17] Doña Lidia uses goat or sheepskin to prepare her 'cloth',[18] while in pre-modern Europe dogskin or 'other skin suitable for making gloves' was used to apply a 'pregnancy girdle' (Gélis 1991: 180). Historical descriptions of the preparation of these skin girdles are very reminiscent of the processes described to us in Sucre both by Doña Lidia and by other women.[19]

The similarities between Doña Lidia's practices and pre-modern European ones extend beyond humoral theory. This is a difficult area, because similarity does not necessarily imply a process of diffusion. At a certain level of generality, some of the practices of midwifery described by Doña Lidia are found much more widely than in Europe and Latin America. For instance, her massage techniques have continuities with traditional European midwifery and with the practice of 'external version' in obstetrics. These techniques were widely used by both midwives and obstetricians in Europe to 'turn' abnormal presentations during pregnancy or before birth, though they are skills that have largely been lost with the rise of the caesarean section.[20] However, a reading of Jacqueline Vincent-Priya's 'conversations

[17] The presence of parsley in Doña Lidia's recipe is unexplained here, as it is more often classified as a 'cool' herb than a 'hot' one (Foster 1994: 211), and the other ingredients, including alcohol and sugar, are unambiguously 'hot'. Note that the 'remedy' or 'medicine' (jampi) that she refers to in Extract 1 (turn 3313) as the 'heat' coming through the veins does not contain parsley.

[18] It would be tempting to see here a connection with the importance of cloth in Andean culture. However, no such connection was made by any of the women who talked of the tiliay process in Sucre, and the use of the Spanish word, tela, would in any case point away from such a connection.

[19] Gélis describes the following process: 'The skin had to be carefully prepared. At the beginning of the seventeenth century, the obstetrician Jacques Guillemeau advised "washing it several times in ordinary water, then in rose-water" and drying it in the shade for two or three days, then softening it by soaking it in the "oils and greases" from St. John's wort or sweet almonds, or in a white-rose unguent, fresh butter, or spermaceti; finally it should be taken out and dried in the fresh air. Then "it can be cut to the size and shape of the belly"' (Gélis 1991: 80). Gélis also describes a post-partum poultice, applied under the bandage (that was normal until recently after birth), consisting of 'tow, moistened with two egg-whites, with cloves and pepper' the idea being, according to Gélis, that the womb would be enticed into its proper place by this 'spicy bait' (1991: 180).

[20] But see Silverton (1993: 385–86) for contemporary debates on 'turning' a breech baby in this way.

with traditional midwives' in Thailand, Indonesia and Malaysia (1991) shows that all of the midwives interviewed in those countries, too, placed a very similar emphasis on the importance of massaging to bring the baby into the correct position for birth.[21] Just like Doña Lidia, it is their massage that they mention first when asked how they attend a birth, and just like her, they see difficulties in birth as arising from an incorrect positioning, which they can correct if the woman comes to them in time.

Similarly, binding the abdomen after birth is a tradition that has been located as far back as Athens in the eighth century BC (Carter and Duriez 1986: 59), and was still practised in England when my own mother was giving birth in the 1940s and 1950s. Doña Lidia ties up the woman's woven belt (faja) immediately the baby has been born and before the birth of the placenta. In many of the south-east Asian areas visited by Vincent-Priya, binding was also practised, though one group of hill-dwellers laughed at it as a 'town' practice, not needed by healthy, rural women (1991: 133). Laderman (1987) writes that in Malaysia, ashes are placed under the sash, and reports a complex of 'warming' practices in the post-partum period that have been labelled 'mother roasting', a phrase which closely parallels the 'suffocation method' for which traditional midwives in Europe were criticised (Gélis 1991: 97). This heating of the mother after birth is still practised in some areas of Bolivia, and involves both thermal warming – keeping her in bed with large numbers of blankets and stopping all doors and windows – and symbolic warming with the requisite food and herbs.

As regards birth positions, Doña Lidia says that she makes the woman kneel, 'sitting like a saint'. Kneeling, squatting, and 'on all fours' are of course the commonest birth positions the world over, and Europe has no special claim on them. Doña Lidia herself sits behind the woman and massages her, 'holding onto her from behind', while she places the woman's husband, if present, in front of her, supporting her. Doña Celestina, who had been attended by Doña Lidia, described herself as sitting on the bed, leaning back against the midwife who was sitting behind her and massaging her. This latter position is the same as that described by Gélis as the commonest in seventeenth- and eighteenth-century France, where the woman 'sat on the lap of another woman who held her arms or the upper part of her body. In remoter places and isolated farms, it would often be the husband who held his wife still' (Gélis 1991: 128). In Thailand and Indonesia, virtually all the midwives say that they hold the woman from behind and massage her stomach, usually while she kneels, again sounding very like Doña Lidia's description.

---

[21] The similarities between the discourses of these south-east Asian midwives and that of the Andean parteras would seem to be prima facie evidence against a diffusionist hypothesis. Yet Foster mentions Malaysia, Thailand and Indonesia as having been subject to the diffusion of humoral ideas, both from the Chinese tradition, and from the Muslim influence, carrying the Greek tradition (1994: 12). This raises the intriguing possibility that midwifery techniques are also the result of diffusion through these traditions.

Other practices seem to be more limited to Europe and Latin America. In Europe, as in present-day Bolivia, there was a great fear that the womb/placenta would move up through the body after birth and choke the mother, and the commonest remedy for this was to tie the umbilical cord to the woman's thigh (Gélis 1991: 163). This practice is still widespread in certain areas of Bolivia, where the cord is tied to the woman's big toe with a thread 'spun to the left' (see below). In cases where the placenta was long delayed, Doña Lidia said she would put the handle of a little tin spoon on the woman's tongue to help her expel the placenta, again a very common practice in Europe, allied with making the woman sneeze or vomit in order to encourage downward, expulsive movements.

Another great fear in Europe was that haemorrhage would take away the mother after birth, and for that reason she was kept awake by her companions for several hours after the birth, or even, according to Louise Bourgeois, for as long as her 'cleansings' flowed (Gélis 1991: 181). This practice is still seen as very important in the several areas of Bolivia where this project worked, and is widely observed in the hours after birth. As Gélis puts it, 'there was a horrid fascination with the idea of death stealing up on the sleeping woman' (1991: 181), so capturing the ambiguity between spiritual explanations and physical ones that was also found in the rural parts of the Bolivian study (Arancibia 1995).

The process known as *manteo*, involving rolling the pregnant or labouring woman from side to side in a blanket, is another staple of Andean birth practices, and it has survived migration into the towns; but it also has resonances with the 'sack-man' who was called in to shake the woman in cases of slow labour in nineteenth-century France (Gélis 1991: 144), and with the nursery rhyme, 'There was an old woman tossed up in a blanket' (Opie and Opie 1951: 434). Doña Lidia likes to take her husband, who is also a healer, along with her to help with the *manteo* before a birth.

Overall, a great many of Doña Lidia's practices have some continuity with ones known and used in Europe, and her theorising around 'heat' and 'cold', as well as around the placenta, and the womb after birth, is also very resonant of European thought. The fact that she cites herbs and recipes of European origin does tend to suggest that her knowledge incorporates much that was brought by the Spanish to Latin America, although it is probable that at a general level, techniques such as massage for 'straightening' the baby are older than this. Possible exceptions are considered in the next section of this paper. Some of Doña Lidia's less physiological interventions, also, such as blowing alcohol from her mouth over the woman's head, or her assertion that she does not look at the blood shed by the woman, which relates to the fear that looking at this blood leads to blindness, have no European relatives that I know of. Doña Lidia also claims that the soul of a baby that was born dead is pursuing her and causing her to 'go mad' when she drinks the ritual offerings of alcohol made to her by the family at a birth. While this recalls Andean beliefs about the soul and the place of alcohol, her daughter's retort that she only attends births as an excuse to get drunk plunges us straight back into the accusations made about drunken midwives in Europe.

Humoral and cultural oppositions

Doña Lidia's knowledge, though based in empirically tested practice and technique, is made systematic by its underpinning in humoral theory. As well as the 'hot–cold' axis already analysed, the concept of the 'dry' birth is crucial in her thinking around difficult births. This 'wet–dry' axis[22] has a clear correlation with ideas about the circulation of the blood from which fertility is thought to derive (Arnold 1999: 48; Arnold and Yapita 1996). Doña Lidia argues that young women – 'those with lots of blood' – have short pregnancies and easier births, and she contrasts them with 'those who have dry births': as a woman gets older, she has less blood, her pregnancies get longer and her births more difficult. Yet while these axes and conceptual oppositions certainly help to understand Doña Lidia's practice and thinking, the *social* oppositions between 'us' and 'them', and the emotions generated, leave a much stronger impression of what is really at stake in her discourse. Indeed, Doña Lidia's whole presentation of her practice to us in the interview can be seen as an attempt to defend the way she does things against what they do in hospital. One senses that this is the way she must probably present herself to anyone nowadays, including to other women from the countryside, who are under a lot of pressure from the medical authorities to go to hospital to give birth.

The local knowledge which, in a sense, 'speaks through' Doña Lidia, incorporates past medical knowledge in a process which aids in discursively creating a sense of identity, where the speakers align with each other through identifying with the *partera*'s practices and opposing current medical ones. The double conversation reproduced in Extract 1 shows this cultural division in multiple ways. The passage itself divides neatly into two, between a first section focusing on the *partera*'s skills, and a second section condemning medical practices. In the two sections, opposing meanings are given to the words 'hand' and 'look'. When the talk is of the *partera*, the hand is the pregnant woman's hand, a sign and source of knowledge for the midwife; when the reference is to doctors and nurses, the hand is primarily a male hand, invading the woman's body in an act of repeated, symbolic rape. The *partera*'s 'look', again, is the means of her knowing the woman's body – indeed is used interchangeably with the word 'know' by the daughter – and is linked to her *feeling* that body and its changes through the pulse. The doctors 'don't look' in this sense; instead, they 'look' at women in the intrusive, sexualised way which disturbs women the world over (Bradby 1998a).

[22] This finding appears to contradict all that has been said about the non-existence in Latin America of the 'wet–dry' distinction of European humoral theory, and which has been used to discredit the theory of European origins (see Foster 1994: 181–84).

Mary's evaluative comment (3318) is the axis that introduces the new sense of 'hand' and provokes the change in theme. Her use of the word 'look' as an exhortation introducing her comment perhaps also encourages its emergence as a key word in the second half of the passage.

As discourse, then, the conversation creates meaning and identity through its use of these mainly binary, opposing meanings. There is an implicit opposition between 'what *they* do' (with their hands, with their looking) and 'what I/she does' (with her hands/the woman's hand, and her knowing-looking). But if the identity of 'they' is very clearly articulated as the doctors and nurses of hospitals and medical centres, the identity of 'I/we/she', is much less clear cut. The next section explores who 'we' may be, again starting from the *partera*'s discourse.

'But that's in the countryside': locating the *partera*

Extract 4

M   *Narí* chaymantá, imawan khuchunki naa, chay tripitan?

M   *And then*, with what do you cut ehh, the cord ?

P   nn Kaypiqa [.] kuchilluwan khuchuchiwan, khuchunku paykuna.

P   ehh Here [.] with a knife I make them cut it, they cut it themselves.

M   aa Paykuna khuchunku ma qanchu// khuchunki?

M   Ah, they cut it, but you yourself don't// cut it?

P   //Má, má khuchuni, noqa j'apiysani piru a.

P   //No, I don't cut it, I'm holding the baby, you see.

M   Aa qan j'apiysanki wawata [.] aaa//

M   Ah, you're holding the baby [.] aah//

P   //Wakin, ñaupaqa kay campuykupeqa [.] k'anallitawan khuchuyku noqaykuqa, kay jina::, //kay jina manka kay, p'akisqueta, i?

P   //Others, before now in our countryside [.] with a sherd of toasting pot we cut it. That's li::ke, // that's like a pot that, broken in pieces, no?

M   //aa aa [.] Ari

M   //Ah ah [.] Yes

P   Chaysitutawan khuchuyku, lloq'e q'aytuwantaq watayku [.] kampupi chayqa.

P   Just with that we cut it, and with a thread spun to the left we tied it [.] That's in the countryside.

M   Lloq'e:: q'aytituwan?

M   With a wool thread, spun to the left?

P   Arí, chayta, chayta lloq'eladu chakinman watayku,

P   Yes, that, that we tied to the left foot,

chay ratu lloqsirqamun parisninqa i?   and right then the placenta came
                                             out, no?

The Quechua language has the peculiarity of having two grammatical forms of the first person plural 'we': one that *includes* the 'you' being addressed, and the other that *excludes* 'you' and differentiates 'us'. The above passage is the only one in the interview where Doña Lidia uses the 'exclusive' form of the first person plural (marked by the suffix *yku*). So here she is clearly differentiating what 'we' do, not only from what 'they' do (in hospital), but also from what 'you', i.e. Mary and I, would do. However, this potential alignment with an 'Andean' rural identity is far from simple, since the *partera* distances herself from it in three ways: firstly, by locating it in the past (I have translated *ñaupaq* as 'before now' but it also means 'long ago'), and secondly, by distinguishing the practice here described from her own current practice (of using a knife). Finally, lest there should be any ambiguity, she emphasises again that 'that's in the *countryside*'. If this describes Andean identity, then the *partera* has already left it.

Now it is possible, and likely, that the characteristics of the potsherd used in the rural areas indicate that this represents the continuation of a pre-Hispanic practice, and Doña Lidia perhaps demonstrates her awareness of its difference from others that she uses, through her location of it in the past. The use of the sherd is also continually brought up by townspeople as an example of a quaint, or backward, rural custom. Townspeople and medical personnel showed no awareness, however, that the toaster is a specially fired clay pot, capable of withstanding the high temperatures required to toast and 'pop' corn, so that when freshly broken it is not only very sharp, but also sterile. The fact that Doña Lidia and so many other midwives have now abandoned the use of the sherd is probably due to the effectiveness of the medical campaigns to train *parteras* in what is arrogantly denominated 'clean birth'. These have focused a great deal on persuading *parteras* to give up the sherd (considered 'dirty') and use scissors instead, enshrined symbolically in the 'gift' of an internationally standard kit containing scissors as the mark of having completed the training course.[23]

Similarly, the use of a woollen thread 'spun to the left' resonates with Andean practices around llamas, wool and spinning, and so may represent an 'old' practice; but the *partera* again differentiates her present self from what 'we' do, or did,[24] in the countryside. On one level, this may simply represent the absence in the town of the raw materials and economic system of

[23] A similar process has occurred in Indonesia, where local midwives (*bidan*) are no longer allowed to cut the umbilical cord, 'because they do not have the right instruments'. The traditional method involved using turmeric and a freshly cut piece of bamboo, both of these having antiseptic qualities (Vincent-Priya 1991: 11–12).

[24] Most of the verbs in Extract 4 are in the tense which is both 'present' and 'near past' in Quechua. 'We cut', in English, captures this ambiguity. However, there is a clear preterite tense at *lloqsirqamun* ('it came out') and the prefacing by *ñaupaq* also suggests a past tense.

the countryside, where there is corn to be toasted, clay for pots, and wool for spinning. On another, it undoubtedly reflects social changes implied in the transition from countryside to town. Indeed, the whole passage quoted in Extract 4 reflects the multiple ambiguities of Doña Lidia's position as a Quechua-speaking, rural midwife, practising in the town under the indirect surveillance of the medical authorities.[25] Nevertheless, even if Doña Lidia has by now taken a step away from the countryside, her discourse implies no disapproval of rural customs. On the contrary, there is a strong sense of allegiance created by the use of the exclusive 'we'. Coupled with the sense of difference and opposition to hospital practices that is expressed throughout the interview, we can perhaps see the passage as incipiently nostalgic rather than rejecting of rural ways.

We then have to ask how widely this 'we' can be extended. This study in Sucre was part of a project that worked in various different areas of the Bolivian highlands, so that it is possible to compare Doña Lidia's thought and practice with those of other, rural midwives. While, in general, much of the philosophy is shared – the psychological approach to supporting women in labour, the physiological approach to 'straightening' the baby, the humoral system of classifying bodily states and herbs – there are details of midwives' practice that differ across different regions. Doña Lidia was the only midwife, for instance, to describe the practice of *tiliay*, and, in all the rural areas, different local herbs were used in childbirth. As regards Doña Lidia's practices around the birth of the placenta – putting the mother to bed and tying the cord to her toe – these were widely known around the region of Sucre and North Potosí, but were quite different from those followed in the community of Inka Katurrapi, in the Department of La Paz. There, an elderly midwife preferred to maintain the mother in the (upright) position in which she had given birth to the baby for the delivery of the placenta (Arnold, Yapita et al. 1995). The 'all-fours' position was also more frequently used than in the Sucre area, and the cord was often not cut until the placenta had been delivered.

These and other regional differences suggest that we cannot assume that Doña Lidia, or the *parteras* of North Potosí, can somehow stand in for a whole such as the Andes. The implication of both Foster's work, and that of his respondents, has been that one can generalise about large unities such as 'the Old World, 'America', or 'the Andes'. Such huge divisions may be useful polemical devices – for both sides in the debate – and there may even be elements in *parteras*' discursive presentation of their practices that encourage a mapping onto such a world theory. However, this paper opens up these unities to questioning, particularly the oft-postulated unity of 'Andean knowledge', both as something unvarying across localities, and as something static and unchanging in time.

---

[25] For reasons of space it has not been possible to describe in detail Doña Lidia's conflict with the nurse in the medical post, which was a topic in the original version of this paper, presented at the *Watanakuy* conference in Cambridge in 1996.

Conclusion: the future of Andean midwifery

This article has dwelt a great deal on the antecedents of Doña Lidia's theory and practice, in part in order to show that her knowledge is not 'traditional' in the sense of representing an unchanging body of Andean tradition; nor is it 'local', if that means that it is entirely rooted in one locality, whether that be Sucre, rural Potosí, or 'the Andes'. On the contrary, the exploration of her knowledge and practices provides ample evidence of the sort of criss-crossing process of knowledge formation in development contexts that is theorised in *Battlefields of Knowledge* (Long and Long [eds.] 1992). As such, her knowledge emerges as both more global and more local than might have been assumed from the generalising heading of 'Andean midwifery'. On the one hand, we have to admit the possibility that much of the theory and practice inherited by Doña Lidia was absorbed from Spanish medicine during the colonial period; on the other, there is evidence that rural midwives from elsewhere in Bolivia have not adopted all of these practices, so that her knowledge is 'local' within Bolivia also. Furthermore, her own practice is changing as her own location has changed: with the move from a rural to an urban area, she no longer uses the sherd to cut the cord, nor regularly ties the umbilical cord to the woman's toe.

But what of the future of her knowledge and practice? Doña Lidia had learned midwifery by accompanying her own mother, who, in turn, had visited a religious site far in the mountains, 'full of authentic *parteros*'.[26] Her own daughter had no wish to take over her mother's trade. As Doña Lidia put it: 'She doesn't understand any of this'; and when Mary asked 'Why not?' the answer came, 'She is studying', formal schooling self-evidently ruling out the idea of being a *partera*. Moreover, the daughter herself, despite her horror of hospital birth, and despite having been attended by her mother for her first birth, was now opposed to her mother continuing to practise in the neighbourhood. This was mainly because of an episode in which the nurse in the medical centre had censured Doña Lidia. A baby had been born dead, according to Doña Lidia and her daughter, because of marital violence during the pregnancy. However, the nurse in the medical post had blamed the death on Doña Lidia, and accused her, in perfect symmetry with her own accusations against the doctors, of 'putting her hand up'. This censure from the medical post had added to the distress Doña Lidia already felt from the episode and the potential threat posed to her by the dead baby's soul. But it had also made her own husband and daughters discourage her from practising, not because they were afraid of

[26] The masculine ending of the Spanish word was used here by Doña Lidia, but would of course include male and female *parteros/parteras*. However, it is significant that she uses the masculine, or inclusive, gender ending here, since male *parteros* generally travel greater distances than female *parteras*. They seem also to be more involved with the spiritual side of healing than women are, which makes sense in the context of pilgrimage to the sacred site mentioned by Doña Lidia.

childbirth or her role in it, but because they were afraid of the medical authorities.

The language politics raised by our 'double conversation' that day in Sucre have already been noted. A little later in the conversation Mary and I suggested to Doña Lidia that we might organise a meeting with other *parteras* in the area, as had been done successfully by the project in La Paz, and asked her if she would like to attend. Her daughter replied, in Quechua, on her behalf, saying, 'She can't speak! She only speaks Quechua.' Together with her mother's assertion that 'studying' (in school) meant that her daughter would not become a *partera*, we have another clear discursive alignment of cultural difference: school education implies the Spanish language, hospital birth, and ability to speak in the public sphere; learning to be a *partera* through a long apprenticeship goes along with the Quechua language, traditional birth, and silent inarticulacy. While it is particularly sad to see these alignments being used in a self-denigratory way by participants in the culture, we can also note how the daughter has resisted the second term in the alignment and rejected hospital birth, or how *parteras* elsewhere have compromised with the medical authorities, taken their short training courses, and now practise under their surveillance. If approached in the right way, Doña Lidia will no doubt do the same. In this way, she and other *parteras* will carry on their long tradition of cherry-picking medical practices that fit their conceptual system, and rejecting those that do not. And Doña Lidia can continue, with more medical legitimacy, to rescue women from the threat of hospital birth:

Extract 5

P   'Uspitalpi upiraykuwanku,

    "Upiraykusqayki," niwanku,' nin.

    Entons, 'Orqhomuy a,
    noqa imanasaqpicha,' nini a.

    Orqhomuwanku,
    qhaqospa unquchini noqa kaypi.

P   'In the hospital they're going to operate on me,
    "We're going to operate on you,"
    they're telling me,' she says.
    So, 'Get her out of there, then!
    I will know what to do,' I say, you see.
    They go and get her out of there,
    and I, massaging her, make her give birth here.

Mindful of Ulf Hannerz's warning (1996: 58) that the right to cultural diversity must not be interpreted as a duty, I am also mindful of my own conclusion that *despite* coercion and heavy persuasion from the authorities, migrant women who go to hospital to give birth in Sucre on the whole do so voluntarily (Bradby 1999: 289). If, at times, the suppression of Doña Lidia's practice by the medical post has seemed to me like an advancing 'iron cage' of not-so-rational Western thought, I take heart from her own courage and example in the face of the power exercised over her, and from the many ways in which migrant women are managing to combine customary practices with hospital birth. These women deserve support from development agencies, as they struggle for such basic rights as upright birth positions, herbal teas, warmth – both thermal and symbolic[27] – and the return of their placentas.[28]

I have argued that the historical process of cultural assimilation of 'old science' at a popular level is cross-cut by the process of the use of cultural traits in ethnic and social differentiation. The historical model is of value in understanding processes of transmission still at work in the present context,[29] and for pointing up the injustice of the current medical power politics. Doctors blame midwives for things they do which actually reflect the medical orthodoxy of yesteryear. But my purpose is not only to make points about social identity and how knowledge is used by the unequal social actors involved. Through the rhetoric and the representations in *parteras'* accounts of their practices, there shines a powerful logic, and an insistence on beneficent practice in the interests of the woman giving birth which resonates with professional midwifery even in its late twenty-first-century, Northern predicament, and with the alternative birth movement. Difficult as this area is, both ethically and politically, it is time that NGOs and other development specialists paid the same sort of attention to local knowledge in childbirth and other fields of health as they do in the area of agriculture and the environment, and took a step back from their obedience to medically dominated health programmes that are justified, if at all, through the discourse of being for the woman's, or the country's, 'own good'.[30]

Acknowledgments

This paper is based on research carried out for the EU-sponsored project, 'Reducing maternal mortality in Bolivia: appropriate childbirth practices in the formal and informal sectors of perinatal care', financed under the STD3 programme of DGXII. I wish to express my gratitude to Doña Lidia, the local midwife who so generously shared her knowledge; to Mary Aguilar, my research assistant and interpreter during the interviewing; and to Jacinta

[27] Women's continual complaints about the terrible 'cold' of giving birth in hospital undoubtedly have thermal as well as symbolic dimensions (TAHIPAMU 1994); nevertheless, Arnold and Yapita have pointed out that metal is extremely 'cold' symbolically, so in part justifying the dread of the caesarean in humoral terms (Arnold, Yapita et al. 1995; Arnold and Yapita 1996).

[28] The importance of beliefs and rituals around the birth and burial of the placenta, and the trauma of their non-observance in hospital birth, are discussed in Bradby 1998b.

[29] An example would be the unlicensed use of ergometrine by local midwives and other people, which is a source of much anxiety to the official medical establishment.

[30] Cf. the title of Ehrenreich and English's book, *For Her Own Good: 150 Years of the Experts' Advice to Women* (1978).

Andrade, who worked with me on the transcription and translation of Doña Lidia's testimony. Thanks also to Rosaleen Howard and to Susanna Rance for their comments on drafts of this paper.

References

Alberti, G., and E. Mayer (eds.). 1974. *Reciprocidad e intercambio en los Andes peruanos.* Lima: Instituto de Estudios Peruanos.

Apffel-Marglin, Frédèrique. 1998. 'Introduction: Knowledge and Life Revisited'. In Apffel-Marglin with PRATEC (eds.): 1–50.

Apffel-Marglin, Frédèrique, and S. Marglin (eds). 1996. *Decolonizing Knowledge: From Development to Dialogue.* Oxford: Clarendon Press.

Apffel-Marglin, Frédèrique, with PRATEC (eds.). 1998. *The Spirit of Regeneration: Andean Culture Confronting Western Notions of Development.* London: Zed Books.

Arancibia, Balbina. 1995. 'Sajt'ay', paper and interview transcription presented to the meeting of the Childbirth Project, Sucre. March.

Arnold, Denise. 1999. 'Introducción'. In D. Arnold, J. Yapita and M. Tito (eds.), *Vocabulario aymara del parto y de la vida reproductiva de la mujer.* La Paz: ILCA (Instituto de Lengua y Cultura Aymara)/FHI (Family Health International).

Arnold, Denise, and J. Yapita. 1996. 'Los caminos del género en un ayllu andino: los saberes femeninos y los discursos textuales alternativos en los Andes'. In S. Rivera (ed.), *Ser mujer indígena, chola o birlocha en la Bolivia postcolonial de los años 90.* La Paz: Subsecretaría de Asuntos de Género y CID.

———, 1998. *Río de vellón, río de canto: cantar a los animales, una poética andina de la creación.* La Paz: Hisbol/ILCA.

Arnold, Denise, J. Yapita, M. Mamani, C. Apaza, M. Tito, M. Villena and Y. Payano. 1995. *Maternidad tradicional en el altiplano boliviano: las prácticas del parto en algunas comunidades aymaras.* La Paz: ILCA.

Austin Alchon, Suzanne. 1995. 'Tradiciones médicas nativas y resistencia en el Ecuador colonial'. In M. Cueto (ed.), *Saberes andinos: ciencia y tecnología en Bolivia, Ecuador y Peru.* Lima: Instituto de Estudios Peruanos.

Bastien, Joseph. 1989. 'Differences between Kallawaya-Andean and Greek-European Humoral Theory'. *Social Science and Medicine* 28: 45–51.

Begley, Cecily. 1990. 'A Comparison of the "Active" and "Physiological" Management of the Third Stage of Labour'. *Midwifery* 6(2): 60–72.

Berkes, Fikret (ed.). 1989. *Common Property Resources: Ecology and Community-Based Sustainable Development.* London: Belhaven Press.

Berkes, Fikret, C. Folke and J. Colding (eds.). 1998. *Linking Social and Ecological Systems: Management Practices and Social Mechanisms for Building Resilience.* Cambridge: Cambridge University Press.

Bolivia, INE (Instituto Nacional de Estadística). 1994. *Encuesta Nacional de Demografía y Salud, 1994.* La Paz: INE/Macro International.

Bolivia, SNS (Ministerio de Desarrollo Humano, Secretaría Nacional de Salud). 1994. *Plan Vida: Plan Nacional para la Reducción Acelerada de la Mortalidad Materna, Perinatal y del Niño, Bolivia 1994–7.* La Paz: FNUAP, USAID, UNICEF, OPS/OMS.

Bradby, Barbara. 1998a. 'Like a Video: The Sexualisation of Childbirth in Bolivia'. *Reproductive Health Matters* 6(12): 50–56.

———, 1998b. 'Community-Level Research within a Reproductive Health

Programme: From Participation to Dialogue'. In A. Hardon (ed.), *Beyond Rhetoric: Participatory Research on Reproductive Health*. Amsterdam: Het Spinhuis.

——, 1999. '"Will I Return or Not?": Migrant Women in Bolivia Negotiate Hospital Birth'. *Women's Studies International Forum* 22(3): 287–301.

Carter, Jenny, and T. Duriez. 1986. *With Child: Birth through the Ages*. Edinburgh: Mainstream Publishers.

Dankelman, Irene, and J. Davidson. 1988. *Women and Environment in the Third World: Alliance for the Future*. London: Earthscan.

Ehrenreich, Barbara, and D. English. 1978. *For Her Own Good: 150 Years of the Experts' Advice to Women*. London: Pluto Press.

Foster, George M. 1994. *Hippocrates' Latin American Legacy: Humoral Medicine in the New World*. Gordon and Breach Publishers.

Gélis, Jacques. 1991. *History of Childbirth: Fertility, Pregnancy and Birth in Early Modern Europe*. Cambridge: Polity Press.

Grattan, John, and C. Singer. 1956. *Anglo-Saxon Magic and Medicine: Illustrated Specifically from the Semi-Pagan Text 'Lacnunga'*. Wellcome Historical Medical Museum, New Series, No. 3. London: Oxford University Press.

Hannerz, Ulf. 1996. *Transnational Connections: Culture, People and Places*. London: Routledge.

Jiménez Sardon, Greta. 1998. 'The Aymara Couple in the Community'. In Apffel-Marglin with PRATEC (eds.): 146–71.

Laderman, Carol. 1987. 'Destructive Heat and Cooling Prayer: Malay Humoralism in Pregnancy, Birth and the Post-Partum Period'. *Social Science and Medicine* 25: 357–65.

Leavitt, Judith. 1986. *Brought to Bed: Childbearing in America 1750–1950*. Oxford: Oxford University Press.

Lehmann, David (ed). 1982. *Ecology and Exchange in the Andes*. Cambridge: Cambridge University Press.

Long, Norman, and A. Long (eds.). 1992. *Battlefields of Knowledge*. London: Routledge.

López Austin, Alfredo. 1988. *The Human Body and Ideology: Concepts of the Ancient Nahuas*. Salt Lake City: University of Utah Press.

Mayer, Enrique. 1994. 'Recursos naturales, medio ambiente, tecnología y desarrollo'. In O. Dancourt, E. Mayer and C. Monge (eds.), *Peru: El Problema Agrario en Debate*. Lima: Seminario Permanente de Investigación Agraria, Universidad Nacional de San Agustín y Centro de Apoyo y Promoción del Desarrollo Agrario.

O'Neil, J.D., and P.L. Kaufert. 1995. '*Irniktakpunga!k*: The Inuit Struggle for Birthing Rights in Northern Canada'. In F. Ginsburg and R. Rapp (eds.), *Conceiving the New World Order*. Berkeley and London: University of California Press.

Opie, Iona, and P. Opie. 1951. *The Oxford Dictionary of Nursery Rhymes*. London: Oxford University Press.

Perroud, Pedro C., and J.M. Chouvenc. 1970. *Diccionario castellano–kechwa, kechwa–castellano*. Santa Clara, Peru: Redemptorist Fathers.

Porter, Doug, B. Allen and G. Thompson. 1991. *Development in Practice: Paved with Good Intentions*. London and New York: Routledge.

Silverton, Louise. 1993. *The Art and Science of Midwifery*. London: Prentice Hall.

TAHIPAMU/Grupo de Solidaridad de El Alto. 1994. *Hagamos un nuevo trato*. La Paz: TAHIPAMU/GS.

Taylor, David R., and F. Mackenzie (eds.). 1991. *Development from Within: Survival in Rural Africa.* London: Routledge.

Tew, Marjorie. 1995. *Safer Childbirth? A Critical History of Maternity Care.* 2nd edn. London: Chapman and Hall.

Valladolid Rivera, Julio. 1998. 'Andean Peasant Agriculture: Nurturing a Diversity of Life in the *chacra*'. In Apffel-Marglin with PRATEC (eds.): 51–88.

Vincent-Priya, Jacqueline. 1991. *Birth Without Doctors: Conversations with Traditional Midwives.* London: Earthscan.

Wertz, Richard, and D. Wertz. 1989. *Lying-In: A History of Childbirth in America.* Expanded edn. New Haven: Yale University Press.

WHO/UNFPA/UNICEF. 1992. *Traditional Birth Attendants: A Joint Statement.* Geneva: World Health Organization.

CHAPTER NINE

Learning and Re-Learning How to Plant: The Impact of New Crops on the Spread and Control of New Agricultural Knowledge in the Ecuadorian Andes

Nicole Bourque

This chapter analyses the process of learning and the possession and distribution of agricultural knowledge in a context of economic and political change. This will be done by investigating the introduction of cash crops in Sucre, a peasant community[1] in the upper levels of the Patate River valley in the Central Ecuadorian Andes, where I carried out anthropological fieldwork in 1989–90 and 1996.

As Barbara Bradby indicates elsewhere in this volume, most of the literature on agricultural knowledge in the Andes has been written by people working on environmental sustainability and/or on agricultural development. This work has questioned the top-down model of earlier development work. It is concerned with examining the interaction between the belief systems and approaches to knowledge of local farmers and scientists in order to make development projects more effective and sustainable (see, for example, Bebbington 1990; Long and Long [eds.] 1992; de Boef et al. 1993; and Apffel-Marglin and Marglin [eds.] 1996). In spite of the emphasis these works place on the value on local knowledge, little attention is paid to the processes by which 'new' agricultural knowledge is evaluated, accepted or rejected in the absence of development workers. As we will see towards the end of this chapter, these processes have an effect on the acceptance or rejection of 'new' knowledge brought in by outsiders.

In contrast, researchers on ritual and religion in the Andes have long been concerned with the processes and politics of knowing. This includes looking at the social implications and dynamics of possessing, transmitting and gaining knowledge (see, for example, Allen 1988; Arnold 1990, 1992; Bastien 1978; Bouysse-Cassagne and Harris 1987; Harris 1986; Radcliffe 1990; Rasnake 1996). These studies reveal that in Andean cultures, knowl-

---

[1] The majority of the population in Sucre identify themselves as Indian. Only a few families identify themselves as *mestizo*.

edge and learning are shaped through people's interactions with the world around them – a world in which one can learn not only from other people, but from the mountains, streams, animals, saints and supernatural beings. Knowledge is embedded in the landscape and in the things created by people, such as houses, weavings and music.

Apffel-Marglin (1998), Vallodolid Rivera (1998) and Rengifo Vasquez (1998) echo this view, but reject the term 'knowledge' as a Western construct that implies a one-way, objectifying relationship between the knower and what is known. They argue that Andean Indians do not have 'knowledge' of the world around them. Rather, they have relationships of reciprocal nurturing which are made possible through conversations between people, mountains, plants, animals, celestial bodies and the elements. In this context, learning does not imply a hierarchical relationship between a teacher and a student. One peasant does not 'teach' another. Rather, people teach through showing and they learn by watching and doing.

The work of Apffel-Marglin (1998), Vallodolid Rivera (1998) and Rengifo Vasquez (1998) provides a valuable insight into Andean modes of thought and raises provocative questions about the nature of agricultural knowledge[2] and the process of learning in the Andes. However, their work is not very helpful in explaining the processes that occur when people begin to accept some Western economic values, agricultural technologies and notions of education.

In this account of agricultural change in Sucre, I will describe how and why cash crops replaced 'traditional' subsistence crops. It will be demonstrated that these changes in production must be understood in relation to changes in patterns of consumption and exchange. I will also consider the role that innovation played in the introduction of new crops and the conditions under which innovative ideas became widely adopted and adapted. This involves a process by which 'outside' knowledge is brought into the village and appropriated and adapted by the people of Sucre to become 'inside' knowledge. Throughout this discussion, I look at how 'knowledge' is bound up with social relationships and with the values, rights and obligations attached to those relationships.

New crops for old

In 1989, the major crop in Sucre was maize. Beans, wheat and lentils were also cultivated to a lesser extent. The annual cycle of planting and harvesting maize, which was closely related to the festival cycle, determined daily activities in the fields and houses. Maize planting began in July and August. Men with oxen ploughed the fields, while men women and children planted

---

[2] Even though I accept the criticisms offered by Apffel-Marglin (1998), Vallodolid Rivera (1998) and Rengifo Vasquez (1998), I will continue to use the term 'knowledge' in order to make my discussion less cumbersome.

the seed. Many households planted their fields with the help of labourers and oxen gained through various types of labour exchanges. During the celebrations of *Finados* (November 1), offerings were made to the souls of the dead to invite them to help the newly planted seed to rise from the ground. Food was also exchanged between households who had exchanged labour during the planting (Bourque 1995a, 1995b). December was dominated by weeding the young maize plants. Families who did not have sufficient maize in storage supplemented their diet with potatoes purchased in the city markets. The money for this came from the sale of small animals and handicrafts as well as from occasional labour on fruit haciendas in the valley bottom. By April, as the maize neared maturation and did not require much care, more men went to work on the valley haciendas. In May and June, fresh maize and beans were harvested. A portion of the maize and beans was set aside for sale. The rest was allowed to dry in the fields to be used for seed and food for the coming year. The feast of Corpus Christi coincided with the end of the harvest of dried maize and beans. During this festival, the Indians in the community thanked San Francisco for helping the maize grow and asked him to bless the seed for next year (Bourque 1994).

In 1989, there was very little variation in the crops that were planted or in the agricultural techniques that were used by households in Sucre. Indeed, agricultural techniques were rarely discussed. Exceptions to this were the occasions when young men were learning how to plough. The ability to plough is very much bound up with notions of masculinity and any failure to control the bulls or to plough in a straight line was greeted with laughter and teasing. Other techniques, such as using the hoe, planting, weeding and harvesting were learnt at a young age by watching, imitating and being corrected by adults. Through working in the fields, children did not only learn about how to care for plants, they also learned about the cultivation of relationships with household members, workers from outside the household and supernatural beings. Thus, learning how to work in the fields does not merely involve acquiring certain agricultural techniques, but also learning a way of life.

When I returned to Sucre in June 1996, maize no longer dominated the village fields. Instead, many fields had tree tomatoes (*tomate de arbol*).[3] Unlike maize, tree tomatoes are not cultivated according to an annual cycle. They take two to three years to mature, after which time fruit can be harvested every two weeks. Tree tomatoes require special care. They need fertiliser. They are also prone to disease and, therefore, need pesticides and fungicides on a regular basis. The introduction of new crops was not the only alteration; there were also changes in the cultivation of maize. Some farmers, seeing the effectiveness of fertiliser on tree tomatoes, began to use it on the maize and bean plants.

---

[3] Tree tomatoes are a subtropical fruit (sometimes known as *tomatillos*). They are quite popular in Ecuador. They are usually peeled and liquidised with a bit of sugar to make a juice.

I was surprised by these changes. In 1989, I had been told that Sucre, at 2800 m above sea level, was too cold for tree tomatoes. Moreover, people did not use chemical fertiliser. They claimed that fertiliser was expensive and burned the plants. In fact, maize was a popular crop precisely because it did not require fertiliser or pesticides. I had been told by a number of informants that years before maize became popular, potatoes had been the dominant crop in Sucre. However, potato yields gradually declined due to the spread of various diseases. These problems could have been overcome by the use of fertiliser and pesticide. However, people were reluctant to spend money and time on this solution. Rather, they shifted their efforts to increasing maize production.

Changing from one crop to another was not a new thing in Sucre. However, the replacement of a subsistence crop (maize) by a cash crop (tree tomatoes) implied greater social and economic changes than the switch from potatoes to maize. The replacement of maize with tree tomatoes was preceded by a gradual alteration in the way people perceived their relationship to money and to the market economy. These changes occurred as people gained more access to money and markets.

For as long as anyone I talked to could remember, the people of Sucre have always obtained some household goods from outside Sucre. This appears to be common throughout the Andes (Larson and Harris [eds.] 1995). However, when a road was built to Sucre in the 1970s, more people began to travel to markets to sell animals, handicrafts, cheese or part of their harvest in order to purchase salt, fat and potatoes. People also went to the valley haciendas to work as wage labourers. Consumption patterns changed as people began to see, desire and purchase clothing, radios and lowland foodstuffs. Other strategies for earning money were also learned as people travelled to the cities. Some households decided to plant a field of onions to sell as a cash crop. Other households opened small dry-goods stores.

In 1989 most households purchased potatoes, noodles and rice to supplement subsistence crops, such as maize, wheat and beans. Most households had radios and people wore clothing purchased from the markets. Some of the wealthier peasant households also had gas stoves. Three households had television sets. One man sold most of his land to purchase a truck, which he used to take people and goods to market. Ten families had a field of onions for sale. Four families had small dry goods stores.

In 1996, most houses had television sets and gas stoves. Rice, potatoes, maize and luxury foods such as bananas and oranges were regularly purchased from the markets. Seven families had dry goods stores. The increased need for transport (to take the tree tomatoes to market) led to a growth in the Sucre transport industry. There were now ten trucks and two minibuses. In the majority of cases, these had been purchased by selling cattle and tree tomatoes.

Knowledge and innovation: how tree tomatoes came to Sucre

In 1986, even though there were no tree tomatoes in Sucre, they were a popular cash crop on the fruit haciendas and *mestizo* farms in the valley bottom, which is at 2000 m above sea level. From their work on haciendas and from trips to local markets, Sucreños became aware of the profits[4] that could be made from tree tomatoes. They were also aware of the production costs and the risks involved. Although people were aware that selling tree tomatoes could bring them more money than raising maize, no one attempted to grow them in Sucre except for Maria, a *mestiza tienda* owner. She had one field of tree tomatoes in a sheltered position at a lower altitude than most fields in Sucre.

The first major tree tomato entrepreneur[5] in Sucre was an Indian woman named Teresa, one of the wealthiest people in the community. In 1991, she decided to try out tree tomatoes in one of her fields, in a sheltered part of Sucre, but at a higher altitude than Maria's field. She purchased baby plants (though they can be grown from seed) and chemical fertiliser. Although she had to wait two year for the plants to yield fruit, her experiment was a success and the plants paid for themselves after one season. The surplus she gained from the crop was invested in buying plants and fertiliser for some of her other fields. By 1996, most of her fields had tree tomatoes rather than maize. She used some of the money from the sale of tree tomatoes to purchase maize, potatoes and rice from the provincial market for daily consumption. She said that growing tree tomatoes was better than growing maize because she could have enough to eat and still have money left over to spend on other items, such as a truck. She also bought cattle that would be sold to buy food and maize seed in the event of her tree tomatoes being killed off by disease.

As people saw the success that Teresa had with tree tomatoes and how this increased her cash income, they began to imitate her and planted one or two fields of tree tomatoes. The techniques for tree tomato cultivation, which include adding fertiliser, pruning and fumigation, were learned by working in haciendas, observing neighbours and asking advice from *compadres* in the valley bottom. Some families, eager to increase their earnings, gradually replaced most of their maize fields with tree tomatoes. In a number of cases, the impetus for change came from young adults, who encouraged their families to grow tree tomatoes rather than maize. Other families, who wanted to use crop diversity as a means of protection from risk, continued to plant some maize and beans (but with the addition of chemical fertiliser). A number of households chose to share the cost and spread the risk of tree

---

[4] Some families were harvesting up to 60 crates of tree tomatoes every fortnight. Each crate was sold for 12,000 sucres. In contrast, one hundredweight of maize could be sold for 25–30,000 sucres (1 $US = 3,100 sucres).

[5] See Gudeman 1992 for a discussion of the importance of entrepreneurs as agents of economic change.

tomato cultivation by share-cropping, a traditional method of risk avoidance.

Agricultural and financial innovation played an important role in the introduction and spread of tree tomato cultivation in Sucre. However, it must be remembered that economic diversification and innovation have long been part of household economic strategies in Sucre and in other parts of the Andes (Zimmerer 1994). Similarly, crop diversification and share-cropping are 'traditional' methods of coping with risk. It is misleading to make a clear cut distinction between what is 'traditional' and what is 'new' since the direction that change takes is influenced by tradition. In fact, the only new strategies that are likely to be widely accepted and adopted are those that are workable within 'traditional' economic and social structures.

Researchers such as Lagos (1994), Gudeman (1994) and Reinhardt (1998) have indicated that a household's ability to adopt innovative economic strategies is limited by financial constraints. However, they fail to note that a further and perhaps more important limitation is people's belief that a particular innovation is a feasible option for them. Innovative ideas are more likely to spread if a local person introduces them to the community. Interestingly, Teresa's experiment with tree tomatoes was not Sucreños first brush with cash-cropping in the community. During the mid-1980s, a Peace Corps couple from Idaho came to teach modern potato farming methods. This was an effort to revitalise potato production, which had fallen into decline due to increased disease. The couple lived in Sucre for two years and initiated a number of share-cropping arrangements with people in the community. They supplied seed potatoes, fertiliser, pesticides and fungicides. Local residents supplied land and labour. The harvest was split equally between the contributing sides. The Peace Corps couple then sold their surplus potatoes to other people in Sucre. They used the money to purchase more fertiliser and pesticides in an effort to demonstrate that potato production could be sustainable and to some extent profitable. However, when the Peace Corps couple left, the majority of people in Sucre did not continue the cultivation of potatoes. They said that fertiliser cost too much and that it was better to grow maize, which did not need any chemical additives.

There are several reasons why Teresa's success with the tree tomatoes was imitated whereas the Peace Corps' potato initiative was abandoned. The first is a very pragmatic difference in profit margins. Tomatoes can bring in a lot more money than potatoes. This provides an incentive to change. Of course, the desirability of earning more money must be understood in the context of Sucre's increasing involvement with the market economy. This includes an increased desire for (and perceived need of) commodity goods. Another factor is a change in people's view on the use of fertiliser. Increased assess to money meant that people could purchase fertiliser without depriving themselves of other necessities. More people chose to spend money on fertiliser when they saw that, if properly used, fertiliser did not harm plants and could significantly increase production. A third reason for the rising popularity of tree tomato cultivation was that Teresa's success proved that it was possible for a local person to grow a new crop without the financial backing and expertise of outsiders, such as the Peace Corps couple.

'Our plants are dying': the need for expert knowledge from the outside

When tree tomato cultivation first began in Sucre, the only necessary chemical input was fertiliser. The root and leaf diseases that plagued plants in the valley bottom[6] were not present in Sucre. People in Sucre talked of the *linda cosecha* (beautiful, abundant harvests) as the trees matured. By 1996, however, these diseases were beginning to appear in Sucre. Diseased plants yield less and less fruit until they eventually dry up and die. I saw several families in Sucre ripping out entire fields of dead plants. Other families were beginning to complain of reduced yields. Nevertheless, some families, such as Teresa's, had predominantly healthy fields. Families who had healthy fields boasted that they had learned how to take proper care of their plants. This required learning how to recognise diseases, knowing which chemicals to use to cure and prevent specific diseases and how to apply remedies effectively. This was something, Teresa said, that you could not learn simply by watching your neighbours or by experimenting. This knowledge came from agricultural engineers.

These engineers are employees of agricultural chemical distributors in the cantonal and provincial capitals. They come to the fields and give a free consultation in return for the purchase of the appropriate chemicals from their company. I spoke with one of the engineers, who said that his aim was not to sell the peasants expensive chemicals that they did not need, but rather to give them good advice. Giving good advice was good business, since he gained new customers through the recommendation of old customers.

By July 1996, very few of the families in Sucre had consulted agricultural engineers. There were two main reasons that people gave for this. First and foremost, there was widespread distrust and misunderstanding of the motives behind the engineers 'free advice'. As one man said to me: 'The *blancos* [whites] have never helped us before, why do they want to do it now? They only come here when they want to take something from us.' A second reason was that the majority of people thought that they were already taking proper care of the tree tomatoes, since during the first few years of tree tomato cultivation the plants gave an abundant harvest and were disease free. As disease became more of a threat, people began to re-evaluate their views on the need for outside advice.

According to the agricultural engineer, it was the increased popularity of

---

[6] By 1996, tree tomato diseases were so widespread in the valley bottom that most hacienda owners turned to other cash crops. This increased the price of tree tomatoes, providing further incentive to grow them in Sucre.

tree tomatoes in Sucre and the desire for a quick profit that introduced the diseases to Sucre and allowed them to spread. Rather than plant tree tomatoes from seed, people in Sucre purchased seedlings from the valley bottom. Along with these plants came root parasites and leaf diseases. The first tree tomato cultivators in Sucre, who were from the wealthier peasant families, would fumigate their plants regularly. Diseases and pests were relatively easy to contain since the tree tomato fields were far apart and the maize fields were not affected. However, diseases became harder to eradicate and began to spread more easily as more families planted tree tomatoes and purchased fumigants only when they thought it was absolutely necessary (i.e. when the plants were dying).

The first person in Sucre to consult an agricultural engineer about his fields was a well respected *mestizo tienda* owner, Frederico. Teresa, who saw that Frederico's fields were improving, went to him and asked for advice. Because he was a *compadre*, she felt that she could trust his recommendation of the engineer. Teresa also discussed the matter with her youngest children, whom she had sent to secondary school in the district capital. They encouraged her to invite the agricultural engineer to see her fields. By July 1996, he was making regular visits to her fields to give the plants a health check and to give advice on what treatment, if any, was needed. She described this as a way of saving money, since she did not waste money fumigating plants that were already doomed to die, unlike many of her neighbours.

It is clear from Teresa's example that the acceptance and adoption of ideas, advice and knowledge from the outside is part of a much wider social, religious and economic web of relationships. People do not feel that they can ask advice of fellow villagers unless they are friends, relatives, *compadres* or trusted neighbours. Although many people knew that Teresa and Frederico had agricultural engineers come to their fields, most people assumed that they paid for these services, since they were both relatively wealthy and it was unheard of for 'white' city people to provide any service for free.

It is interesting to compare the knowledge of agricultural engineers with other types of expert knowledge. The value of 'outside' indigenous knowledge has been well documented in the Andes with respect to shamans, healers and religious specialists (Taussig 1987). This knowledge is usually seen as being more powerful than 'inside' knowledge. People wanting to access this knowledge must travel to the experts. However, outside knowledge from 'whites' is regarded with ambivalence if not outright suspicion. Travel to 'white' dentists, doctors, lawyers or other experts is usually fraught with frustration and deception. 'White' experts who come to Sucre on a regular basis, such as the district nurse or the priest cause tension as they criticise local medical and religious practices (see, for example, Bourque 1995c). By inviting the agricultural engineers to her fields, Teresa demonstrated an openness to outside ideas which she also indicated in other ways. For example, she was one of the first to plant potatoes with the Peace Corps workers and was keen to send her children to secondary school. Teresa's openness to new ideas and her willingness to experiment is not shared by many people in Sucre. The majority of Sucreños are willing to adopt an 'outside' innovation only if they see proof that it is possible for someone in the community, such as Teresa, to make it work.

Community leaders to the rescue: the politics of knowledge

Three weeks before my departure in August 1996, a new element was added to the dynamics of the spread of 'outside' 'expert' agricultural knowledge. A different agricultural engineer from a competing company approached one of the community leaders.[7] He offered to give a free course on tree tomato cultivation to members of the community without any obligation to purchase goods from his company. He claimed that the motivation behind this offer was to give a good impression of his company in the hope of attracting new customers. In approaching Vittorio, the agricultural engineer had made a good choice. Vittorio was well respected within the community and was a former community president and treasurer. On the other hand, he worked as a truck driver (the only one in Sucre in 1989) and had many contacts outside the community. He was active in the provincial indigenous organisation. He was also an active member of one of the national political parties. Vittorio decided that 'outside' 'expert' knowledge about tree tomatoes was indeed necessary and that the engineer could be trusted. He discussed the matter with the current president of the community, Segundo, and with other 'community leaders'. The majority of them fell in with Vittorio's recommendation to accept the offer.

The main reason in favour of allowing the engineer to give a course was the recognition that tree tomato diseases were an increasing problem and that people like Teresa and Frederico were benefiting from the advice of agricultural engineers. Their acceptance was an acknowledgment of the need for outside expert knowledge to be brought into Sucre. However, this outside knowledge was only accepted once assurances were given that Sucreños would be under no obligation to the engineer and his company. Not only did community leaders 'control' the knowledge coming into the community, to some extent they also appropriated it on behalf of the community. The president of the village committee offered the use of the community hall. The committee further added its endorsement by announcing the course during a community minga[8] and by advertising it on the village

---

[7] I use the term 'community leader' (lider) to denote a man who is well respected in the community and who has formal or informal authority. Such leaders are usually past or serving members of the community cabildo. The cabildo is a committee which is elected on an annual basis. It is responsible for running the community, supervising communal work and liaising with officials in the cantonal and provincial capitals.

[8] Mingas are held every two weeks. Every household in the community must send a representative to the minga or pay a fine. During mingas, people work on projects to benefit the community, such as clearing irrigation canals or constructing public buildings.

loudspeaker. As a result, the first evening of the course, which occurred on my final day in Sucre, was well attended.

As this 'outside' knowledge was accepted and turned into 'inside' knowledge, the control of this knowledge became an internal political issue. This happened as national political differences were being played out at a local level within Sucre. The weeks prior to the tree tomato course coincided with the build-up to the second (and final) round of the presidential elections in Ecuador. Representatives from the two remaining parties regularly came to Sucre from the cantonal and provincial capitals to promise various new developments in Sucre, such as paving the dirt road which linked Sucre to the valley bottom. The community leaders were split between the two parties. Vittorio supported Nebot as a national presidential candidate. Segundo, the current community president, supported Adbala (who eventually won the election).

Both Vittorio and Segundo cooperated in supporting and promoting the agricultural course. They both thought that the course would be beneficial and were keen to harness this potential success for their respective political campaigns. Vittorio made it clear to anybody who would listen that this initiative was being offered through his efforts. During a political rally for Nebot, Vittorio went so far as to imply that he had invited the agricultural engineer to Sucre. Segundo, on the other hand, personally made daily announcements about the course over the loudspeaker, emphasising what a benefit it would be for community members. In this way, the knowledge of the agricultural engineer became part of social and political dialogues within Sucre.

Conclusions

This brief investigation of how knowledge about tree tomato cultivation was introduced, accepted and spread among peasants in Sucre raises a number of important points about the dynamics of new knowledge in Andean communities. Many researchers, such as von Barlowen (1995), Godoy (1989), Lagos (1994), Reinhardt (1988), Watters (1994) and Yambert (1989), have portrayed change in peasant villages as something that is initiated or imposed by people and institutions from the 'outside'. As we see from our consideration of agricultural change in Sucre, this is a simplistic view of the processes involved. Even people looking at the role of local agricultural knowledge in the field of development, such as Bebbington (1990), Long and Long (1992) and de Boef et al (1993) lack a thorough consideration of the social and political dynamics of acquiring, possessing and transmitting knowledge.

In Sucre, we have seen that innovation usually relies on contact with ideas from outside the community. For example, Teresa came up with the idea of planting tree tomatoes because she had seen them in fields in the valley bottom and on stalls at the market. The idea of planting onions and opening dry goods stores similarly came from observing how people were making money in the valley. This familiarity makes the process of acceptance easier. Nevertheless, new ideas are more likely to be adopted on a wide scale if the innovator is a local person and if people believe that they will benefit from the innovation. This is also the case for non-economic forms of change. For example, Paerregard (1994) indicates that the growth of Protestantism in rural areas is not due to the activities of foreign missionaries, but rather to the influence of returning migrants who became Protestants while living in urban areas.

The adoption of innovation usually operates within financial and/or ideological constraints. Successful innovations will be those that can be applied using existing social, economic or religious structures. New knowledge spreads through kin contacts and through observing neighbours. This can affect the rate and extent of the spread of knowledge within a community. New knowledge may also be appropriated by people in positions of authority within the community either on behalf of the community or for their own benefit.

Although I have talked about 'inside' and 'outside' knowledge, this dichotomy is not clear-cut. As I have indicated above, 'outside' knowledge can become 'inside' knowledge. The terms 'outside' and 'inside' are more usefully considered as social rather than geographical terms. This is because knowledge is imbedded in, shaped by and spread through social relationships. The legitimacy of and value placed on knowledge is derived from these relationships. What I have called 'inside' or 'traditional' knowledge is that which is shared between household or community members. 'Outside' knowledge is that which is brought to the community through relationships with non-community members. In each case, the social relations and processes of learning are different. For example, children learned how to plant maize by watching and imitating their parents. Tree tomato planting was originally learned by watching and imitating experienced workers in the valley haciendas. However, this process did not give the Sucreños sufficient knowledge to care for the plants when they became ill. As people such as Teresa turned to 'outside' experts, they also had to adapt to new ways of learning. As this generation of peasants learn how to care for tree tomatoes, this knowledge will become part of 'inside' 'traditional' knowledge.

The transformation of 'outside' knowledge into 'inside' knowledge involves making this knowledge part of daily social interactions. However, this process of socialisation is not merely a case of acceptance. At times, it may lead to new conflicts or become part of existing disputes within the community or between community members and outside experts. The 'internalisation' of 'outside' knowledge also occurs as it is connected with other aspects of life in Sucre. For example, in 1996, tree tomatoes were being introduced to the festival of Corpus Christi. In 1989, the festival processions were led by a statue of San Francisco, the patron of the village, who was considered the patron saint of maize. In 1996, he was joined by San Isidro, the patron saint of farm labourers. Teresa and her household used money from the sale of tree tomatoes to pay for the renovation of the statue of San Isidro and for the post-procession feast. I asked her why she had sponsored San Isidro. She replied that caring for the tomatoes required a lot of work. She hoped that in the coming year, San Isidro would reward their devotion by making their work in the tree tomato fields more effective. Thus, in the case of tree tomatoes, economic innovation has led to religious innovation. By making San Isidro responsible for tree tomatoes, Teresa is making tree tomatoes an 'inside' crop and part of Sucre's ever-changing 'tradition'.

References

Allen, Catherine. 1988. *The Hold That Life Has: Coca and Cultural Identity in an Andean Community*. Washington, DC: Smithsonian Institution Press.

Apffel-Marglin, Frédérique. 1998. 'Introduction: Knowledge and Life Revisited'. In F. Apffel-Marglin with PRATEC (eds.), *The Spirit of Regeneration: Andean Cultures Confronting Western Notions of Development*. London: Zed Books: 1–50.

Apffel-Marglin, Frédérique, and S. Marglin (eds). 1996. *Decolonizing Knowledge: From Development to Dialogue*. Oxford: Clarendon Press.

Arnold, Denise. 1990. 'Owners, Borrowers and Weavers in the Bolivian Highlands'. Paper presented at the workshop on Gender Relations, Work and Proprietorship among Indigenous People of South America, Institute of Latin American Studies, London, 7–8 December 1990.

———, 1992. 'La casa de adobes y piedras del Inka: género, memoria y cosmos en Qaqachaka'. In D. Arnold (ed.), *Hacia un orden andino de las cosas*. La Paz: Hisbol: 31–108.

Barlowen, C. von. 1995. *History and Modernity in Latin America: Technology and Culture in the Andes*. Oxford: Berghahn Books.

Bastien, Joseph. 1978. *Mountain of the Condor: Metaphor and Ritual in an Andean Ayllu*. St Paul: West Publishing.

Bebbington, Anthony. 1990. 'Farmer Knowledge, Institutional Resources and Sustainable Agricultural Strategies: A Case Study from the Eastern Slopes of the Peruvian Andes'. *Bulletin of Latin American Research* 9(2): 203–28.

Boef, Walter de, K. Amanor, K. Wellard and A. Bebbington. 1993. *Cultivating Knowledge: Genetic Diversity, Farmer Experimentation and Crop Research*. London: Intermediate Technology Publications.

Bourque, Nicole. 1994. 'Spatial Meaning in Andean Festivals: Corpus Christi and Octavo'. *Ethnology* 33(3): 229–43.

———, 1995a. 'Developing People and Plants: Life-Cycle and Agricultural Festivals in the Andes'. *Ethnology* 34(1): 75–87.

———, 1995b. 'Savages and Angels: Spiritual, Social and Physical Development in Andean Life-Cycle Festivals'. *Ethnos* 60(1–2): 99–114.

———, 1995c. 'Priests and Saints: Syncretism and Power in the Andes'. *Scottish Journal of Religious Studies* 16(1): 25–36.

Bouysse-Cassagne, Thérèse, and O. Harris. 1987. 'Pacha: en torno al pensamiento aymara'. In J. Medina (ed.), *Tres reflexiones sobre el pensamiento andino*. La Paz: Hisbol: 11–59.

Godoy, Ricardo. 1989. 'Small Scale Mining and Agriculture among the Jukumani

Indians, Northern Potosí, Bolivia'. In B.S. Orlove, M.W. Foley and T.F. Love (eds.), *State, Capital and Rural Society: Anthropological Perspectives on Political Economy in Mexico and the Andes*. London: Westview: 247–66.

Gudeman, Stephen. 1992. 'Remodeling the House of Economics: Culture and Innovation'. *American Ethnologist* 19(1): 141–54.

Gudeman, Stephen, and A. Rivera. 1994. *Conversations in Colombia: The Domestic Economy in Life and Text*. Cambridge: Cambridge University Press.

Harris, Olivia. 1986. 'From Asymmetry to Triangle: Symbolic Transformations in Northern Potosí'. In J. Murra, N. Wachtel and J. Revel (eds.), *Anthropological History of Andean Polities*. New York: Cambridge University Press: 260–80.

Lagos, Maria. 1994. *Autonomy and Power: The Dynamics of Class and Culture in Rural Bolivia*. Philadelphia: University of Pennsylvania Press.

Larson, Brooke, and O. Harris (eds.). 1995. *Ethnicity, Markets and Migration in the Andes*. London: Duke University Press.

Long, Norman, and A. Long (eds.). 1992. *Battlefields of Knowledge*. London: Routledge.

Paerregard, K. 1994. 'Conversion, Migration and Social Identity: The Spread of Protestantism in the Peruvian Andes'. *Ethnos* 59(3–4): 168–86.

Radcliffe, Sarah. 1990. 'Marking the Boundaries Between the Community, the State and History in the Andes'. *Journal of Latin American Studies* 22: 575–94.

Rasnake, Roger. 1986. 'Carnival in Yura: Ritual Reflections on Ayllu and State Relations'. *American Ethnologist* 13: 662–80.

Reinhardt, Nola. 1998. *Our Daily Bread: The Peasant Question and Farming in the Colombian Andes*. London: University of California Press.

Rengifo Vasquez, Grimaldo. 1998. 'Education in the Modern West and in Andean Culture'. In Apffel-Marglin with PRATEC (eds.): 172–92.

Taussig, Michael. 1987. *Shamanism, Colonialism, and the Wild Man: A Study in Terror and Healing*. London: University of Chicago Press.

Vallodolid Rivera, Julio. 1998. 'Andean Peasant Agriculture: Nurturing a Diversity of Life in the Chakra'. In Apffel-Marglin with PRATEC (eds.): 51–88.

Watters, Raymond. 1994. *Poverty and Peasantry in Peru's Southern Andes, 1963–90*. Basingstoke: Macmillan.

Yambert, K. 1989. 'The Peasant Community of Catacaos and the Peruvian Agrarian Reform'. In B.S. Orlove, M.W. Foley and T.F. Love (eds.), *State, Capital and Rural Society: Anthropological Perspectives on Political Economy in Mexico and the Andes*. London: Westview: 181–210.

Zimmerer, Karl. 1994. 'Transforming Colquepata Wetlands'. In W.P. Mitchell and D. Guillet (eds.), *Irrigation at High Altitude*. Arlington: American Anthropological Association.

Index

FRANK CHO'S
JUNGLE GIRL®
THE COMPLETE OMNIBUS

SEASON ONE
PLOT AND COVER BY
FRANK CHO
PLOT AND SCRIPT BY
DOUG MURRAY
INTERIOR ART BY
ADRIANO BATISTA
COLORS BY
FRANK MARTIN JR.
LETTERS BY
ZACHARY MATHENY

SEASON TWO
PLOT AND COVER BY
FRANK CHO
PLOT AND SCRIPT BY
DOUG MURRAY
INTERIOR ART BY
ADRIANO BATISTA
COLORS BY
FRANK MARTIN JR.
AND **GIOVANI KOSOSKI**
LETTERS BY
ZACHARY MATHENY

SEASON THREE
PLOT AND COVER BY
FRANK CHO
PLOT AND SCRIPT BY
DOUG MURRAY
INTERIOR ART BY
JACK JADSON
COLORS BY
INLIGHT STUDIOS
LETTERS BY
MARSHALL DILLON

COLLECTION COVER
FRANK CHO
COLLECTION DESIGN
RODOLFO MURAGUCHI
EDITOR
JOSEPH RYBANDT

DYNAMITE®

NICK BARRUCCI:
CEO / PUBLISHER
JUAN COLLADO:
PRESIDENT / COO
BRANDON DANTE PRIMAVERA:
V.P. OF IT AND OPERATIONS

JOE RYBANDT:
EXECUTIVE EDITOR
MATT IDELSON:
SENIOR EDITOR
KEVIN KETNER:
EDITOR

CATHLEEN HEARD:
ART DIRECTOR
RACHEL KILBURY:
DIGITAL MULTIMEDIA ASSOCIATE
ALEXIS PERSSON:
GRAPHIC DESIGNER
KATIE HIDALGO:
GRAPHIC DESIGNER

ALAN PAYNE:
V.P. OF SALES AND MARKETING
PAT O'CONNELL:
SALES MANAGER
VINCENT FAUST:
MARKETING COORDINATOR

JAY SPENCE:
DIRECTOR OF PRODUCT DEVELOPMENT
MARIANO NICIEZA:
DIRECTOR OF RESEARCH & DEVELOPMENT

AMY JACKSON:
ADMINISTRATIVE COORDINATOR

ISBN13: 978-1-5241-1544-9

First Printing   10 9 8 7 6 5 4 3 2 1

SEASON 1
PROLOGUE

COVER BY **FRANK CHO**

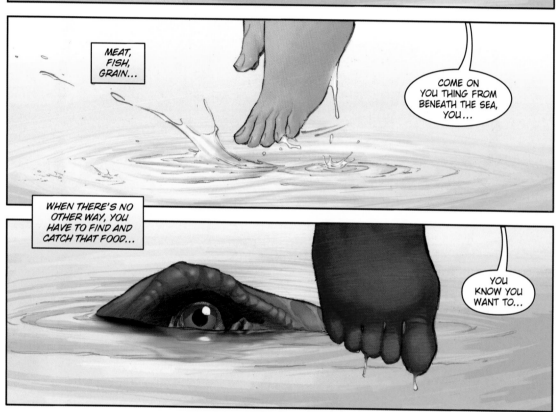
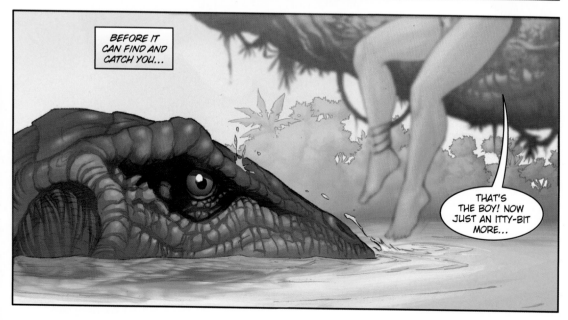

COME ON! I DON'T HAVE ALL DAY!

ROOOAAARRRR

ABOUT TIME!

GOT TO DO THIS BEFORE THE GULPERS GET TOO INVOLVED!

GOT 'IM! ENOUGH FOOD FOR WEEKS!

TOO QUIET AROUND HERE...

I... FEEL SOMETHING... THERE'S--

SOMETHING...

JANA WAS RIGHT. SOMETHING WAS ABOUT TO HAPPEN.

BUT BEFORE SHE COULD MOVE. BEFORE SHE COULD REACT, JANA WAS CAUGHT UNDER A LIGHT BRIGHTER THAN THE SUN. A LIGHT THAT FLOODED THE LAND WITH GLARE, WASHING EVERYTHING IN A BLAZE OF WHITE...

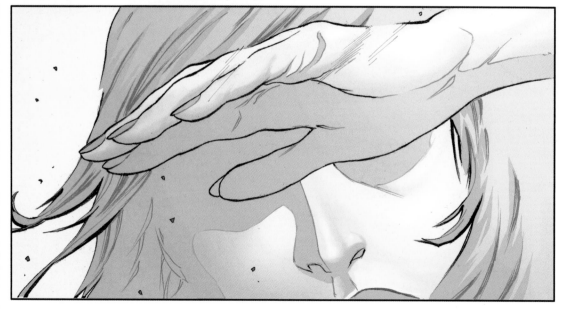

SEASON 1
CHAPTER 1

COVER BY **FRANK CHO**

IT CAN'T BE!

I THOUGHT THE METAL BIRDS WERE JUST STORIES...

WEREN'T THEY?

I'D BETTER TAKE A LOOK...

AND HOPE THERE'S SOME MEAT LEFT WHEN I GET BACK!

EVERYONE OKAY?

SEBASTIAN?

I THINK HE'S OKAY. JUST SHAKEN UP.

DOOR'S JAMMED. MICHAEL? YOU OKAY BACK THERE?

HE'S OKAY—AND HE'S GOT THAT DAMNED CAMERA RUNNING!

PUT THE CAMERA DOWN, MIKE. LET'S GET OUT OF HERE AND SEE WHERE WE ARE.

HEY, MAN—HAND'S OFF! I'M JUST DOING MY JOB.

AND I'M *TRYING* TO DO MINE. LET'S GET THAT DOOR OPEN, OKAY?

THE FIRST ATTACKER IS ONLY A FEW FEET FROM THE FRIGHTENED GIRL WHEN HE SUDDENLY GOES DOWN...

SHLUCCCH

HIS COMPANION HAD NO TIME TO REACT...

WHO IN HELL...?!

LET'S SEE IF I CAN GET A CLOSE-UP...

WHAT'S SHE DOING?

IT LOOKS LIKE...

GET ME OUT OF HERE!

WITH EVERYONE WORKING TOGETHER, IT ONLY TAKES A FEW SECONDS TO FREE THE BIG MAN FROM THE DOWNED PLANE...

WHAT'S GOING ON HERE! WHY DID YOU DROP ME!

THAT THING THERE WAS READY TO KILL CAROLE WHEN SUDDENLY, THIS SPEAR WENT RIGHT THROUGH HIM! THEN THE OTHER HAIRY ONE BACK THERE POPPED UP AND...

SHE STOPPED THEM BOTH!

BGUM

NEVER SEEN ANYTHING LIKE IT!

NO WAY! BEST THING WE CAN DO IS WAIT RIGHT HERE FOR A RESCUE PARTY!

SUIT YOURSELF.

BUT THAT'S GOING TO DRAW ALL KINDS OF ATTENTION—THINGS *YOU* SURE CAN'T HANDLE.

WAIT!

28:50

AS THEY FINALLY GOT UNDER WAY... JANA TOOK SOME TIME TO EXPLAIN THE LAW OF THE JUNGLE AND THE WAYS OF THIS STRANGE NEW LAND...

28:37

DID YOU KILL THAT ONE?

NOPE. WORSE.

28:25

HIS TRIBE BELIEVES THAT YOU'RE NOT A MAN IF YOU DON'T HAVE WHISKERS.

AND THAT MEANS THAT HE CAN'T GO BACK AND TELL HIS PEOPLE ABOUT US...

BUYS US SOME TIME.

28:00

TV—*TELEVISION.* YOU KNOW, YOU HAVE ONE IN YOUR HOUSE AND...CAROLE! MAYBE YOU CAN EXPLAIN IT!

27:32

DON'T TOUCH THAT!

27:31

27:30

27:29

WHAT THE HELL!!

HOPE I GOT THAT! WHAT SPEED!

27:27

DON'T TOUCH *ANYTHING* WITHOUT ASKING ME FIRST!

27:14

THESE THINGS ARE HELL TO GET OFF ONCE THEY LATCH ON...

26:44

26:40

AND THEY'LL DRAIN YOU DRY WHILE YOU TRY.

26:31

THIS IS THE JUNGLE—NOT A GARDEN SPOT! REMEMBER THAT!

NOW, WHAT WERE WE TALKING ABOUT? OH, TV—YOU SAID IT'S IN YOUR HOUSE? WHAT'S A HOUSE?

25:33

...AND THE SIGNALS GO INTO THE ANTENNA—OR THROUGH A CABLE—OR...

LET'S PUT THIS ASIDE FOR THE MOMENT, SHALL WE? IT'S MORE IMPORTANT THAT YOU KNOW WHO EVERYONE HERE IS.

THE LADY YOU SO COLOR-FULLY SAVED BACK THERE IS CAROLE ROSS, THE MAN WITH THE CAMERA IS MIKE...

IS THAT WHAT THE BOX IS? A CAMERA? WHAT DOES IT DO?

LATER. WE'LL EXPLAIN IT ALL LATER.

18:13

TJ THERE IS OUR GUIDE AND PROTECTOR. HE'S VERY GOOD WITH THAT RIFLE...

RIFLE?

—SIGH— LATER, CHILD, LATER! SKY AT THE BACK THERE IS OUR PILOT.

17:15

DAMN!

DOWN!

17:08

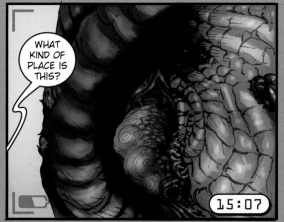

WHAT KIND OF PLACE IS THIS?

15:07

NO TIME NOW. THE BIG ONE MAY COME BACK...

14:44

I'VE GOT A REASONABLY SAFE PLACE NOT TOO FAR FROM HERE.

14:40

ONCE I GET YOU THERE, I'LL HAVE TO SEE ABOUT SOME FOOD...

14:29

...SOME KIND OF SEA CREATURE. I COULD SWEAR I'VE SEEN SOMETHING LIKE IT BEFORE...

DON'T WORRY ABOUT IT NOW—WE DON'T WANT TO LOSE OUR GUIDE.

13:31

LOOK AT THAT!

5:10

3:54

THOSE ARE DINO-SAURS! FLYING DINOSAURS!

1:02

AND THAT WAS SOME KIND OF DINOSAUR TOO! MOSES- SOME-THING.

WHERE ARE WE?!

:33

BUT THOSE *ARE* DINOSAURS! I'M SURE OF IT!

IMPOSSIBLE! DINOSAURS HAVE BEEN EXTINCT FOR, WHAT, MILLIONS OF YEARS!

KA-BOOM

THAT WAS FROM THE AREA OF YOUR MACHINE!

GAS TANK MUST'VE COOKED OFF.

COVER BY **FRANK CHO**

WE'LL HAVE TO MOVE TOO. THAT FIRE IS GETTING TOO CLOSE.

THERE'S WATER THAT WAY. IT SHOULD BE SAFE ENOUGH UNTIL THE FIRE...

MY GOD!

A FIN-BACK!

RUN!

THAT'S RIGHT! I'M RIGHT HERE—COME AND GET ME!

GOOD BOY! HURRY UP NOW!

FAST AS YOU CAN!

TOO SLICK FOR YOU? TOO BAD!

ARROOORRR!

WHAT DID YOU DO?

YES, SKY. WHAT WAS THAT?

WELL, I HAD SOME EXPLOSIVES IN CASE I HAD TO CLEAR SPACE FOR A TAKE-OFF...

WHY IS THE GROUND MOVING?

RUN!

AND I DON'T THINK ANYTHING WILL STOP IT.

JUST AS WELL— THE FIN-BACK SEEMS DETERMINED TO KILL THE STRANGERS...

RAAAHH

THERE'S NOWHERE TO RUN!

WHAT ARE WE GOING TO DO?

WHAT'S THAT?!

THE STRANGERS ARE CLUMSY IN THE TREES. NOT ONE OF THEM EVEN LOOKS UP TO MAKE SURE IT IS SAFE ABOVE HIM...

OF COURSE, JANA KNOWS...

HEY!

WE'VE COME IN A BIG CIRCLE! THERE'S OUR PLANE!

BUT IT CAN'T BE!

IT WAS SUPPOSED TO BURN...!

WHY DIDN'T IT?

THAT'S ODD.

FIRE STARTED RIGHT OVER THERE...

WITH SOME KIND OF, WHAT DID THEY CALL IT? EXPLOSION.

CARRIED BY ONE OF THE DIRT MEN I LEFT BEHIND.

THIS ISN'T BURNT FUEL.

IT'S...

IT'S OPIUM. TOO BAD YOU SAW THAT.

FOR YOU!

JUST KEEP HOLD OF THE DAMN CAMERA.

WITH BOTH HANDS!

IT'S OPIUM! OPIUM IN *MY* PLANE!

IT'S BEEN IN YOUR PLANE QUITE A FEW TIMES— NOT THAT YOU EVER NOTICED, OLD FOOL!

HE WOULDN'T HAVE NOTICED THIS TIME IF IT WEREN'T FOR THAT DAMN WHATEVER-IT-WAS KNOCKING US INTO THIS CRAZY PLACE!

YOU'RE BOTH IN ON IT, THEN! WHAT ARE YOU GOING TO DO NOW?

WE'RE GONNA GET RID OF SOME DEAD WEIGHT.

THEN WE'RE GONNA MAKE THAT JUNGLE GIRL TAKE US WHERE *WE* WANT TO GO...

BUT FIRST, WE'RE GONNA MAKE SURE WE HAVE THE STUFF! DON'T HAVE TO WORRY THAT YOU'RE WATCHING ANYMORE.

THE STRANGERS ARE ACTING ODDLY. AS IF THEY WERE OF DIFFERENT TRIBES...

OKAY, CAMERA-BOY. GET OVER WITH YOUR BOSS.

JANA HAS NOTICED IT TOO...

NOW, ABOUT GETTING RID OF THAT DEAD WEIGHT...

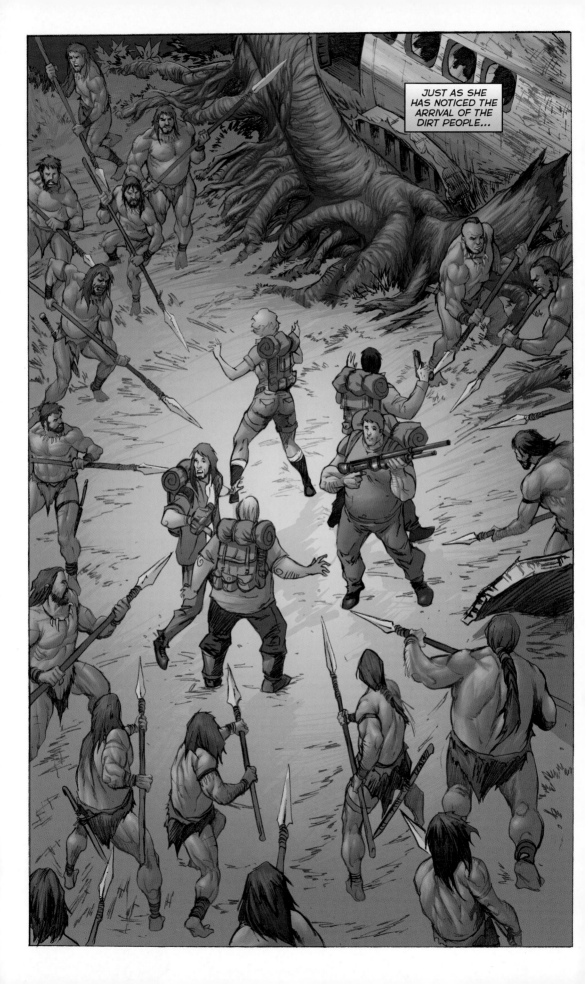

JUST AS SHE HAS NOTICED THE ARRIVAL OF THE DIRT PEOPLE...

COVER BY **FRANK CHO**

HEY, MONKEY BOY! WHAT ARE *YOU* DOING HERE? YOU'RE NOT OLD ENOUGH TO GO WALKABOUT YET!

MEDICINE CHIEF SENT ME TO WATCH OVER YOU—AND DON'T CALL ME MONKEY! IT'S NOT NICE—I DON'T LIKE IT!

OKAY, OKAY. I'LL TRY TO REMEMBER NOT TO CALL YOU MONKEY BOY—MONKEY BOY!

I AM GLAD YOU LEFT THE STRANGERS—THEY ARE IN TROUBLE.

THEN I GUESS I'M IN TROUBLE TOO—THEY'RE STILL UNDER *MY* PROTECTION!

HOLD ONTO MY SPEAR—AND WATCH MY BACK!!

DON'T MOVE! NONE OF YOU MOVE!

LET ME HANDLE THIS.

FWOOGH

CHIEF OF THE DIRT PEOPLE. I AM JANA SKY-BORN OF THE ROCK TRIBE.

KRACK

JANA KNOWS HOW TO MAKE HER PRESENCE FELT— BUT EVEN SHE CAN NOT FIGHT THEM ALL...

YOU ARE TRESPASSING ON OUR LAND.

WE WERE FORCED HERE BY THE GREAT FIRE.

GO. LEAVE THIS PLACE NOW. DO NOT COME BACK.

YOU HEARD THE MAN. PACK UP. WE'RE LEAVING— NOW!

THEY CANNOT LEAVE! WE MUST HAVE THE SKY MEDICINE—AND THE THIEVES MUST BE PUNISHED!

YOU GO. THE OTHERS MUST FACE THE JUSTICE OF THE GODS.

NO. THEY ARE UNDER MY PROTECTION.

MEDICINE CHIEF WILL NOT BE HAPPY WITH ME FOR LETTING HER DO THIS...

BUT WHAT CAN I DO?

BEHOLD THE ENTRANCE TO THE SPIRIT WORLD!

DO YOU STILL DARE TO ENTER?

ONLY LITTLE CHILDREN...

AND THE PEOPLE OF THE DIRT FEAR THE DARKNESS.

I WILL DEFEAT YOUR SPIRITS—THEN I WILL RETURN FOR MY COMPANIONS.

YOU WILL NEVER COME BACK!

NEVER!

SEASON 1
CHAPTER 4

COVER BY **FRANK CHO**

THE STONE STANDS. JANA IS STILL TRAPPED...

HAVE WE ANGERED THE SPIRITS? WAS THE SUN-HAIRED WOMAN RIGHT?

NO! SHE WAS JUST A WOMAN! SHE HAS NOT RETURNED FROM THE CAVE OF THE SPIRTS. THIS IS SOME TRICK!?

THEY KNOW I AM HERE. IT IS TIME TO SHOW THEM HOW A MAN FIGHTS!

I JUST WISH EXPLOSIVE HAD WORKED...

YOU SEE! THERE IS SOME-ONE OUT THERE! HE MUST BE KILLED!

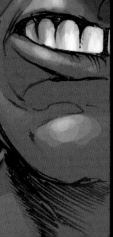

I WOULD LIKE TO SEE JANA ONCE MORE BEFORE I DIE...

HE WAS A GOOD MAN. HE DIDN'T DESERVE TO DIE LIKE THAT.

WE'LL HAVE TO WATCH THE WALLS FROM HERE ON.

THE FLARES MIGHT HELP—WE DIDN'T SEE THESE THINGS WHEN WE HAD SOME LIGHT.

THERE ARE THREE LEFT. DON'T KNOW HOW LONG THEY'LL LAST.

NOT LONG ENOUGH! WE'VE GOT TO GET OUT OF HERE!

SO LET'S GET MOVING. RIGHT?

RIGHT!

INTO THE DARKNESS THEY GO. BUT THEY ARE FOLLOWED AFTER SOME TIME...

COVER BY **FRANK CHO**

I TOLD YOU TO GET THEM *OUT* OF HERE!

HURRY!

TOGG!

LOOK OUT!

TOGG!

I CAN'T RUN AWAY! MEDICINE FATHER WOULD HAVE MY...

DEMONS COME IN MANY FORMS...

THE DIRT PEOPLE'S CHIEF HAS BEEN HUNTING JANA...

WHILE BEING HUNTED BY THE MORE PROSAIC FORMS OF THE DARKNESS-DWELLING GIGANTOPITHICENE...

DEMONS WHO ARE FAR MORE FRIGHTENING...

EVEN TO JANA.

YOU WERE AWFULLY BRAVE TO ATTACK THAT BIG WORM...

IT HAD TO BE DONE.

IT TOOK A REALLY STRONG MAN TO DO SOMETHING LIKE THAT.

YOU THINK *I'M* A MAN?

WELL, AREN'T YOU? NOW IF YOU WERE TO HELP ME GET AWAY FROM THESE OTHERS, I COULD SHOW YOU...

HEY, JANA! I THINK THIS ONE WANTS ME TO MATE WITH HER!

YOU'RE KIDDING!

ALL I HAVE TO DO IS HELP HER GET AWAY FROM YOU. YOU WANT ME TO LET HER GO?

THIS IS ALL YOUR FAULT! I'M TIRED OF DOING EVERYTHING YOU SAY! TIRED OF WATCHING YOUR PRISSY BUTT MOVING IN FRONT OF ME!

REALLY? AND WHAT DO YOU WANT TO DO ABOUT THAT?

I'M GOING TO SHOW YOU WHAT A REAL WOMAN CAN DO!

THAT SHOULD BE VERY EDUCATIONAL...

YEAH— FOR YOU!

WHOOF!

THE STRANGER'S KICK
TOOK JANA BY SURPRISE.
I HEARD THE OTHER ONE
MUMBLE SOMETHING LIKE
'CARROTT-EE', BUT I DON'T
KNOW WHAT THAT MEANS.

I DON'T THINK SHE'LL TAKE JANA BY SURPRISE AGAIN...

IT'LL BE ALL RIGHT AS LONG AS SHE DOESN'T MAKE JANA ANGRY...

JANA'S DANGEROUS WHEN SHE GETS ANGRY.

BITCH!

WHOOF!

THAT LOOKED LIKE IT HURT. MAYBE IT'LL BE ENOUGH...

YOU WANT ME TO FIGHT BACK?

YOU REALLY WANT ME TO FIGHT BACK!

I DIDN'T THINK SO.

COVER BY **FRANK CHO**

WHAT DO WE DO? DO WE FOLLOW THE SHUTTLE? SEE WHERE IT CAME DOWN?

SHUTTLE? IS THAT WHAT IT WAS? TOO FAR AWAY NOW FOR US TO DO ANY GOOD.

I THINK IT'S TIME WE FOUND OUT WHAT'S HAPPENING OUT THERE.

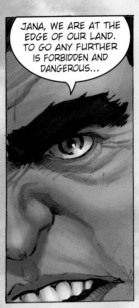

JANA, WE ARE AT THE EDGE OF OUR LAND. TO GO ANY FURTHER IS FORBIDDEN AND DANGEROUS...

I KNOW.

BUT THIS IS SOMETHING I HAVE TO DO!

WE'LL WORK THAT OUT WHEN WE GET THERE.

MIKE— WANT SOME MORE?

I'M FINE.

YOU'D BETTER EAT WHILE YOU CAN— YOU'LL NEED THE STRENGTH.

I WON'T HAVE *ANY* STRENGTH IF I EAT ANY TOO MUCH OF *THIS*.

HAVE IT YOUR WAY.

GET SOME SLEEP— BOTH OF YOU.

TOMORROW LOOKS LIKE A LONG, HARD DAY.

IT WON'T HURT US. IT'S A PLANT-EATER...

BUT YOU DON'T WANT TO BE NEAR THEM IF THEY GET STARTLED.

LOOK!

OH-- THAT'S NOT GOOD! IF THE BIG ONES STAMPEDE OUR WAY...

WE HAVE TO *MOVE!*

AN EXHAUSTING TIME LATER...

WE'RE ALMOST AT THE EDGE OF THE MARSH.

THAT'S GOOD—I DON'T THINK I COULD MAKE IT MUCH FURTHER.

YOU'D THINK I COULD WALK ON TOP OF THE MUCK WITH THESE FEET!

LET'S SEE HOW CLOSE WE ARE TO THE WATER! I COULD USE...

WHAT...?

SOME KIND OF...

DON'T MOVE!

SEASON 2
CHAPTER 2

COVER BY **FRANK CHO**

NOT LONG. LOOK FOR A PLACE WE CAN CAMP.

JANA...

LOOK, ON THE BEACH.

IT'S MAN-MADE. I'M SURE OF THAT. LET'S CHECK IT OUT!

DAMN THIS BEACH! WHERE'S THE SAND? WHERE'RE THE BIKINIS!

BEE-KEE-NI?

NEVER MIND...

LOOK!

THERE'S SOMEBODY ALREADY THERE!

LET'S HOPE HE'S FRIENDLY...

AND SO, WE WERE REFITTED FOR UNDERSEA RESEARCH.

MR. MARSH TRIED TO TAKE HER UNDER THE POLAR ICE SHELF AND SOMETHING... HAPPENED.

WE FOUND OURSELVES HERE, BEACHED AND BROKEN. I SENT A SEARCH PARTY OUT TO FIND CIVILIZATION. THEY DIDN'T COME BACK.

SO YOU SENT ANOTHER PARTY?

NOT RIGHT AWAY. WE TRIED TO MAKE HER SEA-WORTHY AGAIN— THAT'S WHEN WE WERE ATTACKED!

ATTACKED? BY WHO?

JUST HOLD STILL...

THERE!

I WONDER HOW YOU COOK ONE OF THESE?

AND SO, LATER THAT EVENING...

THIS IS *GOOD!*

YAH, IT'S NOT BAD. AND WE GOT A LOT DONE TODAY.

I'LL SAY! THOSE ENGINES ARE REALLY INTERESTING, JANA! THERE ARE WHEELS WITHIN WHEELS AND THEY ALL INTERLOCK AND...

EXPLAIN LATER, TOGG. AFTER WE GET WHERE WE'RE GOING! HOW LONG UNTIL WE CAN GET MOVING?

THAT'S BETTER!

AYE, NOW IF WE CAN JUST CATCH UP BEFORE...

DAMN! IT'S DIVING! GET BELOW— MAYBE WE CAN FOLLOW.

HEAD AFT— MAKE SURE TOGG HAS HIS HATCHES CLOSED!

THE CREATURE'S GONE UNDERWATER, WE'RE GOING TO FOLLOW.

JANA'S CHEST BURNS, HER HEAD ACHES-- EVERYTHING HURTS. THE WORLD IS TIGHTENING DOWN TO A GRAY BLUR...

SHE CAN JUST SEE THE SWIMMING FORM THAT IS APPROACHING. HAD TOGG AND THE OTHERS MANAGED TO REACH HER, AFTER ALL?

NO. IT'S NOT TOGG. NOT ANYTHING REAL. FOR THE FIRST TIME JANA KNOWS DESPAIR...

AND THEN SHE KNOWS NOTHING...

COVER BY **FRANK CHO**

LET GO, DAMN YOU! LET GO!

WHAT DOES IT TAKE TO KILL YOU!

TOGG!

THE LONG-NECK IS ON OUR SIDE!

AND THERE ARE MORE OF THEM!

MANY MORE!

SEASON 2
CHAPTER 4

COVER BY **FRANK CHO**

JANA KNOWS THIS WILL BE HER BEST CHANCE TO FREE HERSELF...

SHE STEELS HERSELF AGAINST THE PAIN AND PULLS WITH ALL HER MIGHT...

UNTIL...

IS THERE ANYTHING WE CAN DO TO HELP?

WE STILL HAVE MORE OF THE TOR-PEE-DOES!

IF WE'RE CAREFUL OF OUR TARGET...

OKAY— LET'S SEE WHAT A LITTLE HIGH EXPLOSIVES DOES TO THIS BIG BUGGER...

FIRE!

SHOULD TAKE ABOUT 3 SECONDS TO GET THERE...

THREE...

SEASON 2
CHAPTER 5

COVER BY **FRANK CHO**

NooOOOoo!

KILL HER! SHE MUST NOT HARM THE DARK ONE!

QUICKLY! KILL HER QUICKLY!!

THERE'S GOT TO BE A WEAK SPOT...

SOME-WHERE...

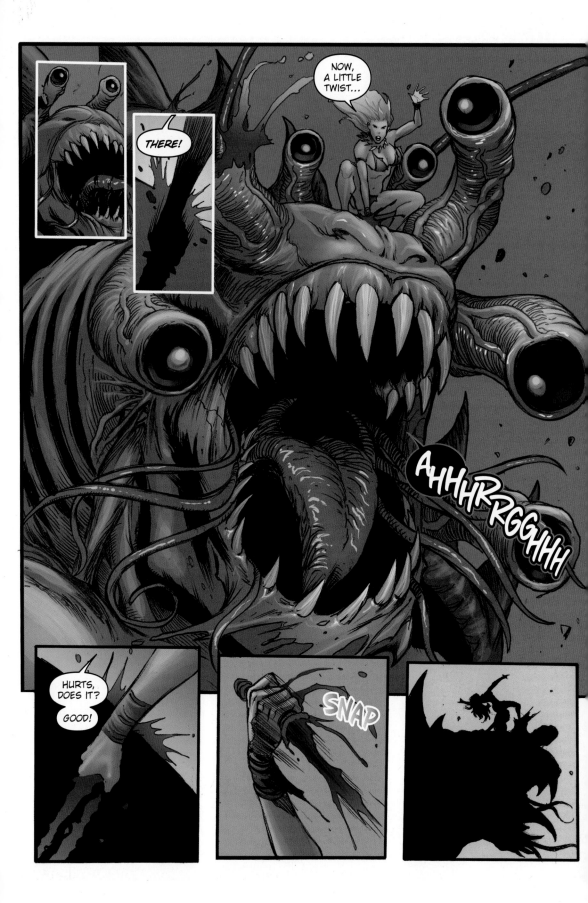

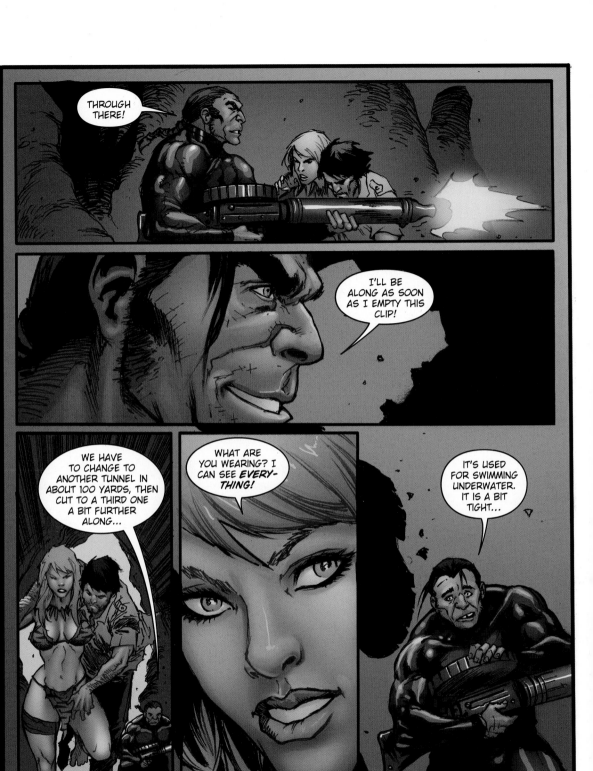

I REALLY **CAN'T** SWIM ALL THAT WELL...

I KNOW JANA IS CONCERNED, BUT AS LONG AS I CAN BREATHE, I'M SURE I CAN MAKE IT...

IT'S NOT ALL THAT FAR...

SEASON 3
CHAPTER 1

COVER BY **FRANK CHO**

TOGETHER, WE FACED A STAMPEDE OF BIG TEETH...

AND THE EVIL DREAM WALKER WHO ATTEMPTED TO LEAD THE DIRT PEOPLE INTO WAR WITH MY FRIENDS...

WE STOPPED HIM AND ESCAPED, BUT WHEN WE DID, WE SAW SOMETHING AMAZING...

SOMETHING THAT HAD TO BE INVESTIGATED...

IS THAT WHY YOU DISOBEYED MY RULES AND TRAVELLED TO THE GOD MOUNTAIN!

HE KNOWS I ALWAYS BREAK HIS RULES! AFTER ALL, I'M HIS ONLY DAUGHTER.

JANA, YOU DIDN'T KILL THE GOD!-- YOU COULDN'T KILL THE GOD! YOU JUST ANGERED IT AND...

NOW...

"NOW IT'S GOING TO DESTROY THIS WORLD!"

DANGER COMES!

LOOK!

"IT IS THE END OF THE WORLD!

THE EARTH IS MOVING...

I HAVE FELT SUCH BEFORE. IT IS...

IT'S A STAMPEDE! WE HAVE TO STOP THEM!

BIG TEETH!

SO MANY!

BUT THIS IS NOT OVER...

DADDY!

WHAT THE HELL...

IT'S ALL RIGHT. I AM NOT REALLY HERE-- I AM INSIDE THE GREAT TEMPLE, SPEAKING TO YOU THROUGH ONE OF ITS DEVICES...

BUT WE DO NOT HAVE TIME TO DISCUSS THIS NOW...

LOOK!

NOT IF I CAN HELP IT!

I WILL FIGHT AT YOUR SIDE!

ME TOO.

IT IS AS I FEARED!

ELSEWHERE, ANOTHER LEADER HAS A DIFFERENT INTERPRETATION...

HAVE NO FEAR!

IT IS THE VESSEL OF THE GODS!

IT IS A SIGN!

IT IS TIME TO TAKE WHAT IS OURS! THE LAND! THE WOMEN!

THE GODS DEMAND IT!

I'VE NEVER SEEN ANYTHING LIKE IT...

IT IS FROM FAR BEYOND THE STARS...

WHAT CAN WE DO?

WE CAN DO NOTHING ABOUT THE GOD-MACHINE NOW...

BUT WE CAN FIGHT THE DIRT PEOPLE-- AND STOP THEM FROM CONQUERING MY PEOPLE!

KILL THE TREE PEOPLE!

KILL THEM NOW!!

HERE THEY COME!

RACING TO THE SLAUGHTER! LET'S GO OUT AND MEET THEM!

SOUNDS LIKE A PLAN!

FOLLOW JANA! DEFEND THE VILLAGE!

COVER BY **FRANK CHO**

THIS HAS BEEN A VERY STRANGE DAY...

ONE THAT STARTED WITH A HOLE IN THE SKY--AND GOT WORSE!

THE BURNING DEBRIS FROM THE SKY HAS STARTED FIRES EVERYWHERE...

THOSE FIRES DROVE THE BIG-TEETH OUT OF THEIR HOME IN THE JUNGLE...

AND INTO THE VILLAGE OF THE DIRT PEOPLE...

THAT MADE THE DIRT PEOPLE TRY TO TAKE THE HOMES OF MY PEOPLE...

JANA! YOU HAVE TO STOP THIS!

FATHER?

YOU HAVE TO GET EVERYONE OUT OF HERE!

BEFORE THAT FALLS ON THEM!

HURRY!

HURRY...

HOW CAN I MAKE THEM LEAVE? HOW...

OF COURSE!

WHAT IS IT?

IT'S A DEVICE FROM BEYOND THE STARS...

IT HAS COME BECAUSE IT RECEIVED A MESSAGE FROM THE OLD ONE WHO WAS TRAPPED INSIDE THE MOUNTAIN.

OLD ONE?

YOU MUST REMEMBER IT--THE FISH PEOPLE WANTED TO SACRIFICE YOU TO IT...

BUT WE KILLED IT...

I AM NOT SURE IF IT CAN BE KILLED...

BUT THE REST OF US CAN!

FOOLISH GIRL! YOU DON'T WANT TO KILL ME!

WHY NOT?

ASK HIM...

DON'T KILL HIM. WE MIGHT NEED HIM.

NEED HIM! WHAT COULD WE POSSIBLY GET FROM HIM?

YOU'RE USING ONE OF THE OLD MACHINES? IT WORKS?

OBVIOUSLY!

WE MUST USE THE WEAPONS THE ANCIENTS LEFT!

USE WHAT?

THE BEINGS THAT BUILT THIS LAND-- THE OLD ONES--USED MACHINES THAT WE CANNOT UNDERSTAND...

THEY ARE STORED IN TWO TEMPLES--ONE DEEP IN THE DIRT PEOPLE'S CAVERNS, ONE AT THE EDGE OF THE TREE PEOPLE'S DOMAIN.

I AM THERE RIGHT NOW...

IT'S TOO BAD HE'S DEAD...

WHAT ARE THEY?

TOGG-- I HAVE A TASK FOR YOU.

OF COURSE, MEDICINE FATHER. ANYTHING...

THERE IS A WEAPON THAT MIGHT SAVE US--BUT IT WAS SPLIT INTO TWO PIECES MANY, MANY SUNS AGO.

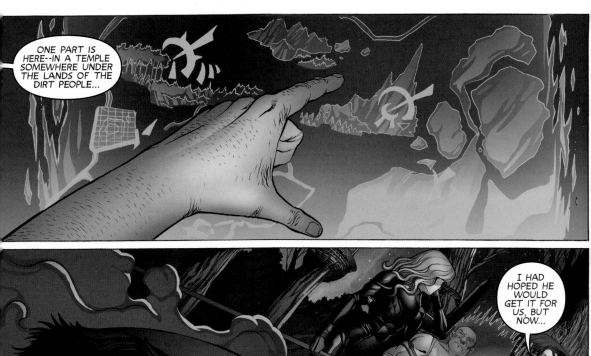

ONE PART IS HERE—IN A TEMPLE SOMEWHERE UNDER THE LANDS OF THE DIRT PEOPLE...

I HAD HOPED HE WOULD GET IT FOR US, BUT NOW...

NOW YOU TWO MUST FIND IT FOR ME.

COVER BY **FRANK CHO**

LEAVE NOW! YOU ARE NOT WELCOME IN THE LAND OF THE DIRT PEOPLE!

BUT YOU'RE DEAD! I KILLED YOU...

RAKASKA! SHE MUST REACH THE TEMPLE IF WE ARE TO SURVIVE!

WHY SHOULD I CARE WHO SURVIVES?

THEY COME FROM BEYOND THE STARS TO RETRIEVE THEIR GOD! WHO ARE WE TO STAND IN THEIR WAY!

BUT IT WOULD MEAN THE END OF ALL!

I KNOW...

YOU'RE MAD!

YOU WILL FAIL, JUNGLE GIRL!

QUICKLY! YOU MUST REACH THE TEMPLE!

WE'RE RUNNING OUT OF TIME!

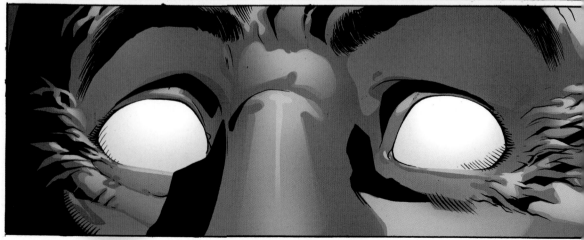

I GOT IT!

I GUESS THAT WAS THE ALPHA!

I COULD HAVE HANDLED IT, YOU KNOW.

YEAH, I KNOW...

LOOK!

I GUESS THAT'S THE TEMPLE.

WE HAVE TO HURRY!

THE LIGHTS...

AUTOMATIC. TRIGGERED BY OUR MOVEMENT.

THIS IS AMAZING! I WONDER...

THERE IS NO TIME FOR WONDER...

LOOK!

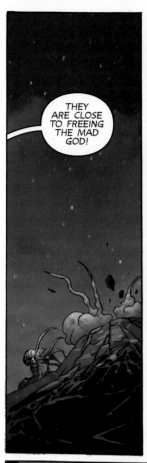

THEY ARE FAMILIAR...

BUT THEY ARE CHANGED SOMEHOW.

THEY MUST LIVE UNDER THE GROUND...

THEY'RE BUGS! HAVEN'T YOU GUYS EVER SEEN BUGS?

BUGS!?!

BIG BUGS!

HEY MONKEY BOY!

MY FATHER SAYS HE NEEDS THIS THING AS QUICKLY AS POSSIBLE...

AND AS YOU ARE THE FASTEST PERSON I KNOW...

BRING IT TO HIM, TOGG...

YOU'RE THE ONLY ONE HE AND I TRUST TO DO IT!

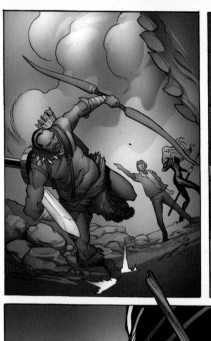

YOU HAVE TO COME TOO! I HAVE A PLANE...

YOU HAVE TO GET TO THE PLANE!

THEY'VE FREED THE OLD ONE! HURRY!

OVER THERE, TOGG!

THE ARTIFACT MUST BE INSERTED INTO THIS CONNECTION--IT'S DELICATE, WAIT JUST A MOMENT...

DON'T BE AFRAID OF WHAT YOU'RE ABOUT TO SEE.

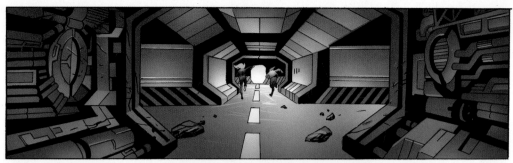

JANA! MEDICINE FATHER IS COMING!

HE SAID NOT TO BE FRIGHTENED...

I WAS INJURED BADLY WHEN OUR PLANE CRASHED...

I DIDN'T WANT YOU TO SEE ME LIKE THIS...

FATHER?

TOGG!

COME ON! WE HAVE TO GO!

BUT MY FATHER...

I AM ALREADY DEAD. I HAVE BEEN SO FOR MANY YEARS...

HANG ON!

I THINK WE'RE SAFE NOW. I'M SORRY ABOUT...

THE OLD ONE HAS NOT BEEN RELEASED. HE SLEEPS IN THE DEEP...

BUT ALL IS NOT WHAT IT WAS...

OR PERHAPS...

IT IS...

AND JANA THE JUNGLE GIRL IS ONCE AGAIN HOME...

THE END!

COVER
GALLERY

SEASON 1 ISSUE #1 VARIANT COVER
ART BY ADRIANO BATISTA AND FABRICIO GUERRA

SEASON 1 ISSUE #2 VARIANT COVER
ART BY ADRIANO BATISTA AND FABRICIO GUERRA

SEASON 1 ISSUE #3 VARIANT COVER
ART BY ADRIANO BATISTA AND FABRICIO GUERRA

SEASON 1 ISSUE #4 VARIANT COVER
ART BY ADRIANO BATISTA AND FABRICIO GUERRA

SEASON 1 ISSUE #5 VARIANT COVER
ART BY ADRIANO BATISTA AND FABRICIO GUERRA

SEASON 2 ISSUE #1 VARIANT COVER
ART BY ADRIANO BATISTA AND FABRICIO GUERRA

SEASON 2 ISSUE #2 VARIANT COVER
ART BY ADRIANO BATISTA AND FABRICIO GUERRA

SEASON 2 ISSUE #3 VARIANT COVER
ART BY ADRIANO BATISTA AND FABRICIO GUERRA

SEASON 2 ISSUE #4 RISQUE VARIANT COVER
ART BY FRANK CHO

SEASON 2 ISSUE #4 BW RISQUE VARIANT COVER
ART BY FRANK CHO

SEASON 2 ISSUE #4 VARIANT COVER
ART BY ADRIANO BATISTA AND FABRICIO GUERRA

SEASON 2 ISSUE #5 VARIANT COVER
ART BY ADRIANO BATISTA AND FABRICIO GUERRA

SKETCHBOOK

BY ADRIANO BATISTA

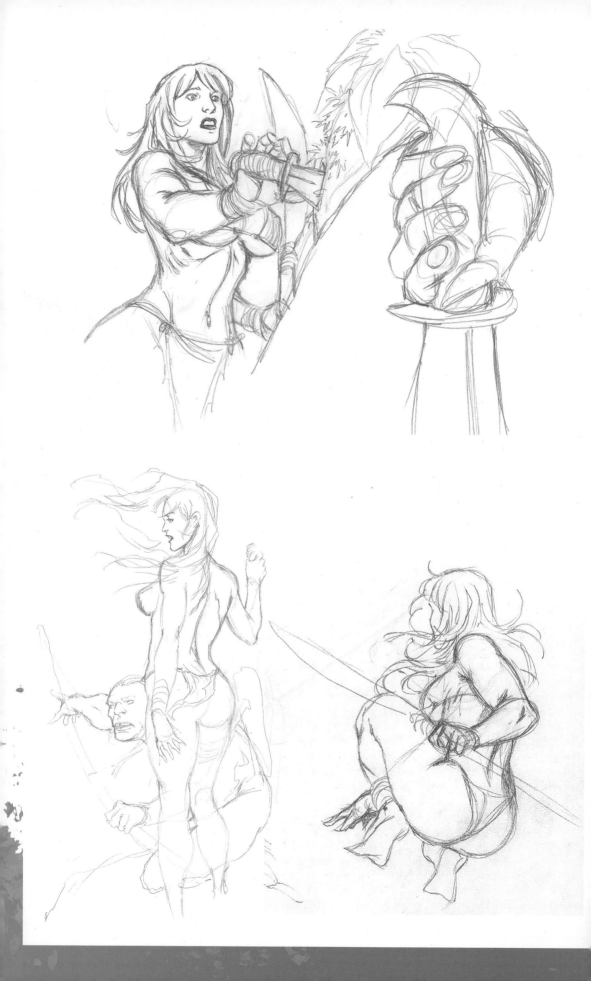